COLEG GWENT
L.R.C. - EBBW VALE
TEL: 01495 333078

EDUCATION, CULTURE AND SOCIETY

EDUCATION, CULTURE AND SOCIETY

SOME PERSPECTIVES ON THE NINETEENTH AND TWENTIETH CENTURIES

Essays presented to J. R. Webster

edited by
GARETH ELWYN JONES

Published on behalf of the
University of Wales
Faculty of Education

CARDIFF
UNIVERSITY OF WALES PRESS
1991

© University of Wales, 1991

British Library Cataloguing-in-Publication Data:
A catalogue record for this book is available from the British Library

ISBN 0-7083-1132-6

All rights reserved. No part of this book may be reproduced, stored in a retrieval system, or transmitted, in any form or by any means, electronic, mechanical, photocopying, recording or otherwise, without clearance from the University of Wales Press, 6 Gwennyth Street, Cardiff, CF2 4YD.

Jacket design by Rhiain M. Davies, Cain
Typeset by Alden Multimedia Ltd., Northampton
Printed in Great Britain by Billings Book Plan Ltd., Worcester

Contents

	Page
List of Contributors	vii
Editor's Foreword	ix
Foreword KENNETH O. MORGAN	xi
J. R. Webster CLIVE WILLIAMS	1
Trinity College, Carmarthen: The Early Years D. CLIVE JONES-DAVIES	11
A Microcosm of the Interaction of Education and Society in Victorian Wales—the Conflict concerning the Education of Girls in Anglesey W. GARETH EVANS	29
Dr J. J. Findlay, First Headmaster of Cardiff Intermediate School for Boys, 1898–1903: Instinctive Traditionalist or Enterprising Empiricist? RON BROOKS	45
The Welsh Committee of the Arts Council in the 1960s ROY BOHANA	63
Welsh Voices—More than Just Talk? BRIAN DAVIES	75
A Period of Change—Working for Progress: Secondary Education in Wales, 1965–1985 ILLTYD R. LLOYD	85

'GWREIDDIAU': Prosiect Creu Deunyddiau ar gyfer yr Ysgol Gynradd   107
INA WILLIAMS

Addysg Uwchradd Ddwyieithog   121
JANEM JONES

Methodology in In-Service Education   139
HYWEL I. EVANS

University and Training College—an Unlikely Marriage?   153
D. GERWYN LEWIS

Thirty Years On—Non-University Teacher Education in Wales   167
M. I. HARRIS

Problems of Teacher Education in the 1990s   177
DENIS LAWTON

The Control of Teacher Education   187
ALEC M. ROSS

Whither the LEA?   203
W. J. PHILLIPS

Sylwadau ar Addysg Gymraeg Heddiw   217
D. GARETH EDWARDS

European Dimensions—Rhetoric and Realities   231
MICHAEL WILLIAMS

The Contributors

ROY BOHANA is Deputy Director and Music Director of the Welsh Arts Council.

RON BROOKS is Lecturer in the School of History and Welsh History at the University College of North Wales, Bangor.

BRIAN DAVIES is Professor of Education at the University of Wales College of Cardiff.

D. GARETH EDWARDS is Senior Lecturer in Education at the University College of Wales, Aberystwyth.

HYWEL I. EVANS is Headmaster of Ysgol Aberconwy and former Chairman of the Curriculum Council for Wales.

W. GARETH EVANS is Senior Lecturer in Education at the University College of Wales, Aberystwyth.

CLIVE JONES-DAVIES is Principal of Trinity College, Carmarthen.

M. I. HARRIS was formerly Principal of the Gwent Institute of Higher Education.

GARETH ELWYN JONES is Professor of Educational Research at the University College of Wales, Aberystwyth.

JANEM JONES is Lecturer in Education at the University College of Wales, Aberystwyth.

DENIS LAWTON is Professor of Curriculum Studies at the University of London Institute of Education.

D. GERWYN LEWIS is Senior Assistant Registrar of the University of Wales.

ILLTYD R. LLOYD was formerly Her Majesty's Chief Inspector of Schools in Wales.

KENNETH O. MORGAN is Principal of the University College of Wales, Aberystwyth.

W. J. PHILLIPS was formerly Director of Education for Dyfed and is currently Chief Executive for Dyfed County Council.

ALEC M. ROSS was formerly Professor of Education at the University of Lancaster and is at present Academic Secretary of the Universities' Council for the Education of Teachers.

CLIVE WILLIAMS is Senior Lecturer in Education at the University College of Wales, Aberystwyth.

INA TUDNO WILLIAMS is Lecturer in Education at the University College of Wales, Aberystwyth.

MICHAEL WILLIAMS is Professor of Education at the University College of Swansea.

Editor's Foreword

J. R. Webster has served education in Wales and outside throughout his working life. He has been a member of the staff of four constituent colleges of the University of Wales Faculty of Education. For some years in the 1960s he had a wider educational brief with the Arts Council in Wales. All his appointments have brought additional commitments, in a Welsh and in a wider context, for example as Dean of the University of Wales Faculty of Education or as a member of the James Committee. I suspect that it would dismay Roger Webster if one were to calculate the number of other committees and bodies on which he has served. Whatever minutes they may have wasted or forced him to read, it is certain that they have brought him to the compensation of the friendship of inspectorate, local authority and academic colleagues by the score. The recipient of these essays is also a distinguished researcher, lecturer and supervisor of research students.

In such circumstances, it may be imagined how invidious was the task of deciding on that small number of contributors who must be representative of such a wide range of interests and activities. To those who have contributed I record my thanks for their readiness to do so and for the speed and efficiency with which they fulfilled their brief. To the many who would wish to have contributed I can only apologize and draw attention to my own self-denying ordinance.

Self denial was not all-consuming, of course, because it has been a delight to act on behalf of the University of Wales Faculty of Education in editing the book. In this capacity I owe a great debt to Ceinwen Jones and Susan Jenkins of the University of Wales Press.

Aberystwyth
June 1991   **GARETH ELWYN JONES**

Foreword

It is a great privilege to be asked to write the foreword to this volume marking the retirement of an old friend, and past and present colleague, Professor Roger Webster. The Education Department at the University College of Wales, Aberystwyth, is almost as old as the college itself. It was founded in 1892, just twenty years after 'Aber' came into being, a symbol of the intimate relationship between 'the college by the sea' and the schools of Wales. It thus pre-dated the creation of 'the county schools', so potent a force in the recent educational, social and political history of the Welsh nation.

Aberystwyth's Education Department has always been highly prestigious and distinctive. It was the first department in England or Wales to have a professor. The holders of the chair have included many eminent figures, notably Foster Watson, the historian of the grammar schools, and, in the more recent past, Jac L. Williams, a leading figure in the Welsh-language educational world. The department has always been active and productive. At the present time, it teaches the three major courses, an undergraduate honours course, primary Postgraduate Certificate in Education and secondary PGCE. It has one of the largest early years/primary courses in Britain. The total number of its funded students is some 300, a figure increased by the Universities Funding Council in 1991; of these about 250 are training to be teachers. There is also a full-time M.Ed. course which attracts many students from overseas.

The Department has never allowed the practical aspects of its work to obscure its commitment to research. Its strength in the history of education and in bilingualism developed in the 1920s. Latterly, it has extended its specialisms to include the pattern and structure of rural education, aspects of policy-making and the special role of Welsh-language teachers throughout the age and subject range. It is also active in the generation of school resources in the Welsh language and the recipient of much funding from the Welsh Office to that end. In the busy, perhaps hectic, educational world of the 1990s and beyond, its activity and distinction are set fair to continue.

In all these developments and many others, Roger Webster has been a major creative force who has given dedicated leadership in the College at a crucial time. The wide-ranging links that Aberystwyth enjoys with overseas schools, colleges and institutions, from Denmark, Friesland and Spain in Europe, to Arizona in the United States, owe much to his initiative. As Dr Clive Williams shows in his biographical sketch here, Professor Webster's career spans Welsh life in many fields. He has lectured in Trinity College, Carmarthen and the University College of Swansea; he was for twelve years professor at our sister college at Bangor. His work at the Arts Council helped regenerate the life of Wales especially in music and the visual arts, while he has maintained a significant output as an historian of Welsh education.

Above all, he has provided inspiration to the Department of Education here over thirteen years and indeed has had a major impact on the profile of the College as a whole. Serious illness neither deflected nor deterred him, and he has come through triumphant. His finest legacy is the robust strength and self-confidence of the Department he has led with such skill and sensitivity. This volume of essays provides a fitting tribute to a career of outstanding achievement on behalf of the schools and the University of Wales.

Aberystwyth,
June 1991   KENNETH O. MORGAN

J. R. Webster

CLIVE WILLIAMS

The prevailing winds of Roger Webster's early career blew consistently southerly and while, with characteristic modesty, he would deny that they brought fame, they certainly brought good fortune in laying the foundations not only of that intellectual and educational perspicacity which has characterized his contribution to education but also of an affinity with Wales undiluted by trace of parochialism, to say nothing of a happy marriage arising from the judicious choice of a Pembrokeshire bride.

A native of Y Gaerwen in Anglesey, and born into a farming community, Roger Webster attended the local primary school before continuing his formal education at Llangefni Secondary School, where he became Head Boy. From here he came south to the University College of Wales, Aberystwyth, where he took Single Honours Geography in the department then under the direction of Professor E. G. Bowen.

In those possibly more parochial days 'Aber' elicited in its students an affectionate affinity with the College and its customs found less frequently among more recent students, many of whom leave Aberystwyth today with the bar unkicked. Roger was no exception to his generation and his later appointment to the Chair of Education at Aber was a most appropriate consummation of an affiliation with the College generated in his student days.

But one example not only of his warm identification with Aber, but also of horizons beyond those of purely professional endeavour, is his well-informed interest in the history and architecture of that labyrinthine edifice known as Old College. Those familiar with Roger's stimulating lecture on Old College and the work of its architect, Seddon, delivered with all the enthusiasm and authority of a latter-day Ruskin (though happily without the vociferous dogmatism), will have found it an uplifting experience, leading the eye as it does to many a hidden corbel, unsuspected spandrel or unfinished decoration, and, less laudably, providing the jaded eye of both lecturer and student with pleasing distraction.

And next to, or rather before, architecture, art—a dominant and lifelong extra-curricular interest developed by Roger Webster during his student days. Initially stimulated by pictures at an exhibition, the Davies (Gregynog) collection, strengthened by early visits to Continental galleries and later confirmed by like-minded colleagues at Trinity College, Carmarthen, his interest in the fine arts has remained an absorbing passion. Later to find tangible expression in his directorship of the Welsh Arts Council, this interest prompted his publication of a number of research articles, held in the highest esteem both in and outside Wales, concerned, in particular, with art and artists, national traditions and visual arts in Wales. Roger Webster has also written reviews, monographs, radio and television scripts, in both Welsh and English, on the arts. He has a particular interest in the teaching of visual arts and music in schools and his research on the changing image of childhood in Western art has resulted in a most stimulating and appreciated contribution to our first-year honours course, 'Childhood in Art and Literature'.

Drawn early to an academic and pedagogical calling, Roger Webster's Baccalaureate was followed by his Diploma in Education, also taken at Aber, Professor Idwal Jones then holding the chair to which Roger was to aspire in his maturity. On this course he was awarded a distinction in practical teaching, primarily on the recommendation of the geography method tutor, Mr W. J. Lewis.

It was, however, the scene of higher, rather than secondary, education which was to witness the bulk of Roger Webster's educational endeavours and in 1948 he was appointed Lecturer in Social Studies at Trinity College, Carmarthen, then an Anglican teacher-training college under the direction of the Revd Principal Halliwell. Here he was concerned primarily with the initiation and development of new courses in geography method and social studies while, at the same time, the Department of Art and its staff, Mr Bob Hunter (on whom he later wrote an article in *Yr Arloeswr*) in particular, did much to consolidate his interest in art.

In 1951, Roger Webster, moving southerly again, was appointed Lecturer in Education at University College, Swansea, the

Education Department being under the professorship of Evan John Jones, and later of Charles Gittins. Here he replaced Mrs Auriol Watkin, whom he was to join later on the staff at UCW, Aberystwyth. At Swansea he was concerned with the teaching of both geography and geology method, in addition to social studies, educational thought and youth leadership.

Here Roger Webster's research potential was early recognized by Evan John Jones who encouraged Roger (who had recently completed his MA dissertation: 'Llanfihangelesceifiog—a study of a rural parish in Anglesey') to undertake further research, initially via the unpublished diaries of Sir O. M. Edwards. This, together with an already present interest in community studies, led to his successful Ph.D. candidature in 1959.

It is from this period on that Roger Webster's formidable record of research and publication primarily dates, a record maintained to the present day in spite of increased administrative and extracurricular responsibilities. Here he has woven scholarly strands of academic and cultural interests into a rich tapestry of educational endeavour. Roger Webster's Ph.D. dissertation, 'The place of secondary education in Welsh society, 1800–1918', has been considered by later researchers as an essential point of departure for further investigations on this theme. Extensive research and publication on the history of education in Wales have thrown particular illumination on grammar-school education, again his recorded investigations being appreciated by both historian and educationist. His main research interests are reflected in the five interrelated areas of environmental studies, history of education, educational administration, curriculum studies and fine arts, interests which in addition to facilitating most worthwhile publication have greatly enriched his teaching. In recent years Roger has focused his attention on the problems of rural schools and bilingualism in Wales, the curriculum and teacher training. The extent and range of Roger Webster's research contribution precludes adequate comment in the current context but I can at least confirm the scholarship, insight and painstaking attention to both detail and documentation which characterize his research. In addition to scholarship his works have a pleasing quality more rare in educational research publication, eminent readability. Bearing in mind Roger Webster's laudable contribution to education in Wales, the title of his most recent publication, 'Education in Wales and the rebirth of a nation'

(*History of Education*, 19 No. 3, 1990) is indeed appropriate on the occasion of his retirement.

Roger Webster's most southerly move, to Cardiff in 1961, was a call less of latitude than of cultural interests which vied with his more formal educational involvements. As Director for Wales of the Arts Council of Great Britain, a post he held for five years, his interest and enthusiastic involvement in the arts were given full rein. In addition to the organization of numerous activities, exhibitions, recitals and concert tours throughout Wales, his period of office saw extended activities of the Welsh and English drama companies which later became *Cwmni Theatr Cymru* and the Welsh Theatre Company. In addition, the Welsh National Opera became a professional company and the first regional arts association was established. In effectively meeting a challenge necessitating considerable administrative and communicative skills, Roger Webster did much to establish what is more generally known now as the Welsh Arts Council as a familiar and worthwhile endeavour for the whole of Wales. Some might see this period as a diversion in the mainstream of Roger Webster's more educational career, but on reflection one sees its relevance as involving aspects of community education, a concept experienced by Roger in his youth and later to be developed by him as a field of educational endeavour and research. Returning north in 1966 to be Professor of Education at University College of North Wales, Bangor, he began, though unknowingly, his second southerly journey, culminating in his present appointment as Professor of Education in UCW Aberystwyth.

The Bangor appointment gave Roger Webster the opportunity to put into effective practice ideas developed over many years in education, particularly in the fields of in-service and teacher training. During his period of office at Bangor, student numbers in the Department of Education more than trebled. Substantial funding was obtained for research and curriculum development projects and, in meeting the needs of in-service training in a scattered rural area, curriculum development projects of a pioneering nature were effectively developed. New masters' degrees in education were established, both within the department and in co-operation with the Department of Psychology, while in the postgraduate certificate Roger Webster encouraged and participated in a pioneering course in outdoor education and pursuits. To those unfamiliar with his love of walking this might come as a surprising adjunct to a career inclined, by its very nature, to be largely sedentary. Canoes, however, are paddled in a sedentary posture and Roger has always been more than willing to paddle his own.

During his years at Bangor Roger Webster undertook increasingly significant committee work. From 1969 to 1978 he was Chairman of the Advisory Committee on Studies in Education at the Open University. During the year 1970–1 he was a full-time member of the James Committee, appointed by the Secretary of State for Education and Science to consider the reorganization of teacher education and training. The James Report led to fundamental changes in the organization and structure of all colleges of education and Roger Webster's co-authorship of an important (minority) chapter was, in particular, a significant contribution.

Towards the end of his tenure at Bangor Roger Webster organized and supervised the amalgamation of UCNW Education Department and St Mary's College of Education. In addition to providing a greatly expanded school of education, the migration of the UCNW Department to St Mary's provided it, for the first time in its history, with adequate facilities and accommodation.

In 1978, as a consequence of the early and untimely death of Professor Jac L. Williams, Roger Webster was appointed Professor of Education at the University College of Wales, Aberystwyth. I first met him at this time and, as a member of staff throughout his current tenure, I turn with relief to more familiar ground. Yet another departmental migration, that from Alexandra Road to Old College, shortly after Roger's arrival, heralded a decade or so of considerable change and adjustment. Change wrought from within has been accompanied, as in all university departments of education by accommodation of and adjustment to obligatory change imposed from without. Rationalization of teacher training in Wales, together with extensive accreditation procedures established by the Council for the Accreditation of Teacher Education have, in particular, resulted in major changes in both the size and nature of teacher-training courses. In addition to the long-established provision of secondary-school training, training for primary-school teaching is now a major concern of the department, our postgraduate certificate in education primary intake being among the largest in the country. A special course in 'Early Years Education' is also now available for intending teachers. The consequential and considerable increase in student-teacher numbers, in PGCE staff and specialist training facilities and accommodation, and in school practice areas (in addition to the bulk of Wales our teaching-practice area now includes several English counties) is such that during Roger's tenure the department has seen an expansion of teacher training far greater than any since its inception nearly a century ago.

Similarly, under Roger Webster's direction, there have been major changes in the nature and extent of in-service education for mature students from both Wales and overseas. In addition, the renewed emphasis on, and consequent extension of, Welsh-medium teaching, involving co-operation and funding from both the Welsh Office and local education authorities, has been a major undertaking. Ever aware of the need to establish and consolidate the viability of the department, Roger Webster has made sterling efforts to initiate and develop research, particularly funded research, meeting immediate and realistic curriculum needs in schools.

These, and indeed many other developments, set against the background of the need to respond to seemingly incessant and obligatory initiatives demanded of university departments of education these days, have made the past decade exceptionally busy and demanding. In times when the outlook for such departments has varied from stormy to uncertain we have been indeed fortunate in having Roger Webster's steady and experienced hand at our helm.

Among his achievements as Professor of Education at Aber, two (at least) deserve special mention: the development of in-service/ higher education courses and his contribution to the expansion of Welsh-medium teaching and facilities. Under his direction the Aber Faculty of Education was the first in Wales to introduce a modular Master of Education degree, combining in-service and higher degree courses. Provided at the College and at school centres throughout our area, these courses, largely in curriculum development, have been centred on the work of schools and the needs of teachers, effective follow-up and continuity also being essential features. These popular, well-subscribed and successful courses are held in increasing regard, not least as a result of the teaching contribution made by Roger himself.

Roger Webster has had a particular concern for the educational needs and general welfare of our overseas students, by whom he is often held not just in mere regard but in affectionate veneration. The immediate educational needs of overseas countries, especially in the Third World, he has borne much in mind in the design of higher education courses. Our M.Ed. courses in 'Educational Technology' and 'Bilingual and Language Education' are now well established and Roger Webster has done much to complement the internationally known pioneering work in these fields of H. T. Conway and Professor Carl Dodson, both now retired. In both funding and recruitment we have benefited here from Roger's excellent relationships with the British Council, both in a personal capacity and as a member of the Welsh Committee for the British Council and of its Commonwealth Committee. Hitherto somewhat *ad hoc*, organization of in-service and higher education courses is now the responsibility of our Centre for In-Service Education, set up by Roger Webster early in his tenure.

The past decade or so has seen a timely and renewed emphasis in Wales on bilingualism, Welsh-medium teaching and the problems of rural schools. In encouraging relevant research, obtaining funding and developing appropriate facilities Roger Webster has made a formidable contribution in a field traditionally associated with the department. Soon after his arrival at Aberystwyth he set up what is now designated the Centre for Educational Studies (*Y Ganolfan Astudiaethau Addysg*), a particularly successful enterprise, substantially financed by the Welsh Office and concerned primarily with the production of Welsh-medium learning and teaching materials. In both quality and quantity the results of this initiative have been highly commendable and widely appreciated in bilingual and Welsh-medium schools.

He is a fluent Welsh-speaker, but the fact that his education in the language came through the community rather than more formally gives him a particular insight not only into the school as a centre of community culture but also into the needs of Welsh-medium education and the problems of learners. Welsh-medium teaching continues as an important feature of the department; while at secondary level the PGCE is available partially in Welsh, at primary level it is wholly so. In continuing education the involvement of the department in external (Welsh-medium) degree courses remains strong.

Bilingualism and rural education have been major concerns of the Aberystwyth Rural Policy Group, set up by Roger Webster and through his involvement producing the model of a bilingual school adapted successfully for Gwynedd. In meeting the need to recruit more Welsh-speaking teachers, Roger Webster played a major part by making a significant contribution to the design and development of the Welsh Office Incentive Bonus Scheme (for intending Welsh-medium and bilingual teachers), centred on Aberystwyth but involving several other colleges. Current research in the department points to the success of the scheme in helping to meet a very urgent need.

In the field of Welsh-medium and bilingual education Roger Webster has both continued and strengthened the policy initiated by his predecessor, Jac L. Williams. In his department there is now more Welsh-medium teaching than ever before and he has done much to establish the centrality of the department's role in Wales.

In the process of partially clearing his library in preparation for retirement, Roger recently presented me with a volume by the Revd Andrew Bell, published in 1823 and concerned with the Madras system of education. In discussing the desirable qualities of the master of an educational institution Bell, quoting from a report, writes,

> His scrutinizing eye must pervade the whole system—his active mind must give it energy—and his unbiased judgement, and equal justice, must maintain the general order and harmony.

Roger Webster had done just this.

In the final analysis appreciation probably arises less from achievement than from personality and personal skills. Gentle in nature and generous in spirit, Roger Webster has a humanity, humour, sympathetic understanding and friendly nature that even his undoubted political acumen cannot hide. A most competent and persuasive communicator, his teaching skills are much appreciated by students. His well-informed though relaxed and informal platonic approach in small-group teaching is held in high regard, though the large-group lecture probably remains his forte (more than one ex-colleague I consulted referred to student ovations at his lectures). Roger's large-group lectures not only generate enthusiasm for the subject but are delivered with that refreshing spontaneity found only in those as well-prepared as they are well-informed. 'All really good teachers are artists', wrote Arthur Pinsent, a former member of the department; 'their lessons have a distinct entertainment value.' In Roger Webster one sees this dictum equally applicable to lecturers, though perhaps entertainment ('agreeable occupation of attention') these days find little place in intense discussion of teaching dynamics. Nevertheless, in days when many pedagogical experts feel that the large-group lecture, like public readings of Dickens, should be relegated to antiquity, it is heartening to know that so worthy an exponent of the genre as Roger Webster still flourishes. With age and familiarity, there is, of course, always the danger of a diminishing concern for standards and procedures in one's large-group lecturing. In my own case, I am less concerned than I was when students arrive late at lectures—provided, of course, that they do not obstruct those leaving early. In Roger Webster's lectures students neither arrive late nor leave early.

In committee work, particularly as chairman, the effectiveness of Roger Webster's personality and personal skills are legendary. A founder member of the Universities Council for the Education of Teachers and senior Dean and chairman of the University of Wales Faculty of Education, Roger Webster's membership of important educational and fine arts committees, in both Wales and England, is too extensive to annotate in detail here. He is, after all, retiring and not applying for another chair. Those familiar with his committee work invariably speak of his insight, immediate grasp of essentials, his remarkable prescience, the persuasive humility of his manner and gifted ability, whether by logic or charm, to convince the sceptic, rally the faint-hearted and elicit co-operation from the hitherto unwilling. (I hasten to add that this is no reflection on the membership of the committees at which Roger presides).

Through his extensive committee work on education committees in both Wales and England, Roger Webster has had an influence for both the good and the sensible. His committee work, coupled with, over the years, external examinerships of a large number of universities and colleges, has done much (as one would expect of a geographer) to put the Aberystwyth Education Department on the map. It is gratifying to find that mention of one's department and its professor at meetings in England rarely elicits the response, 'Roger who?' or 'Aber where?'

Roger Webster's lively sense of humour, which rarely, if ever, deserts him, is a particularly endearing grace, more so because it often contains a gentle and completely disarming self-deprecation. I will let but one anecdote suffice as an example. One day Roger found himself on a bus and in conversation with a young man who evidently had some knowledge of education. As the conversation progressed the young man's face became vaguely familiar and suspecting that he might be an old student, but not wishing to reveal ignorance of his identity, Roger sought a clue by asking 'And what are you doing now?' 'Well,' replied the young man, 'I was in your lecture at nine o'clock this morning.'

I have also found humour, though of a more wry variety, in Roger's response to the plethora of educational initiatives and fashionable excesses of university bureaucracy that plague university education departments these days. His is the wise and essentially good-humoured tolerance of one who has seen it all before, though, as often happens in education, under a different name.

During the years immediately preceding my own retirement, Roger and I shared responsibility for the department, he as Professor of Education and myself as Head of Department. Though in principle a situation fraught with difficulties, it certainly proved otherwise, the result being quite harmonious and, I hope, effective. Again, I think Roger's sense of humour was a contributory factor. Indeed, how could one sustain a difference of opinion with a man who described the arrangement as a 'Morecambe and Wise situation' (except it be about who should be the one with the glasses)? I am pleased to report that throughout my headship of the department Roger Webster behaved himself in an exemplary manner, showed definite promise, and performed his duties entirely to his satisfaction.

To conclude on a more serious note, Roger Webster has made a formidable and lasting contribution to education, particularly in Wales. As Professor of Education his first concern has been the welfare and good name of his department. Yet his has been a wider influence for good; though insular by birth he is insular neither by nature or by achievement. Unique in experience, wide in influence and tireless in endeavour, he is indeed a most worthy elder statesman of education in Wales.

In 1988, in recognition of his services as Chairman of the Post Office Users' Council for Wales, Roger Webster was awarded the OBE. Unable to emulate Her Majesty's gift, I can but tender to Roger, on behalf of staff and students of many colleges with which he is and has been associated, our warmest regards and very best wishes in his retirement.

Trinity College, Carmarthen: The Early Years

D. CLIVE JONES-DAVIES

A history of the early years of the South Wales and Monmouthshire Training College, now known as Trinity College, Carmarthen, which was the first teacher-training college in Wales, reveals a mixture of quaint and homely practices existing within a spartan and sometimes inhospitable regime. Thus, the Welsh Education Committee of the National Society required the first managers of the College to allot 'a fixed annual sum of £50 to their Principal for the supply of vegetables, and in so doing consulted both their own and his dignity in not regarding it "like an annual contract with an ordinary tradesman"'. The students rose at 5.30 a.m. and commenced their private study at 6 a.m. Their day thereafter included 'Industrial Occupations' as well as 'Lectures' and continued until 10 p.m. This 'prudent mixture of manual labour and sedentary employment' was interspersed with periods of prayer and leisure, an allocation of one and a half hours being made in the timetable for both activities during each working day. Her Majesty's Inspector of the time, Revd H. Longueville Jones, commends the College for its concern for the physical and economic, as well as the spiritual and intellectual, well-being of the students by proposing to find them employment indoors since

> it is not prudent to expose young men who are of necessity much under cover, and in rooms, the temperature of which is considerably raised by the heat engendered by their collective presence, to the vicissitudes of a humid atmosphere and damp ground . . . Another very great and serious objection to out-door labour in a wet climate is the wear and tear of clothes, which to poor men, expected to preserve a certain decency of appearance, cannot well be overstated.

The College established in Carmarthen in 1848 was not in the first flush of Church of England teacher-training colleges, some twenty-four of which had already been established by 1848 through the endeavours of the National Society and of a number of the English dioceses. The establishment of the College, although in part motivated by the same concern as led to the founding of the colleges in England, namely the training of young men to be schoolmasters of parish schools, was inspired by a unique set of circumstances which obtained in Wales at that time. From the beginning of the nineteenth century the Church Union Society had sought to promote the interest of leading churchmen in the education of the poor and had been active in the Diocese of St Davids in making small grants towards the payment of teachers. This had, to some small extent, supplemented the monies made available in the will of Madam Bevan and enabled the pioneering work of Griffith Jones to be continued after his death. The Society for Promoting Christian Knowledge had led the way in England during the seventeenth and eighteenth centuries but had had relatively little effect on Wales, and even the British and Foreign Society founded in 1808 and the National Society founded in 1811 had concentrated their efforts during the first half of the nineteenth century on England. When the National Society turned its attention to Wales in 1844 and offered to train young men from Wales in London to return to teach in the Principality the corner seemed to have been turned. However, support from Wales was inadequate to ensure a sufficient supply, which is not surprising since those who would have been selected for training work would surely have found the prospect of up to two years' sojourn in London intimidating. They were, of course, of a different social class from those Welshmen who had attended the Universities of Oxford and Cambridge.

In 1846 the National Society, realizing that the cause of education in Wales could not be effectively served in this way, established its Welsh Committee. The full title of the society unequivocally stated its intentions: 'The National Society for promoting the Education of the Poor in the Principles of the Established Church throughout England and Wales'. Thus it was in 1811 at its establishment; now in 1846 it turned its full attention to the needs of the poor, and, it might be said, to the needs of the Church, in Wales. That the Church had failed to provide for the educational needs of the poor in Wales was made clear in the report of the Committee of Council on Education published in 1847 which had highlighted the abject condition of education in Wales and which had exceeded its brief by impugning the moral condition of the Welsh people. Although the Sunday schools were praised for their work in some areas of Wales, the Commissioners blamed the predominating use of the Welsh language as being the major cause of the backwardness of the nation; its moral condition was directly related to its educational condition. The picture drawn of education in Wales is that of a fitful provision of Sunday schools and day schools depending on the Bible as virtually the only reading book, without equipment and, except for the parish church and a small number of school rooms, largely without suitable buildings for the conduct of lessons.

The Church schools provided by Madam Bevan's charity and by the efforts of some of the parishes, the latter largely at the expense of the incumbent, could boast some degree of training for their teachers, although these were peripatetic. Some schools were established and supported by masters of industry and could at least claim that they were reasonably well housed. They were, however, inadequately provided with teachers and largely served by people who, through injury or illness, could not earn their living at the works at which they were employed. The worst provision of all was at the private adventure schools, ill-housed, ill-equipped and mainly taught by schoolmasters inspired by the profit motive to supplement their income from some other occupation.

In England the situation was certainly better, although the general poverty of rural and urban areas made the work of both the British and Foreign Schools Society and of the National Society difficult. The 'monitorial system' had the advantages of being cheap and of being a 'system' which could be adopted as a regular format for instruction. This gave the schools an orderliness lacking elsewhere and the Welsh Committee of the National Society sought to extend the system to Wales. Prominent churchmen, clerical and lay, saw in the Society an answer to the criticisms of the Commissioners. That they were genuinely concerned about the moral and spiritual state of the populace in Wales is not to be disputed and that they identified a lack of education as being a reason for this condition is to be applauded. However, it is interesting to note that another reason also motivated them in their decision to establish a college in Carmarthen to train teachers for the schools of Wales. This is well expressed in a letter from Sir Thomas Phillips to the SPCK written on 24 November 1848. In it he describes the founding of the College and offers a reason why the SPCK should provide funds for the new institution:

> Public attention has of late been anxiously directed to the condition of the Church in the Principality and to the very large proportion of the people who have forsaken her services and joined themselves to other religious bodies, of whom some are now seeking to disturb her possession and deprive her of the character of a National Church.
>
> The thoughtful friends of the Church best acquainted with the Principality have long been convinced that the only hope of restoring the influence of the Church or even of maintaining her present position in that country must rest upon the establishment of good schools, wherein religious instruction in accordance with the formularies of the Church should be given by Teachers fittly [sic] prepared for the task.

The South Wales and Monmouthshire College at Carmarthen, therefore, was to be a bulwark against Nonconformity as well as a cradle for the nurture of teachers to provide 'sound instruction to the children of the poor'.

Evidence that Sir Thomas Phillips had cause to despair about the condition of the Church is provided by the diaries of the Revd William Edmunds, first Vice-Principal of the College. These are available for the years 1849 (when he took up his appointment), 1850 and 1851.

William Edmunds was a former student of St David's College, Lampeter, who was ordained and was intended for an appointment in the Church. He was in his early twenties when he wrote these diaries and he remained as Vice-Principal until 1854 when he became the headmaster of the Lampeter Grammar School. He later became Vicar of Rhosdie near Llanilar. Edmunds writes of Good Friday, 29 March 1850, that he attended a Communion Service at St Peter's and said that 'There were not many present' and further, that 'I hear the Day was not very strictly observed in Carmarthen'. On Palm Sunday, 24 March, he reports 'a thin congregation at St Davids, Carmarthen'. He attended there the following day and reports again that there was 'a thin congregation'. He is particularly critical of the clergy who did not conform to the proper observances in their preaching or conduct of the service. Thus his entry for the 10 March reads:

> very fine day, never remember finer weather this time of the year. Heard G G William preach at St David's Church.—There was something very odd and unbecoming in his whole behaviour. He did not kneel at all when prayers were said. His demeanour altogether was strange. I

cannot help thinking very often that there is in the Lampeter students a great lack of principle and a want of knowledge of many things which clergymen ought to be thoroughly conversant in.

On Sunday 24 February he reported thus on a service at St Peter's Church:

Archdeacon Bevan tonight read the Collect for St Mathias's Day and that for the Sunday but did not read the Ash Wednesday Collect as he ought to have done. The Collect, Epistle and Gospel for St Mathew's Day was read at St David's instead of that for St Mathias's—the Lessons for the Sunday were read in both places.

He is very sharp in his criticism of individual clergy and obviously his diaries were not intended to be read by anyone else at that time. Thus he wrote on 17 February of the Curate of St Peter's:

Evans is inclined to be Calvinistic and his delivery is far from being free and his attempt at eloquence quite embarrasses him.

The entry for Ash Wednesday includes the observation that he 'heard two sermons—a better one than usual from the Archdeacon'. On 18 March he went to hear the Assize sermon, for which purpose the whole College had been given a holiday on that afternoon. The entry reads thus:

The sermon was preached by the Vicar of Cilgerran and a very good one it was indeed. Cilgerran never wrote it—I suspect it is the production of the Archdeacon of Cardigan's brain.

He was also critical of those who read the lessons in the services and here may lie, in part, the reason for that thin congregation which he reported as being present at St David's on Palm Sunday because for that day he also wrote:

Pugh of Abergwili reading the epistle—what a horrid reader he is. He is enough to frighten anybody.

Despite his criticism of other clergy, including archdeacons, he stopped short of criticizing the Bishop, as we see in his entry for 25 August 1850 when he reports on Bishop Thirlwall preaching at St David's Church at a special service in support of Llanllwch School. He wrote:

a thorough wet gloomy November day—was obliged to change my clothes after coming from Church, but the Bishop's sermon was a sufficient compensation for all our trouble—he is becoming more and more Apostolic and Evangelical continually.

In April 1848, a 'Declaration Deed' setting forth the Trusts of the

South Wales Training Institution was published. It proclaimed that 'natives of each Welsh Diocese shall be admitted and a preference over other candidates be given'. It also stressed that they should 'be possessed of a competent knowledge of the Welsh and English languages'. At the same time, in a significant memorandum to the Committee of Council on Education, the Welsh Education Committee of the National Society drew attention to the fact that there were no inspectors for Welsh schools, no grants for school maintenance as in England and Scotland, and no arrangement for the appointment and payment of pupil teachers. The Committee of Council responded positively to grant what the Welsh Committee had suggested, thus laying the foundations for the teacher-training system in Wales. Doubtless the Committee of Council were impressed by the initiative and commitment of the National Society and by those, like Sir Thomas Phillips in the dioceses of St Davids and Llandaff, who had felt compelled to establish the College at Carmarthen.

A contemporary record states 'the weather on the opening day of the Carmarthen Training College was very unpropitious, heavy rain falling', but then describes a most impressive procession from the Town Hall to St Peter's Church made up of:

> Police Officers, two abreast
> Officers of the Corporation, in their Robes
> Sword Bearer, with the Sword of State
> The Mayor in his Robes
> Councillors who have passed the Chair, in their Robes
> Aldermen and other Members of the Corporation
> The Magistrates
> The Welsh Education Committee
> The Principal and Vice-Principal of the College
> The Archdeacon of Carmarthen and Clergy of the
> Diocese, in Gowns
> The Inhabitants and Visitors

It was 27 October 1848, the first students being admitted the next day. It is interesting to note the requirements placed upon the candidates for admission, who were to be

> not less than 17 years of age, and will be required to read with intelligence, to write correctly from dictation, to work accurately the first four rules, simple and compound, of arithmetic, to be acquainted with the Church Catechism, and the outlines of Scripture, History and

Geography. The terms are £21 per annum payable quarterly in advance, for Board, Lodging, Washing, Tuition Books, etc. There will be no extras whatever.

J. C. Symonds, one of the three Commissioners of the Inquiry into the State of Education in Wales of 1847, reported on the office of schoolteaching as follows:

> No person really qualified for the office of schoolmaster by moral character, mental energy, amiability of temper, and proficiency in all the elementary branches of education, together with aptitude in imparting knowledge, will doom himself to the worst paid labour and almost the least appreciated office to be met with in the country. Were even the means of training schoolmasters as ample as they are defective, and were the number of men adequately trained to the work at hand, the generality of schools would be not one jot the better supplied, for such training would fit men for employment in other spheres, where they would realise four or five times the emolument and enjoy a much higher social position than they can hope for as schoolmasters in Wales under existing circumstances.

The new College at Carmarthen managed to attract twenty-two students in its first year of existence, ten of these came from Carmarthenshire, four from Cardiganshire, three from Glamorgan, two from Pembrokeshire and one each from Breconshire and Radnorshire. The place of origin of one of the students was not recorded. The very first entry in the admission book for the College bears out what Symonds had written a year previously, for Walter Powell, aged 17, from 'Devynnock', near Brecon, the son of Thomas Powell, wheelwright and draper, and his wife Rachel, who had himself been an assistant in a draper's and grocer's shop, is reported in the final column of the entry dedicated to him as 'Gone to Trade'.

Two others during the course of the year also left, one other 'to trade' and one for no reported reason. In the case of eighteen of the twenty-two admitted in the first year, we have records of previous occupations. Five had been schoolmasters, three labourers, three drapers, one a carpenter, one a tailor, one a painter and one an attorney's copy writer. Two are reported as having had no previous occupation, 'being at school', and one, 'being deformed'. The admission of the latter is somewhat surprising in the light of the conditions drawn up in 1846 to govern the qualification of candidates as pupil teachers, which state that 'they ... must not be subject to any bodily infirmity likely to impair their usefulness'. The students at Trinity College, at that time, however, were not pupil teachers and the authorities of the College were not bound by these conditions. However, Thomas Davies, the young man referred to, has nothing recorded against his name in the column reserved for the appointments obtained by the students upon leaving College, although his brother, John Davies, admitted to the College on the same day as Thomas Davies, is reported as having taken an appointment at the National School in Pembrey, before later moving to Aberavon, 'near Neath' and then to north Wales.

The students varied widely in age, six were seventeen, twelve under the age of twenty and ten over twenty, one of whom was aged thirty-two.

By and large these men coped quite successfully with life in College. The entries in the admission book in this first year all appear to be in the hand of William Edmunds, the Vice-Principal, and he takes pleasure in recording their achievements, although from time to time his frustration at their failures shows through. Thus he reports on 8 December 1849:

> In asking Miles last night what case . . . 'three days' in 'and lodged us three days courteously' was, he said 'it was the case of Jonah'.

The Vice-Principal, as in any similar institution, had to deal with problems of discipline amongst this motley crew of students, as is shown in the entry for 29 October 1849:

> Had to make an example of one of the men in my class for telling an untruth (Jenkins). An enquiry going on about some dirt being thrown out of one of the bedroom windows.

The first Principal of the College was Revd William Reed, MA, later Canon Reed, who was appointed from his post as Principal of St John's College, York, of which he had also been the first Principal. The Vice-Principal (Revd William Edmunds) was appointed and the staff was completed by the appointment of a tutor, Mr Field. These three had charge of some forty men, although only twenty-two were admitted in the first year. Relationships between the staff were not easy, according to William Edmunds's diaries, and there was, in particular, some jealousy between him and Field who was also a graduate of Lampeter. The jealousy centred on Field's ambitions for preferment in the Church. On 15 February 1850 Edmunds records in his diary that the curate of St Peter's was leaving the parish. 'Will Field succeed him?', he writes; '*Amser a ddengys*' ('Time will tell'). Time does in fact tell for, after sundry entries in the mean time recording Field's reading of the services at St Peter's, he exclaims in an entry on 7 April, the first Sunday after Easter, 'Field, Curate of St Peter's, as I expected. Shall I ever be curate of any place? I sincerely hope I shall.'

His relationship with the Principal was also strained due, perhaps, to his own self-righteous attitude. Thus he wrote of the Principal on 9 October 1849, 'Don't like the familiar way of talking with the men as it gives rise to false notions of themselves and of their situation', and on 8 December 1849, 'Mr Reed and Mr Field seem to make a great noise with their classes but I cannot make out that they manage to teach much more than I do'.

Their disagreements extended to the organization of the College, as an entry for 8 February 1850 shows.

> Had a dispute with Mr Reed about the Library books. He thought it his duty to put certain books presented by J. Phillips Esq out of the way of the pupils in training. Among others he marked out Owen (a Nonconformist) on the Person of Christ and a collection of papers by Bickersteth—I cannot see that this is fair and proper at all.

And on 6 March: 'Had an argument with Mr Reed about giving the men instruction on school matters'.

These are interesting insights into the atmosphere of this small institution in its first years. Edmunds and Field would have had no preparation for their posts other than their studies at Lampeter and both were in their early twenties. Their responsibilities in the institution were primarily for the delivery of the curriculum, although it is evident that Edmunds had charge of the College during the Principal's absences. These he recorded assiduously with such entries as 'Mr Reed left for London by the Second Mail' (20 April) but, more telling, as 'Mr Reed very scarce', (9 May) 'Mr Reed not in school', (frequent entries) and again 'Mr Reed not in school—saw him in the evening—Rather dry and crusty I thought—Strange. Strange. I don't understand him at all.'

Unfortunately we do not know what effect these somewhat strained relationships between the staff had on the life of the institution as a whole. Were the students aware of their clashes of opinion and their jealousies? The diary adds human dimensions to the records of events which are available and enlivens the entries in the official registers of the time. Harsh though Edmunds's entries appear to be from time to time—and he clearly writes for his own record rather than for the information of others with entries such as

> Met a Mrs Saunders, the Misses Goode and the curate of St David's Church at Llanllwch—Hope I shall never stumble upon them again—

he seems to have been assiduous in his duties at the College. It is interesting to note that the Inspector, Revd B M Cowie, wrote to the Secretary of the Committee of Council on Education on 27 October 1866 to complain of a number of matters relating to the College but including the fact that

> there have been perpetual changes in the staff of teachers. There have been at least four, if not five, Vice-Principals since I have inspected the College, and corresponding changes in the Assistant Masters.

The Principal's reply is direct:

> One would have supposed that Mr Cowie had the means, if he had had the will or the industry, to have ascertained exactly the number of Vice Principals and Masters, whom he had inspected, without resorting to such a vague enumeration as four or five . . . In the eighteen years during which I have held my office, there have been six Vice Principals, and six Assistant Masters.

Five of the Vice-Principals, he points out,

> have held their offices upwards of three years on average, and resigned them either after they had obtained, or had the prospect of equal or better preferment.

We might ask, however, whether Mr Cowie had an inkling of some unhappiness or disagreement existing between the Principal and his staff.

Valuable as the diaries are in informing us of the human relationships within the College, they are, in educational terms, even more important in that they provide a detailed report of the curriculum of the College and of the response of the students to that curriculum. It is evident that the intention of the College was not merely to make the students proficient as teachers but also to provide them with a broad education. This is not far removed from the intention of present-day teacher education, with its dual concern for the professional development of the student as a teacher and his academic development within an institution of higher education. In this the College was fulfilling the wishes of the Committee of Council on Education as expressed in the guidance of Her Majesty's Inspectors. These are well expressed by the views of HMI Revd H. Moseley:

> I am not urging the change of any of the particular schemes or methods

of instruction, which may at any time have been compounded, although I believe that the students at such an institution should be conversant with all of them: I am simply insisting on the necessity of making teaching as an art the subject of study in a training college, in respect to each subject taught; in viewing each such subject under the double aspect, as that which is to become an element of the student's own knowledge, and as that which he is to be made capable of presenting under so simple a form, that it may become an element of the knowledge of a child. It is not the fact that a teacher knows too much which makes him unintelligible to the child but that he knows nothing which the child can comprehend or that he has never studied what he has to teach in the light in which a child can be made to comprehend it.

Revd Moseley inspected the teacher training at the South Wales and Monmouthshire College, arriving, according to Edmunds's diaries, on Friday, 2 May 1851. We need not be surprised in the light of what we know of the relationships between Mr Edmunds and the Principal that the entry for that day commences thus:

> A very fine day—Mr Reed in his class before any of us. The great event of this day is the visit of Mr Moseley—H M Inspector of Schools.

There is much of interest in the account of the inspection and it is important to note that Edmunds had the temerity to ask the Inspector

> to tell us something of more importance to us than anything—the criteria by which Inspectors judge of the lessons given in their presence.

The Inspector's advice at Carmarthen echoes his views expressed to the Committee of Council on Education quoted above. It was, as reported by Edmunds, that

> the first thing looked for, it appears, is that the teacher himself should possess a thorough knowledge of what he presumes to give a lesson upon. No one, said he emphatically, ought to have the presumption to stand before a class and teach them or pretend to teach them what he does not thoroughly know himself. Whatever noise a man may make, however confident he may be in his own mind, if he does not possess this, he falls short in one of the chief things required in a teacher.

The Inspector then went on to compare the educational arrangements made in this regard in America and Germany, praising in particular Germany where, he is quoted to have said,

> the German schoolmaster never dreams of standing before his scholars to give a lesson without previous preparation on every subject—however trifling it may appear.

This is a remarkable statement in the early days of teacher education on the importance of the academic development of potential teachers. Today the Council for the Accreditation of Teacher Education, with its insistence on a minimum of the equivalent of two years of academic study at a level of higher education within the B.Ed. degree, merely echoes Mr Moseley's emphasis on the importance of 'the student's own knowledge'.

The Inspector continued, in answer to Edmunds's question, to indicate that

> the second thing considered is the exposition or the delivery of the lesson—this should be given in small quantities and questioned upon at intervals after it has been given.

Mr Moseley, according to Mr Edmunds, compared this to a mother feeding a child with food:

> She gives the child a spoonful and waits till that has been swallowed [sic] (digested according to Mr Moseley) and so on . . . Such a lesson ought to be. This is a very difficult thing to do and is only acquired by hard study, perseverance and moral courage, but still it is attainable. It is very difficult for a teacher to restrain himself from dealing out more than his pupils are able to receive if he is well acquainted with the subject . . . Mr Moseley has seen teachers plaguing the children (he could not call it anything else) with questions and coaxing things out of them which they had never taught them—when he sees these men leaving their classes with an air of satisfaction he is ready to box their ears—care then must be taken that what has been imparted be carefully recalled and nothing else that none of the lesson be spilt, as he termed it. He compares mere questioning to shaking about an empty bag.

The teacher therefore, needs to have studied 'what he has to teach in the light in which a child can be made to comprehend it.' The Inspector was certainly consistent in the advice given on the processes of teacher training but we can also admire the way in which the Vice-Principal clearly understood and endorsed that advice. For a man who had had no experience of teaching and who had only recently taken up his post as a trainer of teachers, he had enthusiastically grasped the theory expounded and was eager to see it implemented at Carmarthen. This clear expression of the theory of the professional development of teachers and of their academic needs in relation to it and to their own broader education is particularly surprising to read only some four years after the introduction of the pupil-teacher system.

Edmunds, with some satisfaction, concludes this entry in his diary with the statement that 'the lesson given by Wm Thomas, in some degree, came up to the standard'. Later he wrote: 'Upon the whole the Inspector's visit passed off very well' but could not resist a personal observation that 'he is very rough in his manner. Speakes [*sic*] with a Northern accent. The word "whole" is pronounced "wole". He has an impairment in his speech.'

It is pleasing to learn here of the practice of the HMI of discussing with his colleagues the basis upon which the inspection was undertaken and what was required of them as teacher trainers. For Edmunds and Field in particular this would have been a very valuable piece of staff development.

In addition to the record of this particular inspection, the diary makes reference to visits by other Inspectors, particularly by the official College Inspector, Revd H. Longueville Jones. It is from the diary reports of these visits concerned mainly with the examination of the students that we get the best account of the organization of the college course and the curriculum taught. The students were examined in academic subjects and in their practical teaching. The curriculum extended to subjects such as history, scripture, geography, arithmetic, Latin, Greek, French, grammar, logic, English literature and industrial mechanics. In addition the students were set papers on school management. At the commencement of his inspection on 12 December 1849, Longueville Jones had enumerated for the benefit of the students the subjects which they had to pass and what the Privy Council deemed necessary 'before they can grant the lowest certificate of Merit'. At this point, Edmunds reports that

> he also made some equivocal remarks about the Welsh language which the men quite (mis)understood.

On the occasion of Longueville Jones's examination of the students two classes of boys were brought up from the Model School and there is an interesting reference in the report of the first day's examination which highlights the difficulty which pupils, and perhaps the students themselves, would have had with the use of the English language. On the first day of the examination, Edmunds reports that the children referred to 'the poles' as '*y polion*' in Welsh and the inspector shouted '*arall, arall*'. This was with regard to a lesson on the North and South Poles and Edmunds reports, with despair, that 'one said that the North Pole was Welsh'.

The examination of the students seemed to have progressed well on this occasion. Grammar, logic and English literature, according to Edmunds, were 'very creditably dealt with' but Edmunds had his disappointments, reporting that

> their subject was Euclid and that only. My class did not come off as well as I expected. Indeed some of them made a horrid botch of it.

The reference to the Model School provides a direct link with the present-day organization of teaching practice at the College, in as much as pupils of the present-day Model Voluntary Aided School, which is now located much nearer to the College, attend the College for lessons in the practice classroom on the campus where they are taught by the staff and students and where the lesson is observed by other students.

The Model School was established in 1849 expressly to provide the students of the College with a venue for teaching practice. It was organized on the basis of three departments according to the age and sex of the children, namely the infants' department, girls' department and the boys' department. The original school was occupied until 1987 and it is easy for those who knew the old school to imagine the scene in the middle years of the nineteenth century when as many as 350 children would occupy the confined spaces of the building, spaces which in the latter years provided for less than 100 pupils.

It was the pupil-teacher system which was used in the school and the College's records show that the school provided in later years a number of Queen's Scholars proceeding to the College.

The relationships between the College and the school in the early years were not easy, as Nigel Commins reports in his *History of the Model School*. He writes:

> There was clearly a sharp difference of opinion, even possibly professional and personal altercation between the first Master John Davies and the first College Principal Rev Wm Reed.

The difficulties seem to have arisen from an application in 1850 for the College to pay part of the Master's salary at the school. This the Principal was prepared to do only if

> a master had been appointed who shall be satisfactory to the Principal of the College and who shall have made suitable provision for enabling the students in training to practice there as teachers.

The Principal complained to the National Society about the school's inefficiency and eventually decided to keep students away from the school. A reference in Edmunds's diary for 2 May 1851 states, 'I understand that the inspector was not much pleased with the state of the school'. The Inspector referred to was Mr Moseley and doubtless the Principal would have made much of the observations of such an important visitor in his relations with the Master at the school.

So dissatisfied was the College that it proposed that a new model 'Middle School' be established on the College campus and asked the National Society to support this venture. Nigel Commins reports that the National Society's regional organizing master for schools was dispatched to the school and that the Committee of Council on Education sent its inspector for male training colleges to Carmarthen. The outcome was that the school had to bring its Boys' Department up to a standard acceptable to the College and it was also insisted upon that there should be unity between the College and school in the management of their affairs. This brought the two establishments much closer in their organization as was originally the intention when the Model School was founded. To facilitate this closer relationship the College was urged to appoint a Master of Method to its staff. The stipulations were supported by the threat that unless improvements were effected by December 1854, no more Queen's Scholars would be permitted to train at the College. Both the school and the College responded to the demands of the Committee of Council with alacrity and the Principal dropped his insistence that a Model 'Middle' School should be built on the campus.

In its initial years the College seems not to have had any serious problems in the recruitment of students although it was soon found that these could not be recruited exclusively from Wales. The first student from England, a man from Easingwold in Yorkshire, was admitted on 3 April 1849 and he was soon followed by one from Warminster and another from St Albans. It is surprising to see these English names appear amongst those of Welsh men in the very early entries of the admission book but despite competition from other Church of England colleges, the College seems to have been attractive to young men from England recommended by their parish clergy. By 1855, however, it became evident that the funds available for the purpose of maintaining the College were insufficient and there was a real possibility that the new institution would die in its infancy. A local committee was set up under the chairmanship of the then Bishop of St Davids, Dr Thirlwall, which undertook to carry on the work of the College for three years to attempt to secure it on a firmer financial basis. The Welsh Education Committee of the

National Society was appealed to and, from its special funds, contributed £600, and the National Society itself, from its general fund, contributed a further £100 per annum. The crisis had, however, been caused in part by the fact that the subscriptions for educational purposes in Wales made to the National Society had fallen from £2,500 to £1,675. In addition half of the latter sum was required by the National Society for educational purposes in north Wales. Under these circumstances the Welsh Education Committee found it necessary to cut back on spending in Carmarthen and to ask that a local committee be set up to administer the College and to raise what funds they could to support the grant given by the National Society.

An advertisement was placed in the Welsh press in November 1855 in an attempt to raise more money,

> trusting that when it is known that pecuniary aid is required, the inhabitants of the southern portion of the Principality will furnish it.

The appeal was sufficiently successful to allow the College to continue and for the Committee to remain in existence beyond the three years originally envisaged for it. The College survived the period of financial uncertainty between 1860 and 1875 which proved fatal to the existence of a number of the other training colleges. In fact, in 1856 the College invested in a new lecture room which was built in proximity to the Model School and in 1859 an architect was directed to prepare plans for the extension of the two wings of the College at a total cost of £3,199, only one pound short of exactly half of the cost of the original college in 1848. Additional kitchens were added, with a laundry, two classrooms and accommodation for two additional tutors. These, with the original building, proved adequate for the needs of the College until 1896. It was in the light of this moderate security, and in the knowledge of the sometimes traumatic early years of the institution, that HM Inspector Revd H. Longueville Jones could write:

> I am happy to be able to add from repeated personal inspection, and from public examination, that the intellectual condition of the students is highly satisfactory, reflecting, as I conceive, no small credit on the exertions and judgements of the officers of the Institution; and it may be fairly anticipated without any chance of disappointment that lasting and widespread good will be done to the cause of education throughout Wales by means of this Institution.

BIBLIOGRAPHY

Admissions Book, South Wales and Monmouthshire Training College 1848–1883.

C. G. Brown, *A Brief History of the South Wales and Monmouthshire Training College, Carmarthen* (Carmarthen, 1908).

N. Commins, *The History of the Model School* (Carmarthen, 1987).

W. Edmunds, Unpublished Diaries 1849–1852. (Edmunds was the first Vice-Principal of the South Wales and Monmouthshire Training College, Carmarthen 1849–54.)

T. Halliwell, *Trinity College, Carmarthen Year Book and Directory 1848–1948* (Carmarthen, 1952).

J. S. Maclure, *Educational Documents: England and Wales, 1816–1967* (2nd edition, London, 1968).

W. Read, *A Letter to the Lord President of the Committee of Council on Education in reply to the charges of the Revd B. M. Cowie MA HM Inspector of Training Schools, against the management of the South Wales and Monmouthshire Training College, Carmarthen; and to some observations and proceedings on the part of the Committee of Council on Education arising out of those charges* (London, 1867).

R. W. Rich, *Training Teachers in England and Wales during the Nineteenth Century* (Bath, 1972).

A Microcosm of the Interaction of Education and Society in Victorian Wales —the Conflict concerning the Education of Girls in Anglesey

W. GARETH EVANS

During the past thirty years, the history of education in England and Wales has been characterized by the study of educational developments in their sociological setting and the writing of social histories of education. There has been a conscious effort to avoid the social-blindness approach that tended to typify earlier histories of educational legislation and institutions divorced from their overall social context. It is recognized that educational developments do not occur in a social and political vacuum and can only be explained meaningfully in relation to the various political, economic and social factors at work in society at a particular time.[1] There has also been a quest for the utilization of history as a methodological basis for the contemporary study of education. Historical case studies relating to themes and problems such as the subjects of the curriculum, the complexity of curriculum change, the development of technical education, rural education, bilingualism, and the role of sexism and gender-stereotyping are seen as valuable for contemporary, empirical research. A 'sense of history' can inform judgement and underpin research into current educational policies and practices.[2]

For over three decades, students of educational history in Wales have been made aware of these methodological approaches through the pioneering work of Professor Roger Webster. Undergraduate studies in geography at University College of Wales, Aberystwyth imbued him with the philosophy and tradition of human geography established by Professors H. J. Fleure, C. Daryll Forde and E. G. Bowen which highlighted the many relationships between man and his environment. This interest was further consolidated by the sociological writings of Alwyn D. Rees and other scholars on life in the Welsh countryside and the research and writing in 1953 of an

MA thesis on rural life in Webster's native county—'Llanfihangelesceifiog: a study of a rural parish in Anglesey'. Six years later, the doctoral thesis—'The place of secondary education in Welsh society, 1800-1918'—rested on the premise that 'the essential preliminary to explain the development of secondary education is a study of the origin, nature and evolution of Welsh society'.[3] The interaction of education and society permeates the whole work. It marked a turning point in the academic study of Welsh educational history, and for over thirty years has provided generations of researchers with a fine working model. It is no surprise to find that this unpublished work is still one of the most regularly consulted theses in the National Library of Wales.

As well as establishing a valid methodological approach, the meticulous evaluation of primary sources, particularly the endowment and institutional files of endowed grammar schools and the records of the Endowed Schools Commissioners, the Charity Commission, the Central Welsh Board and the Board of Education (Welsh Department) enhanced our knowledge of the rise of the modern education system in Wales. The Aberdare Report of 1881, the Welsh Intermediate and Technical Education Act of 1889, the development of higher grade and intermediate schools as well as the curricular theories of O. M. Edwards were given special attention.

More recently, as befitted the holder of the Chair of Education once filled also by Professors Foster Watson and Jac L. Williams, the importance of infusing a deeper understanding of the educational problems and issues of contemporary Wales through a greater awareness of the historical perspective, generated on-going initiatives concerning curriculum history, bilingualism, rural schools and the education of girls and women. In 1981, drawing on his unrivalled knowledge of education in Victorian Wales and aware of the growing interest in the feminine dimensions of education, Roger Webster encouraged the present writer's research into the quest for secondary and higher education for girls and women in nineteenth- and early twentieth-century Wales.[4]

Every generation rewrites its history. In recent years, numerous books and articles have highlighted the remarkable growth of the study of women's history in Europe and in the United States.[5] In Wales, also, there has been an increasing awareness of the neglect of women's history.[6] The recovery of women's history is making a significant contribution towards restructuring the historical record in its totality.[7] There now exists a dynamic and wide-ranging field of research which seeks to put women back into the historical record. Those who have been described as 'hidden from history' are 'becoming visible'.[8] Currently, there is much academic debate concerning questions of method, data and objectives.[9] Much of the earlier work was closely associated with labour history and made a significant contribution towards broadening the perspectives of working-class women. Their involvement in the Chartist and Labour movements has been highlighted. It has been shown that women's exclusion from the vote was merely the most well-known form of inequality in Victorian Britain. The widening compass of women's history is currently focusing attention on the hitherto neglected themes of the family, marriage, motherhood, domesticity, sexuality, the doctrine of separate spheres, the law and education.[10] Some prominent women such as Emily Davies and Lady Charlotte Guest have been the subject of revisionist biographies whilst other recent research has exploded as myth the long-held view of the nineteenth century as the age of the inevitable and unbroken march of women from the dark ages of total subjection to the daylight of liberation.[11]

The neglect of women's education was a major cause as well as a symptom of their subjection in Victorian Wales. Gradually from the 1870s, a struggle developed to secure a fairer educational deal for girls and women in Victorian and Edwardian Wales. The attempted reform of educational endowments through the agency of the Endowed Schools Commission and the Charity Commission in the 1870s and 1880s marked a significant stage in the increasingly vigorous movement for female emancipation during the late Victorian era.

In August 1878, the *Western Mail* published an optimistic letter from Dr Frances Hoggan[12] concerning the reform of endowments for the education of girls:

> . . . Where, however, their aid is involved, the Commissioners always consider carefully in the first instance, before diverting money from its original purpose, whether it is not possible so to extend its application as to meet what they might reasonably suppose would be the wishes of the donors if they were alive . . . In some instances they have thought fit to recommend that girls should share in the endowments which had become excessive for the needs of boys, or which had been used for the exclusive benefit of boys, contrary to the intentions of the founders.[13]

The Endowed Schools' Act of 1869, and the establishment of the

Endowed Schools Commission which functioned until 1874, initiated a period of reform of school endowments which was continued thereafter by the Charity Commission.[14] Under Section 12 of the 1869 Act, the Commissioners were empowered to utilize endowments of the old grammar schools to establish schools for girls.[15] Though there was much opposition from existing boys' schools and certain localities such as Anglesey in 1871-2 and again in 1878 over the proposal to reorganize the David Hughes' Charity at Beaumaris which included provision for girls, approximately ninety girls' schools were established under the Endowed Schools Act in England and Wales.

The Endowed Schools' Commissioners, in the period 1869-74, and the Charity Commission thereafter, undertook important investigations of educational charities in England and Wales. In Wales, thirteen schemes were introduced between 1869 and 1874 but only six were successful, primarily because of religious opposition.[16] The attempts at the reform of endowments in Wales in the 1870s had not been primarily concerned with the provision of girls' education. The main obstacle facing the Commissioners was the religious division in the Welsh community and the associated question of control of the schools. Eleven schemes were introduced between 1874 and 1880 and the Charity Commission were successful with nine.

Following the Aberdare Report of 1881, and anticipating legislation for intermediate education, the Charity Commission were comparatively inactive in Wales in the 1880s. But by 1889, tired of waiting for a Welsh Intermediate Education Bill, they had published schemes for the reorganization of Abergavenny Grammar School, Jones' School, Monmouth, and Tasker's School, Haverfordwest.

Though it would be a misinterpretation of the work of the Commissioners in Wales to maintain that the educational interests of girls were the main focus of attention, the decisions taken were of importance for the future patterns of girls' education in the Principality. The inquiries also exerted an impact on public opinion.

In north Wales, there was much dissatisfaction with the endowed grammar schools at Bangor and Beaumaris. Friars' School, Bangor, was closed in 1866 for six years because of lack of funds, the failings of the headmaster, and insufficient numbers of pupils:

> ... Yn y blynyddoedd a aethant heibio cynnyrchodd anghyfiawnder Ysgol y Friars ddigofaint aruthrol ym mhlith trigolion Bangor.[17]

(In the years that went by, the injustice of Friars School produced indignation amongst the inhabitants of Bangor.)

Beaumaris Grammar School, with its lack of 'commercial' education, had little appeal to the local population, and its clientele was primarily non-local. It was not regarded as fulfilling its real purpose. It was perceived as a boarding school, offering a classical education similar to the schools of southern England. Only one or two pupils from Anglesey were enrolled.[18] There were allegations of misuse of the David Hughes Charity for twenty-one years—that it had merely served the purpose of enriching headmasters who gave instruction to English and Irish boys, who had no claims whatsoever to the benefits of the trust:

> . . . Through disregard of the rules laid down in the will of the founder, and through the Charity having been long in the hands of one party, the school of late years, instead of serving to provide for the education of poor Anglican youths, has tended to become more and more a boarding school on the model of great classical schools of the South of England.[19]

Having ascertained the situation on both sides of the Menai Straits, the Endowed Schools Commission proposed a scheme in April 1870 to amalgamate both endowments so as to establish a large, efficient boys' school for both counties, located at Bangor, rather than two rival schools. Bangor was the preferred location because it possessed a better site. The Beaumaris building could not accommodate 140 boys. But the Endowed Schools Commission, though 'uncertain about the condition of female education now' had also borne in mind that under the Endowed Schools Act of 1869, they were obliged as far as they could, to make provision for the education of girls. '. . . They considered that in Wales, and in these parts especially, there is not a provision for the education of girls which one would have desired to see.'[20]

Consequently, it was proposed that the school building at Beaumaris be converted into a school for approximately forty girls. It would be 'of a similar character to the boys' school' and 'subservient to the interests of the same class of parents'. Boys who would otherwise have enrolled there would be given free scholarships to the new school at Bangor.[21] It was now hoped to attract to Beaumaris the daughters of professional men, clergymen, farmers and tradesmen of Anglesey and Caernarfonshire. The scheme required the initial approval of the governing bodies, and objections would be considered. Eventually, the scheme would have to be approved by Parliament.

When the proposals were first revealed at a meeting in Bangor on 13 April 1870, they were, unsurprisingly, welcomed. The main interest focused on the arrangements for boys' education which were viewed in terms of the founding of 'a Harrow or Rugby for North Wales'.[22] But the significance of the proposal for girls' education was also much appreciated:

> ... One of the greatest boons ever had by Wales would be to have a girls' school established at Beaumaris ... Great difficulty was now found in obtaining girls' education in Wales; there were few schools of that class in the Principality.[23]

It was felt that there was no girls' school of the proposed standard nearer than Howell's at Denbigh and 'that was not so open as this would be'.[24] The *Carnarvon and Denbigh Herald*, which viewed the proposed girls' school as compensation to Beaumaris for the loss of its boys' school, welcomed the whole scheme as conferring '... the greatest education boon on North Wales that it has ever received'.[25]

In Anglesey, however, there was immediate opposition to the proposals. On 14 April 1870, in a meeting at Llangefni 'with influential gentlemen', J. L. Hammond, the Assistant Charity Commissioner, said that the feoffees of Beaumaris School had, by resolution, declared that they had no objection in principle, though they wanted to ascertain the feelings of the inhabitants of the island before giving a definite answer. Nevertheless, it was clear that there was strong opposition to the removal of the David Hughes Charity from Anglesey. A girls' school was seen as a doubtful benefit: '... the proposed girls' school at Beaumaris which seems to be thrown in as a sop to the inhabitants of Anglesey to console them for the loss of David Hughes' endowments must also be regarded as an experiment'.[26]

On 28 April 1870, a public meeting purporting to represent the whole county was held at Llangefni and voiced its unanimous opposition to the removal of the David Hughes Charity from Anglesey. It was argued that it ought to be reorganized in accordance with the wishes of the island, and a County Committee of thirty-six, representing Anglicans and Nonconformists, was formed to safeguard the interests of the inhabitants. There were further protest meetings in the county, and resolutions sent to the Endowed Schools Commission.

On 5 July 1870, at a public meeting at Beaumaris, Assistant Commissioner J. L. Hammond endeavoured to justify the proposal to convert the existing building in the town into a girls' school for thirty to forty boarders, together with an unspecified number of day pupils. It was admitted that the Endowed Schools Commission regarded the proposed school as an 'experiment', and were as yet unclear regarding its precise nature: '. . . With regard to girls' education, the problem is so difficult, the want of experience is so great; that it is quite possible that this plan which must be an experiment may be a failure.'[27] But it was their considered judgement that they were duty-bound to provide for the education of girls as well as boys. They did acknowledge that a portion of the David Hughes endowment might be used to finance 'better modes of supplying this want' and their proposals were open to modification: '. . . if it is not the place for girls, and if it can be shown that the £250 can be utilised in a better way, the Commissioners might adopt another plan'.[28]

It was felt, however, that Beaumaris would be a most acceptable location for a girls' school. A 'retired spot' was needed for such an establishment. Beaumaris's remoteness and general characteristics made it very suitable, and it was deemed to be '. . . a significantly nice place for girls, as it was rather a fashionable and luxurious place, and a place where girls might be trusted to go about'.[29] The school buildings were most satisfactory, and significantly, in contrast with boys, the lack of a playground would cause no problems for a girls' school.

The meeting was unimpressed with this judgement, even more so when it was argued that Beaumaris was suitable for girls for the very reason that made it unfavourable as the location for a boys' school. Hammond claimed that suitable lodgings for boys were unavailable, and the town's four to five miles' distance from the nearest railway station was a major obstacle for a successful boys' school. On being pressed regarding the consultations held, Hammond admitted that he had been influenced by Sir Richard Williams-Bulkeley, but also by the trustees of the school, who had maintained that for financial reasons, the town's inhabitants would much prefer to take in visitors for the season rather than lodging boys all the year round for a small weekly sum.

A resolution was passed stating that the proposed scheme was 'unadvisable and impracticable'.[30] In the face of such opposition, and also aware that a school providing a sound commercial education at a reasonable charge was required in Anglesey, the Endowed Schools Commission now modified their scheme. It now incorporated a 'third-grade, middle-class, commercial school' offering a sound English education including modern languages, sciences, drawing and Latin, but not Greek. It would be partly supported by the David Hughes Charity and be conveniently located in a central position in Anglesey. Together with the schools at Botwnnog and Llanrwst, it would feed the first-class school for north-west Wales that would be located at Bangor. Part of the David Hughes endowment would now be deployed towards establishing first-class exhibitions for Anglesey boys enabling them to acquire free, or partially free, admission to the high-class school. Welcoming the proposals, the *Carnarvon and Denbigh Herald* said: 'We require a Rugby or a Harrow in North Wales'.[31] Hammond was now contemplating the educational reorganization of the whole of north Wales on the basis of eastern and western divisions, with a first-grade school in each, which would be associated with lower-grade schools through scholarships or exhibitions financed from their endowments.

However, secondary education for girls remained an integral part of this amended plan. When he revealed his changed plans, Hammond made it clear that '. . . on this, the Commissioners considered themselves morally, if not legally bound'.[32] It was still felt that the adoption of the Beaumaris school and its financing from the David Hughes Charity would provide the most economical and desirable arrangement. In spite of doubt being cast upon the logic of this argument, the Assistant Commissioner insisted that, though Beaumaris's remoteness from a railway station was a drawback for a boys' school, it was not the case as regards a girls' school. Revealing a perception of feminity steeped in Victorian social conventions and morality, he argued:

> . . . The question of girls' education was a difficult one, and they had no experience upon it, although they knew something about boys'. The most sanguine reformer of girls' education was not able to say what the future would be. It seemed that a secluded place was rather better for a girls' school than a largely populated place . . . The commissioners rather looked at Beaumaris as a place corresponding in some way to Bath, Cheltenham and Brighton: a rather refined population, an extremely pleasant town . . . where girls could walk about without any fearful rudeness being exhibited to them. Beaumaris was a place where people might be induced to reside for the advantages of female education, and the commissioners were not without hopes that the school

would have a larger number of girls even as day scholars than it has had of boys of late.[33]

Though the amended proposals were more favourably received, there was still opposition, particularly to the deployment of part of the charity outside the county of Anglesey. On 16 July 1870, at their annual meeting, the Anglesey Baptists passed a resolution claiming that the income of the David Hughes Charity, which amounted almost to £1,000 per annum, was quite sufficient to maintain a first-class classical and commercial school on Anglesey. Opinion seemed divided regarding the feasibility of a girls' school at Beaumaris, but there was no outright opposition to the principle of secondary education for girls. It was seen by one observer as a welcome alternative to having one's daughters educated away from home in Cheshire and by another as 'a great boon to North Wales and the commencement of a new era in education'.[34]

As yet, no formal scheme had been drafted. The situation was changed in August 1870 when Robert Davies, a wealthy timber merchant, and chairman of the County Committee, announced that, in order to retain the David Hughes Charity '. . . in the county which the donor intended it',[35] he would subscribe £2,000 to enlarge the Beaumaris School if the Endowed Schools Commission chose it as the site for a first-grade boys' school. But if they decided it would be more advantageous to move it to another location in Anglesey, he would donate £5,000. It was stipulated that the school, where fees would be moderate, would be controlled by a popularly elected governing body. The offer was welcomed in various meetings throughout Anglesey.[36] Significantly, there had been no reference to the implications for girls. The main concern was the retention of a school of status on the island.

The Endowed Schools Commission now reconsidered the position. In a meeting with Hammond, Davies questioned the expediency of establishing a girls' school, though he thought that the David Hughes Charity would not be violated if such an institution were located in Anglesey. Hammond revisited the area and found very little local interest in the proposal to establish a girls' school. Eventually, on 13 July 1871, the Endowed Schools Commission published their draft scheme concerning Beaumaris Grammar School and the David Hughes Charity.[37]

It was made clear that 'the general object of the scheme is to supply a liberal and practical education to both boys and girls by means of schools in Anglesey'. A new governing body of fifteen members—two ex-officio, six representative, seven co-opted—was to see that a new boys' school for 150 was located at a convenient spot in the county, whilst the Beaumaris school was to be converted into a girls' school for day pupils and boarders. No girl under eight years would be admitted, and the tuition fee would range from £3 to £8. Exhibitions would be available. In both schools, the curriculum would include reading, spelling, writing, arithmetic, English grammar and composition, literature, history (ancient and modern), geography, politics, physical training, drawing, vocal music, natural science, Latin and French. Whilst the boys' school would also offer maths, mensuration and land surveying, in the girls' school elements of algebra and geometry, instrumental music, domestic economy, laws of health, and needlework would be offered. There could be further differentiation, with Greek and German taught in the senior department of the boys's school, and other modern languages besides French might be available in the girls' school.

Reactions to the scheme were somewhat predictable. Attention focused primarily on the composition of the governing body. In general, Nonconformists were favourable to the scheme, though their failure to persuade the Endowed Schools Commission to increase the number of co-optive members caused a reluctant Davies to retract his offer.[38] The Anglican party were particularly critical of the omission of the Bishop from the scheme and objected to what they regarded as an Anglican school being 'taken out of the hands of the Church'. The feoffees of Beaumaris School also viewed the scheme as a charter for Nonconformist control. But they also objected to the proposed conversion to a girls' school. Not only was the whole of the David Hughes Charity needed for a boys' school, but a girls' school at Beaumaris was not required:

> ... There is no question that, to say the least, a considerable part of the parents who might otherwise be expected to use the school, and wish to give their daughters a sound education would prefer to give it them in England where they may mix with English girls, imbibe new ideas and get rid of their Welsh accent ... There exists no kind of general desire or wish in the county for such a school for girls.[39]

Others also doubted the viability of a girls' secondary school. In otherwise supportive editorials praising the liberal spirit of the scheme and the recognition of the preponderance of Nonconformists in Anglesey, the *Carnarvon and Denbigh Herald* commented:

'... Let us hope that this part of the scheme will not turn out a failure.'[40]

The scheme was approved by the Education Department on 29 April 1872. However, opposition still continued, particularly from the feoffees of Beaumaris School and the Bangor Diocesan Congress, whose petitions against the scheme were presented to the House of Lords on 26 July 1872 by Bishop Campbell of Bangor.[41] The exclusion of the Diocesan from the governing body, which was claimed to be contrary to the will of David Hughes, was the main area of contention. But it was also a time of legal controversy regarding the interpretation of Section 17 of the Endowed Schools Act. It had been interpreted by the Endowed Schools Commission as excluding clerics from *ex-officio* membership of the governing bodies of endowed schools. In moving an address in the House of Lords to Her Majesty to refuse her assent to the scheme, the Bishop voiced his objections to the exclusion of the Diocesan Bishop from an *ex-officio* appointment to the governing body and he also objected to the removal of the boys' school from Beaumaris. After a short debate, in which the Marquess of Salisbury said that the 1869 Act was not intended to be '... the instrument of a system of Dissenting raids upon the Church of England endowments', the motion was carried by 65 votes to 50. Significantly, there was no reference to the education of girls in that debate.[42] In Anglesey, the rejoicing of Anglicans was accompanied by some protest but mainly a surprising acquiescence by Nonconformists in a 'fait accompli'.[43]

Five years were to elapse before the arrangements for secondary education in Anglesey were subject to further investigation. Since 1874, the duties of the Endowed Schools Commissioners had been transferred back to the Charity Commission and it was their Assistant Commissioner, R. Durnford, who in October 1877 visited Beaumaris to ascertain the condition of the school and the attitudes of the feoffees.[44]

Durnford told them that the transfer of the school to Holyhead, and the conversion of the existing Beaumaris Grammar School into a girls' school needed to be considered. He was advised by Dr Briscoe, Vicar of Holyhead, that Beaumaris would be a suitable location for a girls' school. It was 'much wanted in the district', with many girls obliged to attend schools as far away as Chester. However, there was no consensus, and the feoffees were opposed to the transfer of the grammar school to Holyhead. He was also told that it was premature to convert the existing grammar school into a girls' school, but the feoffees did favour a girls' school at Beaumaris.

Deliberately avoiding lengthy discussions and agitation, Durnford advised the immediate publication of a new scheme. A new draft *Scheme* was published by March 1878, proposing the erection of a new school for 150 boys at Holyhead and the use of the buildings at Beaumaris for a girls' school or its location in any other suitable building provided by the governors. The governing body would include, amongst others, the Bishop, the Mayor of Beaumaris and the two local Members of Parliament and three women appointed for five years.[45] At the girls' school, the tuition fees were to be in the £4–10 range instead of £3–8 as in the 1871 scheme. Scholarships, in the form of total or partial exemptions from payment of tuition fees, were to be available for up to 10 per cent of the girls attending the school.[46] The headmistress would be paid a stipend of £100 per annum together with a capitation payment of not less than £2 per pupil.

The main reaction focused on the proposed transfer to Holyhead. At a public meeting in Beaumaris on 26 March 1878, strong opposition was registered.[47] At Holyhead, there was enthusiastic support for the proposal to locate the boys' grammar school there. In particular, it was maintained that it enjoyed excellent communications with Beaumaris, where a boys' school was unlikely to flourish within such a short distance of another grammar school at Bangor.[48]

Though the protagonists were primarily concerned with the location of a first-grade school for boys, the education of girls inevitably figured in the deliberations. Though some showed little sympathy towards female education, and claimed that to substitute a girls' school was contrary to the will of the founder, there appeared to be no evidence of outright hostility to the principle of educating girls. Dr Orme, headmaster of Beaumaris Grammar School, said '. . . assuming that it is desirable to make the experiment of a girls' school at Beaumaris, there would be little difficulty in finding suitable premises. Some masters at the grammar school could service it.' In an editorial on 6 April 1878, the *Carnarvon and Denbigh Herald* showed considerable support and responded to the criticisms voiced in a most enlightened manner:

> . . . We may dismiss the objection founded on the silence of the testator as to girls because in the sixteenth century, the education of women was something more than neglected, and was not the object of charitable

dispositions. The commissioners are expressly directed by statute to extend to girls the benefits of endowments . . . an extension, the propriety of which, seeing that there is no school for girls either in Anglesey or in Caernarvonshire, no reasonable being will contest. If a Girls' School may be expected to supply a want long felt, and to stimulate a desire to afford to girls a higher and a better education than what they now receive, that is so much to the credit of the new scheme as contrasted with the present.[49]

The Charity Commission responded to the situation in February 1879 by modifying the scheme through giving the governing body the role of choosing the site for the boys' school. However, the feoffees demanded that the boys' school should remain at Beaumaris for at least five years, during which period a girls' school might be established at Menai Bridge.[50] Following another visit by Durnford to Beaumaris, the feoffees' proposals were accepted by the Charity Commission, and embodied in the scheme finally approved and submitted to the Education Department on 4 May 1880.

Strong disapproval was voiced by supporters of Holyhead concerning the location of the boys' school in Beaumaris,[51] and also by the Beaumaris feoffees concerning various parts of the scheme.[52] But there was no recorded opposition to the proposed girls' school because of a lack of convenient access to the railway station. By the summer of 1880, in the face of growing pressure from Welsh Members of Parliament, Gladstone's government was about to instigate an all-Wales inquiry into the condition of intermediate and higher education in Wales—the Aberdare Inquiry. In these circumstances, action concerning the scheme for secondary education in Anglesey was deferred. By then, the Charity Commission had advised that separate boys' and girls' schools at Beaumaris were not financially feasible. The need for a more centrally located boys' school, and a girls' school either at Beaumaris or at Menai Bridge, were to be recommended in the Aberdare Report. But another decade and a half were to elapse before provision was made for girls' secondary education—in dual schools at Beaumaris, Llangefni and Holyhead —in the arrangements for intermediate education in Anglesey in 1894.[53]

Though the proposed reforms of the David Hughes Charity and Howell's Charity proved unsuccessful, the establishment of the Dr Williams' School at Dolgellau in 1878, and the changes introduced in the case of Tasker's Charity at Haverfordwest, Jones' Charity at

Monmouth, and Lewis School Pengam, were to have a significant effect on girls' secondary education in Wales.

It is also true that the reform of endowments in the 1870s and 1880s made a greater impact on girls' education in England than in Wales. Addressing the first meeting of the newly established 'Association for Promoting the Education of Girls in Wales', at Cardiff in January 1887, Douglas C. Richmond, Charity Commissioner, noted that in sixteen years, eighteen intermediate or higher girls' schools with endowments had been established in London and thirty-nine in other parts of the country, but only two in Wales. Whilst recognizing the importance of the Endowed Schools Act of 1869 in activating the reform of endowments, he also acknowledged that

> ... it was like offering to the girls crumbs falling from the boys' table, but a good deal was being effected in that way little by little.[54]

The failure to provide equal educational opportunities for girls in Anglesey in the 1870s highlighted the many impediments in Welsh society—prevailing perceptions of femininity, tradition, conservatism and prejudice—which exerted a profound influence on the campaign for a fairer educational deal and female emancipation in late Victorian Wales.

REFERENCES

1. J. W. Tibble (ed.), *The Study of Education* (London, 1966); Ivor E. Goodson (ed.), *Social Histories of the Secondary Curriculum: Subjects for Study* (London, 1985).
2. Lawrence Stenhouse, 'Case study and case records: towards a contemporary history of education', *British Educational Research Journal*, 4 No. 2 (1978), 21–39.
3. J. R. Webster, 'The place of secondary education in Welsh society, 1800–1918' (University of Wales Ph.D. thesis, 1959).
4. W. Gareth Evans, *Education and Female Emancipation: The Welsh Experience 1847–1914* (Cardiff, 1990).
5. B. S. Anderson and J. P. Zinser, *A History of Their Own: Women in Europe from Prehistory to the Present*, 2 vols. (London, 1988); Robin Morgan (ed.), *The International Women's Movement Anthology: Sisterhood is Global* (London, 1985).
6. Deirdre Beddoe, *Discovering Women's History* (London, 1983); idem, *Women between the Wars, 1918–1939* (London, 1989); Angela John, *By the Sweat of their Brow: Women Workers at Victorian Coal-Mines* (London, 1980).

7. R. J. Evans, *The Feminists* (London, 1977); M. Vicinus, *Women in English Social History 1800–1914* (London, 1987).
8. R. Bridenthal and C. Koong (ed.), *Becoming Visible: Women in European History* (Boston, 1988); Dale Spender, *Invisible Women* (London, 1982); Sheila Rowbotham, *Hidden from History* (London, 1983).
9. Aringa Angerman (ed.), *Current Issues in Women's History* (London, 1989); Jane Rendall, 'Women's history: beyond the cage?', *History*, 75 No. 243 (February 1990), 63–72.
10. M. Vicinus (ed.), *A Widening Sphere: Changing Roles of Victorian Women* (Indiana, 1977); Carol Dyhouse, *Feminism and the Family in England 1880–1939* (London, 1989); Susan Mendus and Jane Rendall (eds.), *Sexuality and Subordination* (London, 1989).
11. Daphne Bennett, *Emily Davies and the Liberation of Women* (London, 1990); Revel Guest and Angela V. John, *Lady Charlotte* (London, 1989); Patricia Phillips, *The Scientific Lady: A Social History of Women's Scientific Interests 1520–1918* (London, 1991); Sylvia Ann Hewlett, *A Lesser Life: The Myth of Woman's Liberation* (London, 1987).
12. The first Welsh and the second British woman to graduate in medicine, she was a leading supporter of the women's cause in the 1870s and 1880s.
13. *Western Mail*, 20 August 1878.
14. Peter Gordon, *Selection for Secondary Education* (London, 1980).
15. *Carnarvon and Denbigh Herald*, 16 April 1870.
16. Webster, op. cit., 289.
17. *Baner ac Amserau Cymru*, 27 April 1870; H. Barber and H. Lewis, *The History of Friars' School* (Bangor, 1901).
18. Ibid.
19. *Carnarvon and Denbigh Herald*, 12 June 1880.
20. Ibid., 16 April 1870.
21. Ibid.
22. Editorial, *North Wales Chronicle*, 16 April 1870.
23. Ibid., quoting Mr Lloyd Jones.
24. Ibid., quoting Mr Douglas.
25. Ibid.
26. Letter from J. Ll. Griffith, Holyhead, in *Carnarvon and Denbigh Herald*, 23 April 1870.
27. *Carnarvon and Denbigh Herald*, 9 July 1870.
28. Ibid.
29. Ibid.
30. Ibid.
31. Editorial, ibid., 23 July 1870.
32. Ibid., 16 July 1870.
33. Ibid.
34. Ibid., 23 July 1870.
35. *North Wales Chronicle*, 20 August 1870.
36. D. Pretty, *Two Centuries of Anglesey Schools* (Llangefni, 1977), 271.
37. *Carnarvon and Denbigh Herald*, 20 July 1871.

38. Pretty, op. cit., 273–4.
39. PRO Ed. 27/6287: letter, 25 October 1871.
40. *Carnarvon and Denbigh Herald*, 22 July 1871. See also 16 September 1871.
41. Pretty, op. cit., 274.
42. *The Times*, 26 July 1872.
43. Pretty, op. cit., 275.
44. Ibid., PRO Ed. 27/6290: R. Durnford's report, 18 November 1877.
45. *North Wales Chronicle*, 30 March 1878; *Carnarvon and Denbigh Herald*, 23 March 1878.
46. *Carnarvon and Denbigh Herald*, 6 April 1878.
47. Pretty, op. cit., 278.
48. Editorial, *Carnarvon and Denbigh Herald*, 6 April 1878.
49. 6 April 1878.
50. PRO Ed. 27/6290: letter from feoffees.
51. Pretty, op. cit., 280–1.
52. PRO Ed. 27/6291: letter from feoffees.
53. PRO Ed. 27/6290.
54. *Western Mail*, 18 January 1887.

Dr J. J. Findlay, First Headmaster of Cardiff Intermediate School for Boys, 1898–1903: Instinctive Traditionalist or Enterprising Empiricist?

RON BROOKS

'The first headmaster of the Cardiff Intermediate School for Boys', wrote J. R. Webster in 1959,[1] 'was J. J. Findlay, a great admirer of Thomas Arnold and the Public School system. His ambition was to create at Cardiff a Public School for day boys.' Subsequent studies[2] of the implementation in Cardiff of the Welsh Intermediate Education Act of 1889 have confirmed the disparity between the wishes of some of its authors that 'schemes should be ambitious, comprehensive, (and) expansive',[3] and Findlay's narrow interpretation of his task. They also generally agree that Findlay's conservative approach to implementing the Act was largely the inevitable and expected outcome of his years as a teacher in some of England's most prestigious public and proprietary schools.[4] This essay aims to take the study of Findlay's years at Cardiff further by showing that his 'traditionalism' was sometimes more profound but always less instinctive than has hitherto been supposed. It was more profound in that, in addition to imposing the public-school model on intermediate education in Cardiff, he gave full and active support in *The Times*[5] and elsewhere to the essential feature of the class-based education system, what J. R. Webster terms 'the principle of grading schools according to their curriculum, fees and leaving age'.[6] He showed himself as anxious to use this principle to distinguish Cardiff's intermediate schools from their chief rivals, the higher grade schools, as he was to use it to assert the position of Cardiff Intermediate School for Boys as a first-grade school within the intermediate sector.

But more important than the issue of whether Findlay was more or less 'traditionalist' than is commonly supposed is that of the very nature of his approach to educational reform. The few friends who knew of his involvement in other educational experiments while he was at Cardiff would scarcely have seen him as a 'traditionalist' at all. During his Cardiff headship he helped to inaugurate elsewhere in Britain reform movements which were openly opposed to the kind of education which he was vigorously introducing into his own school. In the period from 1897 to 1903, he was employed by the independent progressive school movement in Hampstead, north London, and by the garden city education movement at Letchworth, Hertfordshire, as an educational consultant to devise radically different schemes of education from those on offer in the traditional public school and in the emerging state sector.

This was not simply a case of a person who failed to practise at Cardiff what he preached at Hampstead and Letchworth. The schemes which he carefully devised for the Hampstead and Letchworth experiments took fully into account the requirements of the commissioning body and the expectations of the social groups which they were intended to serve. His contribution to the first Welsh experiment in secondary education was no exception; the only difference was that his task at Cardiff Intermediate School for Boys was more carefully defined. The Welsh Intermediate Education Act laid down what an 'intermediate education' should consist of, and an intensely class-conscious Cardiff insisted on its implementation within a public-school model. Findlay was appointed headmaster in the face of stiff competition precisely because he seemed best suited for that task. But from Findlay's point of view, as this essay aims to show, it gave him another opportunity to engage in a practical, educational experiment, albeit of a very different kind from those at Hampstead and Letchworth.

Findlay and the King Alfred School Society, Hampstead

At the time of his interview for the Cardiff headship, Findlay was not anxious to publicize his contribution to other reform movements, except, that is, for his service in 1894 and 1895 on the Bryce Commission which recommended the introduction in England of the kind of secondary education which the Welsh Intermediate Education Act of 1889 had provided in Wales. Prior to moving to Wales in the late summer of 1898, he was a lecturer in the College of Preceptors in London, where he, and his wife who had previously trained student teachers in Froebelian techniques in Sheffield, became involved in the independent progressive school movement. They were drawn, in particular, into the work of a small group of Hampstead intellectual grandees who intended to set up a secular society whose aim was to found a number of 'rational schools' in which examinations and punishments were banned, in which 'bookish education' and 'separate subjects' were reduced, where the manual arts and integrated subjects were promoted and where individuality and all-round character were developed through the 'scientific study of child nature'.[7] There was to be no religious teaching of any kind. The preliminary circular for the Society, which Findlay in 1898 was officially to name the King Alfred School Society because of the approaching millennial celebration of King Alfred's death,[8] stated clearly that it intended to offer an alternative form of education to that found in the developing 'High Schools and Private Schools' which were 'out of touch with the broader and healthier views of the training of children that science and the scientific study of child-nature have roused'.[9] The society was, in many ways, an offshoot of the Ethical Union and the Moral Instruction League which was set up in London in 1897 (in the same year as the King Alfred School Society was launched), 'to substitute systematic non-theological moral instruction for the present religious teaching in all State schools, and to make character the chief aim of school life'.[10] The London School Board was their chief object of attack. It was natural for Findlay as lecturer and researcher in educational theory and practice at the College of Preceptors to become involved in these London-based movements. But what was an achievement in curriculum reform and design for a London college lecturer in the winter of 1897 and the early spring of 1898 could become a potential embarrassment to an aspiring Cardiff headmaster in the late spring and summer of 1898.

Part of Findlay's achievement in London lay in helping to establish the independence of the Society from state interference so that it could, in the words of the Memorandum of Association and Incorporation,

> establish and carry on schools to give practical expression to the best theories extant, and particularly to the theories enunciated by educational reformers, such as Pestalozzi, Froebel, Herbert Spencer, Louis Compton Miall[11] and others working on similar lines.[12]

Given that a few years earlier the Bryce Commission, upon which

Findlay had served, had recommended the setting up of state secondary schools, the Society believed that its independent status would enable it to pioneer new aims and teaching methods to serve as a possible model for them. 'In view of secondary education soon coming further under state organisation', wrote Findlay in a note appended to the 1898 Society prospectus, 'the King Alfred School Society is anxious to have many of its schools established to demonstrate the great advantages of reform.'[13]

Findlay's greatest contribution to the work of the Society was to devise a novel curriculum for its first, and as it turned out, its only school in Hampstead. His 'concentrated curriculum', part of which is reproduced below, stands in marked contrast with that which he pioneered in Cardiff. He was greatly influenced in its design by the wishes of the founders of the movement, who included Cecil Sharp, Principal of the Hampstead Conservatoire of Music, Sir Hamo Thornycroft, a distinguished sculptor of the age, Alice Mullins, wife of another sculptor Roscoe Mullins, Isobel White Wallis, wife of E. White Wallis, a distinguished scientist, and F. W. Miall, a journalist and brother of Professor L. C. Miall, biologist and educational reformer of Leeds. Graham Wallas,[14] Dr Michael Sadler,[15] Alice Woods,[16] and C. F. A. Voysey, the author of *Individuality*,[17] soon added their names to the list of those who 'sympathized' with the aims of the movement.

The curriculum which Findlay designed for the King Alfred School Society in 1897 combined six unusual features, many of which have survived to the present day. This resulted in a curriculum, to use the words of Amabel Williams-Ellis, the wife of Clough Williams-Ellis of Portmeirion, which was 'irregularly bold'.[18] Its first and essential characteristic was that it was 'a concentrated curriculum' based on an 'areas-of-experience' model. The lengthy list given in the Memorandum of Association of educational innovators to whom the Society was indebted was reduced to two in Findlay's preliminary prospectus of December 1897; these were the two German philosophers, Herbart, whom he studied whilst at Jena and Leipzig and from whom he derived the notion of the concentration of studies, and Froebel, upon whose ideas he and his wife based their emphasis on experiential learning through observation and free expression. The influence of Herbart was seen in the curricular arrangement for older children of 'severe intellectual studies' being 'confined to morning lessons' with 'the older children returning in the afternoon for lighter occupations'.[19] The influence of Froebel was particularly evident in the education of children between four and nine in the stress on sense experience. A second characteristic of the Findlay curriculum, which accorded very much with the ideas of the founding fathers, was that there should be parity of status between all areas of experience. For example, Group C ('arts of expression in speech and music'), but especially Group D pursuits ('the manual arts'), were considered as important as Group A experiences (the study of humanities). Book learning was to take second place to 'practical work' where, for example, 'Geography would be studied through maps and plans of the locality and field work, and Geometry through surveying'.[20] History would involve field excursions. A third feature of the King Alfred School curriculum was its rejection of a subject-based model in favour of the co-ordination of studies by which it was said 'time is saved and interest strengthened'.[21] 'The studies in Literature and Geography are selected so as to help the lessons in History, in the same way the lessons in Science, Mathematics and Geography help each other and receive help from workshop occupations.'

These three distinctive features, which at the turn of this century challenged much contemporary practice in state and independent schools, were reinforced by three other, no less unconventional, characteristics, the rejection of examinations and of religious instruction, and a belief in the extension into the school life of the best practices of the home, including coeducation and parental involvement. The antipathy to examinations was expressed by Findlay's unambiguous statement in the prospectus that the Hampstead school 'intended to avoid the preparation of pupils for any entrance examinations and to minimise home lessons'. In any case, the rejection of the single-subject curricular model left few examinations for pupils to enter. One of the founders, Isobel White Wallis, explained the Society's fundamental objections to examinations. She rejected 'the great juggernaut of modern education, the examination craze which encouraged the medieval method of cramming with juiceless facts, names and dates'. But it was not simply to the effects of examinations on teaching methods that she objected.[22] Above all, 'by means of examinations, children are ground in a mill where individuality is repressed and where humanity is minted into pieces as like each other as the coinage'. The hand-written (rather than printed) school magazine, the 'Alfredian', joined in the chorus of

JUNIOR SCHOOL | Commencement of SENIOR SCHOOL

	EARLY CHILDHOOD (Kindergarten)	LATER CHILDHOOD	EARLY BOYHOOD OR GIRLHOOD
AGES	About 4, 5, 6	About 7, 8, 9	About 10, 11, 12
Group **A** — THE HUMANITIES (Story, History, Literature.)	Fables, simple stories *not* limited by time, space, or other sense experience. (Varying with the seasons and months of the year.)	Stories (from simple but classic literature) leading from Legends to authentic history, *e.g.*, The story of The Patriarchs, Ulysses, Norse Sagas, Robinson Crusoe; finally, The Settlement of England, St. Augustine, Alfred, Canute and Harold. The Story of the Exodus.	Great English Heroes and Kings from 1066 to 1700 and ending with the connections between French and English History. (Compare Groups **B**, **C**, **D**, below.) The Kings of Judah and Israel.
Group **B** — NATURE KNOWLEDGE (including Geography)	Collection and observation of all kinds of simple objects, related, week by week to the story in Group A.	Geography of England, beginning with that of the neighbourhood. Study of familiar animals and plants (associated partly with the life of our forefathers in the woods and fields of old England. See Group A). All examined at first hand from Nature, and classified in an elementary way.	Geography of France and S.W. Europe. Beginnings of Physiography and simple experiments in Physics (compare Columbus, Bacon, etc., connected with Group **A**).
Group **C** — ARTS OF EXPRESSION IN SPEECH AND IN MUSIC	Songs and Speech chiefly connected with the stories in Group A and the Nature Knowledge in Group **B**.	Reading and Writing and Tonic-Sol-fa singing commenced. The subject matter sought from Groups **A** and **B** chiefly. Simple Composition: oral and written.	English Reading, Writing, Composition continued. French commenced and made very prominent in the last year. The subject matter sought from Groups **A** and **B** chiefly. Singing.

Group **D** — ARTS OF REPRESENTATION AND OTHER MANUAL ARTS	The Kindergarten Gifts and Occupations: representing, in a variety of forms, objects from Groups **A** and **B** and other interests of the child.	The Kindergarten Gifts and Occupations continued and developed. Drawing from nature, etc. Subject matter from Group **A** and **B**. Gardening connected with the botany lessons.	Drawing, Modelling, &c., Gardening, Cardboard work, or Carpentry. Beginnings of Geometrical Drawings, Maps, Diagrams: All connected with Groups **A** and **B**. Drawing from nature and from Norman and Early English decoration to be found in the neighbourhood.
Group **E** — ABSTRACT SCIENCES NUMBER, FORM, LANGUAGE	Beginnings of Number—up to 10. Recognition of simple Geometrical Forms (according to Frœbel's doctrine)—all in the concrete from Group **B**.	Beginnings of Arithmetic. Number up to 100 or beyond. Geometrical ideas further developed—all in the concrete from Group **B**. First ideas of Theory of Music.	Number beyond 100. Ideas of time from History, of space from Geography. Definitions of Geometry. First ideas of Grammar, in French and English. Music continued.
Group **F** — RECREATION	Physical and Musical Drill. Kindergarten Games. Short walks. Free play between lessons.	Physical and Musical Drill. Continuation of Kindergarten games. *Short* excursions and walks (see Group **B**). Free play between lessons.	Physical and Musical Drill. School Games. *Short* excursions and walks (connected with Groups **A** and **B**). Free play between lessons.

Note—After 12 years of age a large number of hours per week will be given to Latin, if boys are entered with a view to proceeding to a Public School. The previous thorough pursuit of French will make the approach to a second foreign language far more easy. The French teaching will be planned so as to conduct the lessons *wholly in French*, as soon as possible.

The Curriculum as laid down in the Preliminary Prospectus, December 1897.

condemnation shortly after the school was opened.[23] It was also a basic tenet of the Society that there should be no religious instruction in its schools. The school prospectus circumvented the issue with the single statement: 'The education will be conducted in a religious spirit . . . but free from connection with any religious or political organisation.' The Bible could be used as a source of stories but was not to be used for the purpose of religious instruction.

The final characteristic of the curriculum and school organization as laid down by Findlay was the introduction in the King Alfred School, Hampstead, of the best practices of the home. The school was seen to be the natural extension of the good home—hence, unlike other progressive schools, it was neither a single-sex nor a boarding institution. The practice of boarding was denounced as 'cuckooism' and that of creating single-sex institutions as encouraging unnatural relationships. The King Alfred School was to offer coeducation on a day basis, was to give careful attention to health matters, including strictly limiting school hours to avoid overwork, and was deliberately to foster links with parents. One of the objects of the school and Society as laid down in the prospectus was

> Co-operation between Teachers and Parents. Frequent informal meetings are arranged to afford parents and teachers opportunities for conference and consultation. Also, provision is made for parents (who are members of the Society) and for members of the teaching profession to form part of the governing body of the School.[24]

When Findlay drew up the first draft of the school prospectus and curriculum towards the end of 1897, there was no indication that he intended to move to Wales, or to leave the College of Preceptors for elsewhere. The founding of the King Alfred School in Hampstead fitted in well with his personal plans and professional interests. In October 1897 he put before the founding committee of the Society a plan which would solve his imminent London accommodation problem, provide paid employment for his wife, and education for 'our own two little ones'.[25] He proposed a three-year plan in which their own scheme 'to start a small school for little children teaching others along with our own two little ones' would fuse with the plan of the Society to establish its first school by Easter 1898. The Findlays would move from Connaught Square to Hampstead where they would set up home in a house shared with the new school. 'If a large enough house were taken on a three years lease, we could take part of it for our own private use—you could take the rest for the school.'

By January 1898, Findlay was revising his plans. He was still anxious to share his house with the new school but, in a second letter to the Society, he made the point that

> I cannot at present bind Mrs Findlay to be at your disposal as a mistress for more than six months. Nor ought I to hide from you the possibility of my being called away from London after next September. Things will be very uncertain—far more so than when I previously wrote to the Committee.[26]

However, he was still willing to move to 'the proposed house' in Ellerdale Road, Hampstead, with the Society paying Mrs Findlay 'whatever salary you can afford'. The details of the sharing of the costs of the house between the Findlays and the Society were discussed and agreed by the end of January 1898. Findlay was to act as director of the project, a headmaster was to be appointed by the Society and the school was to open at Easter. Findlay urged caution, adding in a third letter to the Society:[27]

> In accepting the post of Director, I must adhere strictly to the policy of not engaging to do more than we can really hope to perform. Our zeal for reform makes us liable to commit the Society to obligations which are beyond our powers . . . I trust that my zeal for reform is genuine but I have witnessed many efforts at reform which have failed because the reformers have been too ambitious.

By March, Findlay's application for the Cardiff headship had been joined by over a hundred others and the school governors there were working on a shortlist of eight. At a meeting of the Society's newly created council on 5 March 1898, Findlay requested in a letter that 'all printed proof of (the) draft prospectus bearing his name might be considered confidential'.[28] This may have been because the interview panel in Cardiff could have viewed the prospectus more as a personal statement of belief than as an experimental, workable curriculum commissioned by a society to meet its ideological needs. His success in securing the post in the face of stiff competition from a Bangor professor, a Cardiff lecturer and three headmasters, including the favoured local candidate Waugh, was in part due to his recognition that the reform of Welsh intermediate education was very different from the kind of reform envisaged by the Hampstead rationalists. His Nonconformist background and his friendship with the Bishop of Hereford, who wrote an introduction in 1898 to Findlay's book on Arnold and who later invited Findlay to provide an educational scheme for Letchworth, gave him a broad basis of support within the appointment committee. His service on the Bryce Commission was evidence of his enthusiasm for the cause of state secondary education. His public-school background and his reputation as a scholar confirmed by his recently published book on Arnold of Rugby were of particular importance to those on the appointment committee who aimed at making Cardiff Boys School a first-grade intermediate school on classical lines. In an age which demanded a variety of grades within the intermediate system, the religious, political and social forces in Cardiff insisted that the intermediate schools of 'the principal city in Wales' should belong to the first grade. Waugh, the favoured local candidate, who topped the first ballot and tied with Findlay on the second, was not, as headmaster of the higher-grade school, as well qualified as was Findlay to fulfil such expectations. He thus lost to Findlay on the third ballot by twelve votes to nine and the latter thus secured the headship.

Findlay and Cardiff Intermediate School for Boys 1898–1903

It would be wrong to interpret Findlay's involvement in the 'rational experiment' in Hampstead, his headship at Cardiff Intermediate School for Boys and his 'education consultancy' at Letchworth Garden City as three distinct chronological steps in his career, for he was engaged in developing curricula for all three reform movements during his five-year sojourn at Cardiff. However, what is remarkable about the years 1898 to 1903 is not that he was able to find time to become involved in several reform movements simultaneously but that the curricula he devised for implementation at Hampstead and Letchworth contrasted so sharply with that which he implemented in Cardiff.

Findlay's move to Cardiff in the early summer of 1898 did not end his association with the Hampstead venture. Whilst his duties as headmaster meant that he was too busy to take any official part in the running of the King Alfred School Society or its Hampstead School, he maintained contact with the venture and advised the school's first headmaster, Charles Rice,[29] on the implementation of the 'concentrated curriculum' he had devised a few months earlier. Rice reported on the progress made in the implementation of the Findlay curriculum to the first general meeting of the Society in October 1898. By that time, 'the coordination of studies' was said to be well under way on both the science and arts sides of the curriculum.[30] He reiterated Findlay's concern that the curriculum should not be based on abstract theory. 'All theory', Rice declared, 'should be drawn from practical or personal experience.' Findlay's role during the next five years was that of unofficial adviser; it was not until after he left Cardiff for Owen's College, Manchester, in the late summer of 1903, that he allowed his name to be put forward for election to the Council of the Society. Apart from giving general advice on curricular matters, he also helped to choose the successor to Rice, who, by 1901, had become increasingly frustrated by the Society's close control of the day-to-day running of the school. Rice was succeeded by John Russell, who, as an authority on Pestalozzi,[31] had given occasional lectures with Findlay at the College of Preceptors and who joined with him in the plan to introduce 'reformed education' in Letchworth from 1903 onward.

Findlay's task at Cardiff was markedly different from that of Rice and Russell at Hampstead. It was not simply that he was appointed to a single-sex school to introduce a separate-subject curriculum. Intermediate education in Cardiff, as elsewhere in Wales, operated within an entirely different set of parameters, which prevented any radical innovations. 'It can be seen, therefore,' writes J. R. Webster, 'that despite the attempt to give the intermediate schools a new character, underlying the whole structure was the ever-present consideration of grading.'[32] The Commissioners insisted that grading should form the basis of the 'new education', and Findlay heartily concurred in a letter to *The Times* in 1900. However, he was more concerned in his letter to distinguish his school from Cardiff's higher-grade school, which he blamed for the very slow expansion of his own, than he was to establish the position of his school in the first of the three grades of intermediate school. He thus supported a rigid, hierarchical arrangement in which schools and their curricula were geared not to individual need as in Hampstead but according to leaving age and occupation:

1. Secondary school, leading to professional and higher business careers, for pupils remaining at school till 16 or 17 years of age or beyond.
2. Higher elementary schools, for pupils remaining at school at least until 13 years of age, and often until 14 or 15 (artisan, retail trades, etc.)
3. Primary schools, to pupils looking only to the lower forms of

unskilled labour; these, unhappily, are often removed from school before 13 years of age.[33]

He praised the Commissioners and government for their wisdom in realizing that 'the future career of the pupil is the leading thought to guide us in determining the duty of the school'. The higher-grade schools should recognize 'the limits of the course' and should not offer education of an intermediate kind. He attempted to reply to the accusation made by the higher-grade schools that the intermediate schools did 'not meet the aspirations of the working classes' by pointing to the 'abundant supply' of scholarships.

Cardiff Intermediate School for Boys was not, however, founded primarily to meet working-class aspirations. Its high fees[34] and large percentage of pupils who had previously attended private schools[35] meant that it catered largely for Cardiff's middle classes. It developed into a first-grade school largely for the sons of the middle and upper-middle classes for whom an education based on the traditional public-school model was deemed to be appropriate. The house system was seen by Findlay as a principal instrument for achieving the goals of a first-grade intermediate education. 'I venture to say that if a boy spends a number of years in the school as an active member of his house, he will leave us in nine cases out of ten, as a young man of wholesome active temperament, imbued with habits of public service and duty.'[36]

Findlay's desire to turn his school into a day public school led him to adopt several practices which the Hampstead experiment had deliberately sought to avoid, and for which he was criticized by Sir Philip Magnus.[37] The subject-based curriculum had been largely laid down in the Welsh Intermediate Education Act in a deliberate attempt to distinguish it from elementary education. Hence his school followed a curriculum which was common to most intermediate schools aspiring to first-grade status. Its core subjects included English, mathematics, scripture, chemistry, French, physics, geography, singing and drawing. As the school aimed to prepare students for university, all pupils began Latin in the fourth year and Greek was included in fifth-year options with German, Spanish and a commercial course which encompassed book-keeping and shorthand designed for those not staying on to the age of eighteen or nineteen. But it was not so much the subject-based curriculum which contrasted with the Hampstead scheme; it was Findlay's approach to its implementation which differed so greatly.

The curriculum was criticized by Sir Philip Magnus for being 'somewhat bookish in character', and for downgrading the kind of practical subjects and experiences which were ranked so highly at Hampstead. He employed students from Oxford and Cambridge to teach the compulsory academic subjects; woodwork and music classes were held outside school hours and were voluntary, with the former being taken by the school caretaker.[38]

Examinations, deplored by the King Alfred School Society for putting too much pressure on students, became the chief curricular focus of Cardiff Intermediate Schools for Boys. Magnus complained that in Findlay's school 'the pupils work at too high pressure, and the attention of the masters is distracted from the true aims of school teaching by the necessity of preparing pupils for so many different tests'.[39] Findlay set up a special examination department charging an additional fee to give extra tuition in subjects necessary for qualifying for particular forms of employment. In the upper school, students were entered for examinations with the Central Welsh Board, and for the Matriculation and Scholarship examinations of a number of universities (including Wales and London), in addition to the great number of specialist examinations for professional bodies. The overworking of students which was assiduously avoided at Hampstead became a dominant feature of his Cardiff curriculum. School was held on Saturday mornings, compulsory games each Tuesday and Thursday afternoon and the customary inter-school matches most Saturday afternoons. The traditional public-school model against which Findlay's Hampstead curriculum was a protest formed the basis of his Cardiff experiment in intermediate education. But then the clientele of the schools and their expectations were so very different and Findlay had the gift of developing curricula to meet the requirements of the market.

Findlay and Letchworth Garden City Education

Just before he left Cardiff to take up the Sarah Fielden Chair of Education at Owen's College, Manchester, Findlay became involved for a short period in a third educational reform movement, garden city education. In 1898 Ebenezer Howard had launched the garden city movement with his book *Garden Cities of Tomorrow*. The movement, designed to avoid the slum conditions of many industrial towns, had made such rapid headway that by 1902 the Garden City Association was preparing to purchase the Letchworth Estate in order to build the first garden city. In the autumn of that year,[40] the Association began to consider the question of the type of education which was best suited for Letchworth Garden City. A small subcommittee to expedite discussion was set up in 1903 under the Bishop of Hereford, who, as we have seen, had contributed an introduction to Findlay's book on *Arnold of Rugby*. John Russell, the headmaster of the King Alfred School, Hampstead, was also a prominent member of the subcommittee and later succeeded the Bishop of Hereford as its chairman. In order to give a focus to its discussions, the subcommittee invited Findlay to prepare a paper on garden city education.[41] This he did during his last few weeks at Cardiff. He presented it to the Letchworth subcommittee on 7 July 1903. His scheme of education contained elements of both the Hampstead and Cardiff curricula but differed from them in significant ways.

In his 'Suggestions for the education of children dwelling in Garden City',[42] Findlay placed an asterisk alongside those aspects of the scheme which he believed reflected the 'reformed principles of education' to which the people of Letchworth 'will be more open'. These included smaller classes than were usually found in state schools, coeducation, open-air studies, manual work being given a more dignified status than was found in many schools, and the liberal use of visual aids and field trips. He was particularly concerned that the Garden City should establish mixed schools (in contrast with the school he ran in Cardiff). 'My own conviction (from many years' observation)', he declared, 'is entirely in favour of mixed schools.' He was equally anxious that the curriculum should not be too subject-orientated. 'The chief danger I foresee may lie in the attempt to introduce too many "subjects",' he warned the crowded Letchworth meeting, though he strongly favoured the retention of separate provision for 'religious instruction', arithmetic, geometry, music and languages. He realized that a curriculum based upon such principles would require additional finance through voluntary contributions by parents, and a strong measure of local control; hence he argued in favour of 'a special Body of Managers, at least one third (of which) should be elected by pupils' parents to supervise the experiment'. In addition, there would be 'ex-standard work' for pupils who wished to stay on after the compulsory leaving age, and the system of pupil-teachers whose 'evils . . . are widely recognised' would be avoided throughout the system.'

Perhaps Findlay's most radical departure was to consider part-time continuation schooling for those who had left full-time education, an issue which was moving to the centre stage of educational debate in the first decade of this century. Following a line of argument similar to that of Percy Nunn[43] he put the case for combining provision for full-time and part-time education. He urged that 'the Continental system of providing instruction for apprentices on one or two mornings or afternoons (instead of in the evenings as at present)' be given serious consideration. Such 'instruction' should be based on technical and liberal studies, which should include economics 'in view of the socio-ethical basis of the Garden City life'.[44]

His suggestion that the Garden City Association should 'at an early date select a Head Teacher in sympathy with the aims of the Garden City' was acted on in November 1905 when C. A. Pease was appointed to take charge of the temporary school in 'The Sheds'. However, John Russell's annual reports, as chairman of the Garden City Education Council, from 1906 onwards show the collapse of the Findlay scheme (which had been developed in 1904 by Dr Foat). The lack of sufficient voluntary contributions necessary to maintain the school and its 'reformed curriculum' led to the school's transfer to county authority control. Only vestiges of the 1903 scheme survived when the school was moved to a permanent site in Norwood Road under its old headmaster. Purdom, Letchworth's first historian, concludes that under the influence of the Findlay 'scheme' the 'committee, like most of the pioneers, thought of Garden City as so much superior to the ordinary conditions of twentieth century life that they looked for greater perfection than was even remotely possible'.[45]

Conclusion

If Findlay's activities at Cardiff are viewed in isolation from his involvement in reform movements elsewhere, it is difficult to interpret his approach to reform as anything other than that of an ex-public school teacher and headmaster imposing on intermediate education in Cardiff the model which had served him so well in his previous career. However, the preceding review of his contribution to reform movements in London and Letchworth suggests an alternative interpretation—that his actions were not those of the unthinking traditionalist but those of an educationist who was acutely aware of the limitations imposed on educational experiments by the social, political and economic environments in which they operated. When he warned the King Alfred School Society of the dangers of 'overambition', he was urging its members not to develop a form of education which was unlikely to win the support of the people of Hampstead upon whose fees the ultimate success of the rationalist experiment depended. Similarly he realized that intermediate education in Cardiff had to meet the various aspirations of those who would pay the fees.

Findlay was criticized by Magnus in his report on secondary education for turning Cardiff's Intermediate School for Boys into a forcing house for examination entrants. However, as Findlay's book *Principles of Class Teaching* (published in 1902 while he was at Cardiff) shows, he was well aware of the difference between intermediate education, which provided 'an intermediate stage between the Primary School and the University'[46] with its consequent examination pressures, and secondary education. Unlike Magnus, Findlay interpreted the term 'intermediate' in its strict sense and produced a curriculum to fit that purpose. In Findlay's view, secondary education was altogether different; the basic principle upon which the secondary school curriculum should be based was, in his view, that 'the ground should be covered slowly, that no haste should be displayed in commencing new studies, that the education should . . . be "liberal", liberal in its scorn for haste—raw haste, half-sister to delay . . . leisure is one mark of a good secondary school.'[47] Magnus was thus, in Findlay's view, wrongly criticizing intermediate education using criteria appropriate to an entirely different form of education.

In 1903, Findlay moved to Manchester where, as Professor of Education, he continued to set up 'demonstration' or 'experimental schools' of different kinds. He published the results of his experimental curricula and teaching methods in *The Demonstration Schools Record* from 1908 onwards. It was this area of his achievement which H. C. Barnard commented upon in his standard history of education[48] nearly fifty years ago, and which has formed the basis of recent research[49] into Findlay's work at Manchester.

REFERENCES

1. J. R. Webster, 'The place of secondary education in Welsh society, 1800–1918', (University of Wales Ph.D. thesis, 1959), 457.
2. See especially A. C. Impey, 'The development of state-provided secondary education in Cardiff, 1870–1939' (University of Wales M. Ed. thesis, 1973), 58–60.
3. T. Ellis and E. Griffith, *A Manual to the Intermediate Education (Wales) Act, 1889, and The Technical Instruction Act 1989* (London, 1889), 55.
4. At Bath College (1884–5) and at Rugby (1888, 1893–4), with headships of two Wesleyan proprietary schools, Queen's College, Taunton, and Wesley College, Sheffield (1885–91).
5. 25 May 1900.
6. Webster, op. cit., 371.
7. The preliminary circular of the King Alfred School Society, July 1897. This and the following documents are to be found in the Society's archives at its Hampstead School in North End Road, Hampstead, north London.
8. The choice was between the New Century School Society and the King Alfred School Society.
9. Preliminary circular entitled 'The Proposed Rational School', p. 1.
10. See F. H. Hillard, 'The Moral Instrument League 1897–1919', in *The Durham Research Review*, 3 No. 12 (September 1961), 53–63.
11. Miall was included because he was the brother of the Society's first chairman, F. W. Miall; he later became president of the society.
12. Memorandum of Association and Incorporation of the King Alfred School Society, first draft, December 1897.
13. 1898 Revised Prospectus, appended note.
14. Author and member of the Fabian Society and London School Board and lecturer at the London School of Economics.
15. In 1894, Sadler became head of a special inquiries section of the Education Department to report on systems and methods of education abroad, and became a member of the Board of Education.
16. Principal of Maria Grey Training College and a key figure in the provision of educational courses for the Ethical Union.
17. Chapman and Hall, London, 1915. Reprinted by Nadder Books, 1986.
18. Trevor Blewitt (ed.), *The Modern Schools Handbook* (with an introduction by Amabel Williams-Ellis) (Gollancz, 1934), 12.
19. Preliminary Prospectus, December 1897–9, 3.
20. Ibid, 2.
21. Ibid, 4.
22. *Daily News*, 6 February 1898.
23. The first verse of the poem entitled 'Matriculation' written in the first volume of the school magazine (Autumn term, 1898) ran as follows:
    Matriculation
    Before King Alfred's blessed the nation
    And charmed the rising generation
    Folk had preferred decapitation

> Or other sure extermination
> Or torture slow, of long duration
> Or lands in state of devastation:
> Than cause such general consternation
> And tales of strange prevarication
> About their huge self approbation
> By sending in an application
> To enter for Matriculation.

24. School Prospectus, second draft, February 1898.
25. Letter accompanying founding committee minutes, 25 October 1897.
26. Committee minutes, 10 January 1898.
27. Ibid.
28. Ibid., 5 March 1898.
29. Rice was previously an assistant master at Bedales, the second progressive school to be founded in the late nineteenth century. Findlay wisely refused to let himself be drawn into the stormy relationship between the Society and the school's first headmaster, between 1898 and 1901.
30. Minutes of the Ordinary General Meeting, 20 October 1898, p. 2.
31. Russell translated Roger de Guimps' *Life and Work of Pestalozzi* in 1890.
32. Webster, op. cit., 375.
33. *The Times*, 25 May 1900.
34. Its fees of £7.10s. per annum were among the highest in Wales.
35. At Cardiff Intermediate School for Boys 32 per cent, compared with 27.1 per cent and 21.4 per cent for Swansea and Newport Boys' Intermediate Schools respectively.
36. Welsh Intermediate Education Act (Cardiff Scheme) Minutes, p. 357.
37. P. Magnus, *Report on the School System of Cardiff*, with special reference to the provision of Evening Technical Instruction (Cardiff 1907).
38. W.I.E.A. (C.S.) Minutes, p. 316.
39. Magnus, op. cit., 19.
40. *The Garden City Education Council*, First Report, 1906 (signed by John Russell), p. 1.
41. C. B. Purdom, *The Garden City* (London, 1913), 170.
42. First Garden City Heritage Museum Papers, Letchworth.
43. J. R. Brooks, 'Labour and educational reconstruction 1916–1926: a case study in the evolution of policy', *Journal of the History of Education Society*, 20 No. 3 (September 1991).
44. 'Suggestions for the education of children dwelling in Garden City', p. 2.
45. Purdom., op. cit., 170.
46. *Principles of Class Teaching*, 233.
47. Ibid.
48. H. C. Barnard, *A History of English Education from 1760* (London, 1947), 308–9.
49. 'J. J. Findlay: an early professor of education and reformer of teaching training', a paper delivered by A. Robertson at the annual conference of the History of Education Society, Liverpool 1990.

The Welsh Committee of the Arts Council in the 1960s

ROY BOHANA

The section on Wales in the twenty-second Annual Report (1966/67) of the Arts Council of Great Britain ends thus:

> The Director for Wales, Dr J. R. Webster, resigned on the 30th September, 1966, having been appointed Professor and Head of the Department of Education at the University College of North Wales, Bangor. He was the Welsh Committee's chief officer for five most formative years, and his work for the arts in Wales will have lasting and beneficial results.

The members of the Welsh Committee responsible for his appointment on 10 December 1960 had been Professor Gwyn Jones (Chairman), S. Kenneth Davies, Sir Emrys Evans, Alex Gordon, Dr D. Dilwyn John, Eileen Llewelyn-Jones, Wynne Ll. Lloyd, Alun Llewelyn-Williams, Lady Amy Parry-Williams, Robert E. Presswood, Frances Rees, Dr. D. E. Parry-Williams, and Iolo Aneurin Williams. M. J. McRobert, then Deputy Secretary-General of the Arts Council, was also present. They would have been relieved to have attracted such a strong candidate. There had been staffing problems, and when Dr Webster took up his duties on 1 April 1961, he found a far weaker instrument of patronage than the one he left on returning to academic life in the autumn of 1966.

In all but name the Arts Council of Great Britain had been set up in 1939, on the outbreak of war, when the Council for the Encouragement of Music and the Arts (CEMA) was founded. Its first Chairman, from 1939 to 1943, was Lord MacMillan (Minister of Information and Chairman of the Pilgrim Trust) and Lord Keynes succeeded him. Three of the four founder members were Welsh—Sir William Emrys Williams, Dr Thomas Jones (whom Sir William once described as 'the Nestor from the Rhymney Valley') and Sir Walford Davies (born in Oswestry of Welsh parentage) who had spent seven years, from 1919 to 1926, as Professor of Music in University College, Aberystwyth. The fourth member was Sir Kenneth Clarke.

During the war years CEMA was deeply involved in promoting and funding the arts, both amateur and professional, embracing music, drama and the visual arts. In six years its work had clearly revealed that there was a continuing role to be fulfilled in increasing accessibility to the arts, and on 12 June 1945 the Chancellor of the Exchequer, then Sir John Anderson, announced that the Government was to incorporate CEMA, under the name of the Arts Council of Great Britain, to be responsible to, and financed by, the Treasury. The Arts Council, in inheriting CEMA's aims and ambitions, continued to pursue most of its policies, with the notable exceptions of the amateur arts (which were entrusted to other bodies) and the direct promotion of music and drama in England. However, in the more rural areas of Scotland and Wales, and in the field of visual arts, direct promotion continued. On 9 August 1946, King George VI granted a royal charter to the Arts Council. Ever since, it has enjoyed an official status, yet retains autonomy. Its members throughout the United Kingdom are chosen as individuals, not as representatives, and its staff are not civil servants. Yet it enjoys a government grant, and senior civil servants attend its meetings as assessors.

It would be appropriate to record progress made in developing the Arts Council's work in Wales prior to Dr Webster's arrival. Although an advisory Welsh Committee had been appointed from June 1945, it had no authority for the actual expenditure of the Council's funds in Wales until 1953/54, when it was granted the privilege and problems of autonomy. A block grant of £30,000 was negotiated for that year and it increased over the next seven years; £32,000 (1954/5), £33,650 (1955/6), £35,250 (1956/7), £42,910 (1957/8), £43,950 (1958/9 and 1959/60), and £60,823 (1960/1). By 1966/7, when Dr Webster resigned from his post, he and his chairman, Professor Gwyn Jones (who served as Chairman of the Welsh Committee from 1957 to 1967—his predecessors having been Lord Harlech from 1945 to 1948 and Wyn Griffith from 1948 to 1956) had negotiated an astounding fivefold increase to £305,000.

Before Dr Webster, there had been two Directors of the Welsh Committee. Huw Wheldon served from 1946 to 1949, when he was seconded to London to act as the Arts Council's representative in the organization of the 1951 Festival of Britain. Subsequently, he moved to BBC television. From 1947, the Welsh Committee supported an office in Wrexham where the supervising officer was Myra Owen. During the war she had been chief instructor in an ordnance factory and eventually became Director of Training for the Royal Ordnance factories when the war ended. A Welsh-speaker who had trained as a musician, she became acting Director of the Welsh Committee in 1949 and Director in 1951. Intermittently during the 1950s, there had been assistant directors responsible for drama, music and the visual arts, but when Dr Webster assumed his duties in April 1961 it was with the knowledge that his predecessor had been obliged to resign and the Deputy Director (who assumed responsibility for music, and who had been a short-listed candidate for the post of Director) was about to leave for Australia, thus leaving the newly appointed Director with the sole support of Tom Cross, assistant director for visual arts. Staffing problems had clearly produced unfortunate circumstances, but they eventually became a blessing in disguise. The Director was now able to make new appointments to suit the needs of the progressive arts policies which he was determined to pursue; assistant directors for music and drama were appointed within a year.

Artistically, the Welsh Committee's work from 1946 to 1961 had been valuable, but painstakingly slow in developing. In the late 1950s its commitments had a settled appearance, drifting along in a curiously repetitive pattern. Welsh National Opera, though receiving critical acclaim particularly for its amateur chorus, continued to operate on an *ad hoc*, short-season basis—very much as it had done since 1946. Festivals receiving funding included those of Swansea, Llandaff, the combined choirs festivals of Dee and Clwyd, Montgomeryshire County and Brecknock County, and the Anglesey Music Festival. Subsidies of small amounts were offered to music clubs and societies for chamber music, and there were sporadic and short orchestral tours. The Committee organized drama tours by companies which it had set up specifically for the purpose, or by those provided by the Arts Council centrally. Support was given to Welsh-language drama, both amateur and professional. The art department arranged exhibitions originating in Wales and outside, but the sole support for literature was a grant of £100 in 1958/9 to the literary and poetry magazine, *The Anglo-Welsh Review*. Whilst all these activities had certainly increased the audience for the fine arts in Wales over fifteen years, when Dr Webster arrived in Cardiff he would have found a noticeable absence of strategy or any kind of structured forward planning. The Welsh Committee's work from 1946 to 1961 naturally reflected the general trends of the Arts Council's activities throughout the United Kingdom. During the 1950s the Council's subsidies had been crucial to the sustenance of its clients but, at times, many of the country's leading arts organizations had been treading on thin ice. The 1956/7 Arts Council annual report was entitled *Art in the Red*, and that for 1958/9, *The Struggle for Survival*. Even though the Council's overall expenditure had grown from nothing to £1.745 million in fifteen years, it appeared that in a 1961 investigation (carried out by the International Theatre Institute) relating to national and civic expenditure on theatres and opera houses in fourteen European countries, Britain came tenth —three places lower than Bulgaria and only a trifle higher than the small nations of Denmark and Finland. Expenditure on the fine arts in Britain in 1961 amounted to ten old pennies (around four new pence) per head of population, whilst subsidy for egg producion came to ten shillings (or fifty new pence) per head!

It was clear that the pace of patronage needed to accelerate, and the Arts Council said so. It was fortunate, therefore, that Dr Webster's five years with the Welsh Committee coincided with significant increases in government funding for the arts. For 1962/3 the Chancellor of the Exchequer, Conservative Selwyn Lloyd, announced an increase of 24 per cent, bringing the Council's grant to £2.190 million. The annual report was entitled *A Brighter Prospect*. However, in return for its increased investment, the Government clearly intended that the arts should attract complementary increases from local authorities. Since the introduction of the 1948 Local Government Act (section 132), authorities had been empowered to raise money for the arts from the rates, but their actual commitments had been a fraction of what was permitted.

The Government now required the Arts Council to develop its relationships with local authorities to a far greater degree and, during his years as Director for Wales, Dr Webster became increasingly preoccupied with the task of developing local responsibility for the arts. Within months he had produced a survey of the support given by Welsh local authorities in 1961/2. A total of £6,900 was on offer to Welsh National Opera, being £3,000 from Glamorgan

County Council, £1,000 from Swansea Corporation, £2,000 from Cardiff, £1,000 from Monmouth County and £700 in smaller amounts from twenty other authorities. The music festivals received modest amounts and the Welsh Committee's drama tours attracted support from the boroughs of Colwyn Bay, Aberystwyth and Caerffili (where the borough council was the only authority in Wales to be responsible for organizing an arts festival). In Pembrokeshire, the authorities 'pooled' contributions towards the costs of orchestral concerts. These contributions were helpful, but the harsh reality was that the majority of Welsh authorities were giving no more than token assistance to the arts. The Welsh Committee of the Arts Council, and its Director, now needed to seek a more clear-cut formula for sharing responsibility for the arts in Wales between central and local funds.

At a Welsh Committee meeting in January 1963, the Director and his assistants gave a comprehensive presentation on the subject of local authority participation in funding and local organization. The Director recommended the concept of an arts trust as a useful vehicle for receiving funds from the Arts Council, local authorities, and other grant-giving bodies, and for being responsible for organizing and funding the arts in a given geographical area.

He had developed a close working relationship with J. O. Jones, Secretary of the Anglesey Rural Community Council, whose work in organizing the arts was one of the best examples of local initiative. In addition to providing local organization for orchestral concerts, plays and exhibitions, the Community Council had developed its own Welsh Drama Festival and County Music Festival. It seemed an ideal situation for testing the arts fund experiment. In 1964, J. O. Jones, co-operating with Dr Webster, established the Anglesey County Arts Fund with the object of co-ordinating, organizing and financing the major artistic projects on the island. The Welsh Committee contributed £2,100 to the fund, Anglesey County Council gave £300, the eight district councils provided a total of £300 and the Gulbenkian Foundation promised £1,000 annually for three years. With these resources, the Community Council continued to organize the music and drama festivals, but added visits by the Royal Liverpool Philharmonic Orchestra, the London Philharmonic Orchestra and the Welsh Theatre Company. Art exhibitions were arranged in co-operation with the Arts Council and the South Wales Group. Subsidy was given to Theatr Fach, Llangefni, and the Anglesey

Music Club, and works of art were purchased for a county collection. The partnership between the Welsh Committee and the Anglesey Rural Community Council proved such a success that in November 1964 the Director suggested the possibility of establishing an arts trust which would be representative not only of Anglesey, but of all five north Wales counties. In May 1965, in the first instance, a North Wales Arts Advisory Panel would be formed to review the organization and financing of the arts in the area, to co-ordinate Welsh Committee-sponsored activities, and to co-operate with local authorities and other organizations towards establishing a North Wales Arts Trust. J. O. Jones would be the Panel's secretary and would be based in Bangor. An immediate grant of £2,500 from the Welsh Committee would be provided to cover the Panel's administration until 31 March 1966.

The first meeting of the Panel took place on 17 June 1965, when Sir Ben Bowen Thomas accepted the chairmanship. Following consultations between the Panel and local authorities, the newly founded North Wales Arts Association, funded by county councils and the Welsh Committee, began its work in April 1967. Arts associations for west Wales and south-east Wales followed in 1974 and 1976. The three associations have done much to increase local authority involvement in the organization and funding of the arts, and have been able to orientate activity to suit the needs of their individual communities.

The Government's challenge to the Arts Council in 1962, to seek financial partnerships with local authorities, was positively taken up in Wales, and the substantial increases in monies for the arts in the Principality during the period 1961–6 reflected not only increase in demand from a growing audience, but also the determined effort which Dr Webster and his Committee made to develop local responsibility. The Welsh Committee's grant from the Arts Council increased annually; £108,290 (1962/3), £140,432 (1963/4), £155,575 (1964/5), £209,922 (1965/6), £305,000 (1966/7). These resources enabled significant artistic developments to take place.

Within a year following his appointment, the Director presented a comprehensive survey of arts activities to his Welsh Committee. Whilst admitting that the cultural life of Wales would be greatly impoverished without visits from internationally known orchestras, conductors and soloists, London-based opera, dance and theatre companies, and without art exhibitions originating outside Wales, he nevertheless held a strong belief that Wales should support its own major artistic companies, thereby making an indigenous contribution to the arts in Britain. An avid supporter of Welsh National Opera, he consistently argued for additional funds for the full professionalization of the company with its own chorus and orchestra, together with a greater share of performances in the United Kingdom as a whole. He played an important role in preparing the way for these developments to take place from 1970 to 1973 onwards.

In drama, the Welsh Committee had for many years been arranging two short tours by Welsh and visiting companies of the Arts Council of Great Britain. Whilst appreciating that anything was better than nothing, that the tours had brought professional drama to Wales and had increased audiences, the Director knew that the time was ripe to form a permanent touring company. It would be the first step towards the establishment of professional theatre in Wales, encouraging Welsh dramatists, actors, producers and designers. In the autumn of 1962, the Welsh Committee founded the Welsh Theatre Company with Warren Jenkins as Artistic Director. On his own admission, Dr Webster recognized the act of faith implicit in forming a drama company without a theatre base, workshops or adequate storage facilities. But the brave decision had been made.

The initial tour lasted nine weeks, with two plays: Alun Owen's *The Rough and Ready Lot* and Molière's *The Miser*. One-night stands were carefully avoided, the tour opening with a week in Colwyn Bay, followed by a fortnight in Cardiff and a week in Swansea. Over the Christmas period the company played for five weeks in Cardiff, with an adaptation of R. L. Stevenson's *Treasure Island*, the première of a play by the Cardiff poet Dannie Abse, *The House of Cowards*, and Tennessee Williams's *Period of Adjustment*.

In the autumn of 1963 the company was for four weeks at Cardiff's New Theatre with a spectacular production of *War and Peace*, followed by Anouilh's *Antigone* and Gwyn Thomas's *The Keep*. The latter two plays later went on tour, together with a production of Shakespeare's *Macbeth* which had been substantially assisted by co-operation with local education authorities. Whilst the company was attempting to serve Wales nationally, its work was obviously being influenced by the chronic shortage of properly equipped venues, and it was not easy to attract actors to improvised premises to endure 'the rigours of guerrilla exercises in diffusion of the arts', as Sir William Emrys Williams had called similar activity in England. In order to concentrate on a small number of the better theatres, where the public could see performances at their best, the Welsh Committee introduced a transport subsidy scheme which served to encourage audiences to travel some distances to performances.

The Welsh Theatre Company inevitably felt the need for a medium-sized theatre for its base in Cardiff, since the New Theatre, with over a thousand seats, was too large for the scale of its work (much of which toured to smaller venues). In his attempt to secure a smaller theatre, the Director's tact and patience came under severe pressure, as he strove to cope with the demands of the St David's Trust, a group of well-known figures (Lord Aberdare, Clifford Evans, Sir Cennydd Treharne and Saunders Lewis) who envisaged a new national theatre building, with varying capacity of 950–1,500 seats.

By 1965, Dr Webster had a precisely clear view of how progress could be made. The Welsh Theatre Company would develop into a national theatre company with permanent organizational and artistic staff, performing in Welsh and English, providing for new writers and new audiences—creating a truly national movement. It would need base theatres in Cardiff and Bangor for its work in English and Welsh respectively, as well as four or five other properly equipped theatres in other centres.

In 1966, these ambitions were greatly assisted by the publication of the Council for Wales and Monmouthshire's report on *The Arts in Wales—a Study of the Organisation, Finance, Accommodation and other Provision for the Arts*. The report received wide public exposure and discussion. The pioneering work of the Welsh Theatre Company and the pressure it exerted for the need for new theatres eventually led to far-reaching results. Within years, the country boasted nine such new buildings—Theatr Clwyd in Mold, Theatr Gwynedd in Bangor, Theatr Harlech, Theatr Hafren in Newtown, Theatr y Werin in Aberystwyth, the Torch Theatre in Milford Haven, Theatr Taliesin in Swansea, the Dolman Theatre in Newport and the Sherman Theatre in Cardiff.

Dr Webster's realistic approach to national theatre applied equally towards the need for a permanent national orchestra. There had been two attempts to found such an orchestra, the first in the inter-war period, the other in 1950. Both had failed due to the lack of a concert-going tradition, the absence of strong local organization and the dearth of concert halls. A third attempt would need to wait for better circumstances, but in order to create new audiences and acquire more skilful promoters, the Director lost little time in persuading the Welsh Committee to take on the responsibility for financing, planning and co-ordinating orchestral concerts from 1962 onwards. Between then and 1966, large orchestras visited Aberystwyth, Bangor, Barry, Cardiff, Fishguard, Haverfordwest, Llangefni, Llandudno, Merthyr, Rhyl, Swansea and Wrexham, whilst chamber orchestras appeared in Abergavenny, Port Talbot, Brecon, Cross Hands, Narberth, Dolgellau, Menai Bridge, Monmouth, Pembroke, Pontypool, Ystrad Mynach and Connah's Quay. The list of symphony orchestras taking part in this touring programme over the period was formidable—the four London Orchestras (the Royal Philharmonic, London Philharmonic, Philharmonia and London Symphony), four regional orchestras (the Hallé, Bournemouth, Liverpool and Birmingham Orchestras) and distinguished orchestras from abroad, including the Leipzig Gewandhaus, Munich Philharmonic, Warsaw Philharmonic and Salzburg Mozarteum. Conductors included Barbirolli, Dorati, Monteux, Susskind, Prichard—all leading figures internationally at the time.

The Director's prediction of the value an effective touring programme would have on the prospects for an eventual national symphony orchestra proved to be entirely accurate. By the early seventies, audiences and promoters had been developed to such a degree that the Arts Council and the BBC were able to provide joint funding to expand the 44-player BBC Welsh Orchestra to full symphonic strength of 88, to take it out of the Cardiff BBC studios to give public concerts throughout Wales, and to enable it to serve as a national symphony orchestra in providing a platform for Welsh performers and composers.

One might perceive Dr Webster's deep involvement in mainstream performing arts activities as an indication of a more casual approach to the visual arts. Nothing could be further from the truth; indeed, his knowledge of the visual arts was extensive and his interests widespread. He wrote about them and talked about them regularly on television. But since the Welsh Committee had been served by three assistant directors for art since 1955 (John Petts, Philip Jones and Tom Cross), he would have found a more ordered structure in the Welsh Committee's visual arts activities, and there was less call on his own time. Even so, the growth that characterized music and drama found equivalent exposure in art. The number of exhibitions arranged by the Welsh Committee increased from forty-seven in 1961 to ninety-eight in 1964, but the major problem in implementing an enlightened art policy was the paucity of exhibition rooms with adequate facilities and supervision.

As mentioned above, between 1961 and 1966 the Arts Council's expenditure on the arts in Wales had increased fivefold. Welsh National Opera's grant had grown from £31,000 to £100,000, expenditure on the Welsh Theatre Company from nothing to £63,000, and orchestral music from £1,900 to £21,000. Thus, mainstream performing arts provision had been transformed. A new arts buildings programme had been put in place. Publicity about arts activity was being disseminated through Welsh Committee bulletins and publications. The Arts Associations' arts funding structure had been inaugurated. It had been correct to record in the 1966/7 annual report that the Director's work would 'have lasting and beneficial results'. It had been the most productive period of growth in the history of the Arts Council.

Over the years, some have believed that the Arts Council should have put greater emphasis on the diffusion of the arts in the geographical sense to spread the arts on the widest possible scale. Dr Webster was firm in his view that standards should come first. This had also been Sir William Emrys Williams's philosophy throughout his twenty-seven years of association with the Arts Council. I quote from Sir William's last contribution to an annual report, that of 1961/2:

> In the long debate between 'Raise or Spread?' the decision adopted was to put standards first. Widespread diffusion is liable to produce the dry rot of mediocrity. High values in the arts can only be maintained on a restricted scale. They cannot be secured, for example, by gallant but ill-equipped teams of strolling players performing one night stands in village halls.

Dr Webster's own disbelief in the 'strolling players' way of doing things was the key to his eventual success.

On 7 February 1967 the Queen granted a new royal charter to the Arts Council. Clause 8(i) read as follows:

> The Council shall, with the approval respectively of our Secretary of State for Scotland and Our Secretary of State for Wales, appoint committees, to be called the Scottish Arts Council and the Welsh Arts

Council, to exercise, or advise them on the exercise of, their functions in Scotland and Wales.

The change in title from Welsh Committee to Welsh Arts Council was as significant as it was deserved, since it recognized the remarkable achievements of the previous few years.

Welsh Voices—More than Just Talk?

BRIAN DAVIES

I have known for over forty years that Welsh history was quite different from its English counterpart. For a start, it began from the back of your 'best book' while English started from the front. This fact alone carried two messages in stirring contradiction. The English version was obviously authoritative and 'correct', while the Welsh, beginning where you were supposed to finish up, promised to be both more authentic and subversive. The lived experience of working from both ends toward the middle in lower secondary school (I have not the slightest recollection of being taught any history in primary school) never quite lived up to this promise, though it afforded other delights. Welsh history was taught by passionate irregulars, catching turns from other subjects, full of the sounds of recurring treachery and the sights of the undersides of descending conquerors' soles and heels. The highlights remain indelible: Llew Last forced to kneel on Rhuddlan Moor, which was not convenient for anyone, but humiliating for us; Henry VIII fixing the courts and the rustlers; Gruffydd Jones and his marvellous circulating schools where the views from the windows must have changed, unlike ours, by the minute; those terrible commissioners turning the air and the books blue with their dreadful lies. All was loss, from the abandonment of the wonderfully socialistic-sounding principle of gavelkind to the Welsh knot (*sic*) hung round our grandfathers' necks, with only a few pulsating fightbacks like the men of Rebecca who looked like a cross between Old Mother Riley, the transvestite males of every beery Christmas party and a tidy pack on a night out. Continuity was clearly in our bones.

Coming to this very welcome opportunity to appraise the social vision in Roger Webster's history is not only a pleasure in its own right but forces upon me a reappraisal of my own relation to a Welsh past and present that is also difficult, even painful. There are more things than I can find in the books. This is partly how it has to be. Inimitably, Gwyn A. Williams tells us: 'There are whole areas of human experience, among them the most significant, which lie too deep for the historian's plumb line.'[1] The picture of historian as mason (or at least builder and decorator to the social sciences) evokes precisely the issue with which the historian and all of us interested in the past struggle. All crafts are unnatural and none more so than the historian's, though the view that history is 'there for the taking' is one of the most beloved of those who wish to appropriate a version of it. The notion that history is simply where today has been is robustly commonsensical. However, as anyone with the slightest interest in its welfare will tell you, having waited up for its return from a night on the tiles is no guarantee of being in the right state to ask it useful questions or to hear what is being said by a voice which may be misleading. Williams's allusion to the historian's plumb-line should remind us that there is much in the Welsh educational past which affords a specific and endearing version of that old question, 'How long is a piece of string?'

That Roger Webster is a historian with the strongest sense of the social is evident throughout his corpus. While the overriding scholarly virtue of his doctoral thesis centring on the 1889 Act[2] remains its detailed historiography of individual school foundations in relation to changing policy and social conditions, it places itself squarely within the sociological discourse of its era. His thesis is that the 'interaction of education and society may be best appreciated from a study of secondary education, for it is the availability of secondary education that most significantly determined the extent of social mobility at any particular time',[3] and that in relation to Wales, 'social mobility and anglicisation are complementary aspects of the same social change'.[4] Estates of the realm give way to class and, in time, the educational ladder gives way to the 'as yet unrealised ideal of providing the same educational facilities for all'.[5] And beneath the surface, Welsh educational evolution, in comparison with English, 'displays fundamental differences due in some measure to the different origins and evolution of the societies in the two countries'.[6] He attempts to show that nineteenth-century Welsh education is influenced by the social structures of a previous age. On the evidence of the 1847 Commissioners, he argues that the *tyddynwyr* (peasant subsistence farmers) transplanted their kin-based, classless relationships with ease from west Wales as far as clan-filled Merthyr. The social and educational distinction that emerged was between the 'passed over', Anglicized aristocracy and professional middle class on the one hand, and *y werin* on the other, the latter including 'all who thought in Welsh terms'.[7] But there is a further, vital distinction to be made. At one definitional extreme he acknowledges the position where it is held that '*y werin* is the society or nation in the totality of its life', in contrast to 'every class that demands privileges that are not subordinated to the highest good of the nation'.[8] This will not do. For Webster, those who 'go' in class terms find it 'exceedingly difficult' to remain *gwerinwyr* ('even if they later renew their interest in Welsh affairs'), because they have adopted English values.[9] This permits exclusion of those nineteenth-century migrants to England, who were in fact much the most potent source of change and revival in Welsh education, from the vanguard of educational reformers. Three decades later, much of this reads like routine paradox and post-colonial position-seeking, albeit on a canvas as worn and criss-crossed as Wales. Leaving home and moving place is deemed fatal by those who have not done at least one of them. In post-modern terms, this version of *y werin* reads like black consciousness meets the Exclusive Brethren, Celtic-style.

Y werin did not welcome early nineteenth-century attempts to school them. Even towards mid century, they 'had yet to realise the economic value of education, indeed they had not yet begun to think of "class" or "social advancement" at all; they were still thinking in tribal terms, and thus they could find no purpose in secular education',[10] reserving their enthusiastic support for their Sunday schools. In his analysis of the fate of the old endowed grammar schools and their revival and augmentation after 1889, he divides the country into north, centre and south and details particular district and school trajectories. In each, it is not until the 1860s that *y werin* quicken their interest either in such schools or in the new exile-driven and Nonconformity-fuelled university they were to feed. The 'alien puritanism' of Nonconformity was to split *y werin* into *buchedd* (way of life) A and B groups, the thrifty get-ons, future Liberals who grasped 'that without capital, the only way in which they could gain "positional social status" was to gain an education that was more advanced than that given in the elementary school',[11] and the no-good Bs, 'more easy going, readier to spend money, less regular in religious attendance, less strict in Sunday observance'.[12] The former responded to economic changes such as the development of the railways and increased industrial unit size, as a result of which 'the "scale" of the society was increasing, and social relations were becoming more tenuous and impersonal'.[13] The latter become invisible in Webster's discourse.

We are left with two images of Welsh pre-1870 provision—of its general relative backwardness, and of the endowed schools providing for the eminent scholar of humble origin in a way that such schools outside Wales failed to do. Religion and localism ensured that little happened with respect to endowed schools between Taunton and Aberdare. The tripartism and the 'ladder' which the former foreshadowed were, in Webster's view, 'different' in Wales from the start. As the commissioners found 'in Wales the lower middle and working classes merged to form *y werin* and it was difficult to make a clear distinction between second and third grade schools, and between these schools and elementary schools'.[14] The total increase in grammar-school numbers between 1867 and 1880 was very limited, though the character of the grammar schools probably became more homogeneous. Compliant Wales, content to cut its own tongue in its elementary and secondary schools, even before the measures of Lowe and Forster, was to be deemed worthy of reward by Aberdare for being 'content with maintaining the continuity of national life, preserving the traditional sentiments of the race', its loyalty contrasting with Irish sedition and 'protests against the supremacy of a dominant race'.[15] Mam-driven Mundella —and we must take Allsobrook's injunction to treat the biographical seriously as cause—thought Welsh conditions ripe for the production of 'a complete model of educational organisation worthy of the imitation of the English people',[16] whose centre-piece was to be the 'intermediate' schools, spearheading an advance whose main thrust would be through locally-adapted elementary and higher grade schools.

Webster's celebration of the Intermediate Education Act and its results symptomatizes his age and an educational culture fixed by and fixated on the 'gram' (grammar school) that grew from 1889, rather than on the 'standards' of the elementary school which the majority of our foreparents knew, those elementary schools for which Mundella was sending us the advanced model brochures from 1882. It is the 'whipped cream' of Grade One schools like Cowbridge which makes up modern Welsh educational history rather than the greasy *cawl* of Machynys or Splott. We have no Lowndes to catalogue the waste of talent, let alone Bill Taylor, eminent educationalist and eleven-plus failure. Our 'Wusstory' is still to be written.

The issue of language and the theme of urban-rural contrast are dominant categories in Webster's analysis, widely echoed in the shape of the attention given to modern schooling in recent histories of Welshness such as those of Williams[17] and Morgan.[18] His pre-parturition nation, by early this century (Labour was close but not started), had 'educational provision (which) reflected the cohesion of a more traditional society in rural Wales, [than] the growing complexity of the social structure of industrial South Wales'.[19] Because its chief aim everywhere was 'to facilitate economic and social mobility', Welsh was excluded from both the elementary and the secondary curriculum without protest in the nineteenth century; 'it was seen as an entirely natural and, indeed, desirable development'.[20] Reinsemination could only commence when Welsh political reproductive activities were displaced from the Nonconformist position. The sterility of the intermediate curriculum provided the text for Owen Edwards's rural romanticism. This latter wooed few in the bastions of an increasingly 'normal' class politics of a dominant south, even in the uniquely expansionist period up to around the century's turn, when south Wales was outranked only by the USA as a world centre of immigration.[21] In Webster's view, Edwards (although he achieved little more than putting his picture on every school wall) was the 'only educationalist in the early part of the century who really understood how. . . [A]n individualistic literary curriculum had a particularly traumatic effect on Welsh culture and society. . . The main purpose of the secondary school in Wales was to equip more able pupils to find posts outside their communities. The secondary school thus became a major cause of the impoverishment of Welsh life, especially in rural areas.'[22]

Williams precisely locates such accusatory voices as Webster's in the 'other Wales' simultaneously marginalized and made possible by the massive late-nineteenth-century expansion of inward migration to the south, without which Wales would have come to some variation on the southern Irish fate.

> What has come to be thought of as 'traditional' Nonconformist, radical, Welsh-speaking Wales in particular, that Wales which created so many of the characteristic Welsh institutions, notably the education-

al, was in some basic senses a by-product of this industrialisation, its ideology growing from a marginalised rural society, most often through the agency of displaced and upwardly mobile middle classes who had climbed out of that populist tilth.[23]

The dependency of this 'traditional' Wales on the deeply penetrated industrial south-east defined its contradictory soul. Our grandparent twin nations (and their several cousins), destined shortly to place separate orders for *Y Cymru Coch* and *Tit Bits*, begin round about that time. Webster the Arts Council saw 'the decrease in the vitality of indigenous Welsh culture as being not only the major responsibility of the Welsh educational system but also of the communications revolution'.[24] The nob when turned which made the world Wales's oyster revealed only the second-hand. A channel later, the Japanese protuberance affords us *Sgorio* to *Hel Straeon* to be watched (at least in the case of the former) by all codes within our speech groups — those who neither went nor lost the Welsh language, not quite our tiniest but certainly our most vocal minority; those rather more numerous who stayed and mutated into patois forms; those who have lost the language, joined by those who came without it who are determined to privilege their children with it (one of the wonders of the suburban south); those children, joined by their media-attracted rural cousins, who will become a new force in southern politics; the talkers tidy and untidy, by far our largest force; and inward migrants who most completely span the social and linguistic scales from the planning-consented ICCIEs (international corporate capitalism is 'ere) of the Vale to the thirty non-English-language bearers of the Cardiff schools located by Baird and Harris,[25] among the non-Welsh-speaking element of which are our least privileged minorities, crying out for an as yet unrealized application of 'some of the educational principles which have been evolved in successfully implemented Welsh/English bilingual education programmes'.[26]

The 'bilateralism' which Webster discerned in interwar Welsh secondary schools —

> there were in most schools far more places available than in English secondary schools but, once the pupils were admitted, all the attention was given to the dedicated 50 per cent who might obtain a school certificate, the rest were merely tolerated[27]

—still persists, remarked on by the Welsh Schools' Council as late as the 1981 Loosmore Report which saw it manifested in underachievement induced by an earlier surfeit of grammar-school places. Reynolds and Murgatroyd, using Assessment of Performance Unit data, developed the Loosmore thesis as a particular Welsh variation on a world-wide system failure to address the needs of the ordinary and less able in the 'schooled for failure' debate which followed. The virulence of this debate, a decade of disillusioned teachers later, can only be understood by empathizing with how the accused feel to be victim of the unnatural practices of their judges. Reynolds is right to tell us that, protests notwithstanding, not enough has changed, with Welsh no-qualification rates for leavers stubbornly staying above English rates and nearer to those of our riven cousins in Ulster. Beneath our national rate, there is the more telling reality of 'difference between Welsh LEAs in the relative performance of their schools which can now be seen as the most important educational issue confronting Wales'.[28]

Only two years into our new ERA of LFM for all and GMS for the quick, the issues for policy may be even more complex. At the grass roots, some of our least advantaged secondary schools are asking whether they can afford to stay with their LEAs under present conditions. The truly remarkable product of Thatcher's drive for real enterprise in the home is the aspiring southern parent, racked with the choice for her four-year-old between going Welsh or private. Few feel the need to take the latter, drastic step. Needs are served by sending young Craig to the Welsh school to be baptized the elective bilingual of the family.

No figure can be more keenly awaited than the self-assigned 'speak Welsh' return from this year's census. The tails-up and/or heads-down scenarios are no doubt already written (I simply want to say 'what a lousy question') and now have a post-1988 context which has made the vital shift from spectacular, positively discriminating voluntarism to unenforceable compulsion. Khlief's unpalatable thesis[29] concerning the dual purpose of the 'post-1945 ethnically assertive middle class' in seeking the hegemony of their Welshness which served for them as 'an expression of upward striving as well as a context for social bonds and solidarity'[30] ought to be alive and well. Just as most punters get to Joe Coral's rather than Ascot, so most Welsh 'nationalists' experience the trammelled ecstasy, glass in hand, of the boys on the box rather than the alcohol-free dampness of the National in August. There is no doubt still a 'knowable community' of the kind which Webster refers to as meeting at the

National Eisteddfod, given only to deeply legal acts in public with their LEAs, usually involving the exchange of extra money from the Welsh Office. Not only is Reynolds[31] seeking rhetorical leverage in regarding as 'quite extraordinarily irresponsible' the lack of planning activity toward producing the teachers to meet the core and foundation needs of National Curriculum Welsh (a probable tripling of Welsh-speaking teachers, duly redistributed), he is wrong on several counts. He misrecognizes the elasticity of the curricular elements of the Education Reform Act, tacked on to provide 'the same thing' to test, by a standards lobby now painfully getting its nose (and Act) back into joint, having been tweaked and tomfooled by TGAT (Task Group on Assessment and Testing). National Curriculum compulsion will turn out to be optional except where the marginal cost of enforcing it is virtually nil. Compare and contrast the current experience of Year VI teachers with our secondary-modern linguists. He also loses sight of the fact that the success of Welsh-medium schooling and learning Welsh as a modern language to date is predicated on the reality of its additive nature and electiveness, involving 'voluntary attendance by children whose families were committed to the notion of bilingual speakers in a bilingual country'[32] and where both languages have high status. That the progenitors of Welsh-medium/ Welsh-language schooling have achieved this through children being trooped voluntarily through our classrooms is one of the more remarkable sociolinguistic feats of our educational age. Its space and authenticity is guaranteed only while it works within a post-modern pluralism of style-sign and competitive persuasion and positioning. At one moment in the late twentieth century, one child in Merthyr could be living in a materials-rich, language-immersed, *athrawon bro*-tended, level-busting, Key Stage 1 *dosbarth*, while another could be living in a fractionated new-middle-class-capped world of educational support whose resources were fixed by the Section 11 plans of a local education authority some way down the expenditure table. Disconcertingly, they have the same formal educational entitlement, more likely to be served in a world of citizens (how the word has fallen into disuse!) than nationals. Morgan[33] is right to remind us that 'history was something that happened' to the Welsh, so long as that history is regarded as unnatural and multifarious. My Welshness was cold class-rolled, saw Saunders Lewis as a foreign body, saw Plaid (before its conversion to greener forms of local state enterprise) as rule by the theocratical, knew which way to point their aerials after the planner took away — and before the switches gave us back — our choice, and regarded the description Anglo-Welsh as an arrogance designed to cover a rumbled attempt at appropriation of the control of the means of enunciation. If Wales is 'reborn' in Webster and Morgan's terms rather than suffering yet another of the serial phantom pregnancies poeticized by Williams, then it must, if it is to avoid being a monster, realize that its world is the polyvalent, multi-past, many-tongued twenty-first century. Webster would also ask: 'What future is there for Welsh-language programmes if all we can provide is talk?' The encouragement, in a lively contemporary way, of the visual arts, music, drama, dance, film-making and other creative activities in our schools and colleges is as important as the encouragement of Welsh and teaching through the medium of Welsh'.[34] The agenda which this prospects is not media studies in clogs but one of international and cross-cultural access to differentiated experience which does not see a need to separate issues of identity, equality and worth. Here again is the Roger Webster we should all take seriously.

REFERENCES

1. G. A. Williams, *When Was Wales?* (London, 1985), 181.
2. J. R. Webster, 'The place of secondary education in Welsh society, 1800–1918' (University of Wales Ph.D. thesis, 1959).
3. Ibid., 1.
4. Ibid., 42.
5. Ibid.
6. Ibid., 3.
7. Ibid., 42.
8. Ibid., 43, quoting D. Lewis.
9. Ibid., 44.
10. Ibid., 55.
11. Ibid., 176.
12. Ibid., 173.
13. Ibid., 176.
14. Ibid., 211.
15. D. Allsobrook, '"A benevolent prophet of old. . .": reflections on the Welsh Intermediate Education Act of 1889', *Welsh Journal of Education*, 1 No. 1 (1989), 14, quoting Lord Aberdare.
16. Ibid., 16, quoting A. J. Mundella.
17. G. A. Williams, op. cit.
18. Kenneth O. Morgan, *Rebirth of a Nation: Wales 1880–1980* (Oxford and Cardiff, 1981).

19. J. R. Webster, 'Education in Wales and the rebirth of a nation', *History of Education*, 19 No. 3 (1990), 186.
20. Ibid.
21. Williams, op. cit., 178.
22. J. R. Webster, *The Arts and Education in Wales* (North Wales Arts Association, 1979), n.p.
23. Williams, op. cit., 180.
24. Webster, *The Arts and Education in Wales*, n.p.
25. A. Baird and J. Harris, 'Second language acquisition among Cardiff primary school children', *Education for Development*, 8 No. 1 (1984), 3–27.
26. Ibid., 26.
27. Webster, 'Education in Wales', 189.
28. D. Reynolds, 'The wasted years: education in Wales, 1979–89', *The Welsh Journal of Education*, 1 No. 1 (1989), 42.
29. B. B. Khlief, *Language, Ethnicity and Education in Wales* (The Hague, 1980).
30. Webster, 'Education in Wales', 191, quoting Khlief.
31. Reynolds, op. cit., 43.
32. Baird and Harris, op. cit., 21.
33. Morgan, op. cit., 420–1.
34. Webster, *The Arts and Education in Wales*, n.p.

A Period of Change—Working for Progress: Secondary Education in Wales, 1965–1985

ILLTYD R. LLOYD

The 1944 Act was born of a desire to ensure that all children were afforded opportunities to develop their educational potential and to play their part in the improvement of society. The idea of the provision of a full education, variously defined, for all children — including those from deprived as well as privileged backgrounds, those of low intellectual ability as well as those of high achievement, girls as well as boys — was to continue to feature prominently in educational debate in the years following and up to the present day. Not all accepted the primacy of schools as the instruments of achieving the nation's goals, but the importance of education as a means of encouraging personal satisfaction and meeting the individual's own needs, and as a means of responding to the demands of industry and commerce and to the nation's requirements, was increasingly recognized.

The call for an improvement in the quality of educational provision resulted in many changes in the content of, and the arrangements for, the education of our children, especially during the twenty years between 1965 and 1985. Many of the actions taken during this period, although sometimes leading into cul-de-sacs or failing to produce the benefits envisaged at the time, did in general assist towards a deeper consideration of underlying principles. The firmer understanding engendered gave rise to more coherent schemes during the later years. It is this period which will be the subject of this chapter, in particular in the context of secondary schooling.

The 1944 Act saw education as a continuous process with the formal provision beginning in the primary school but continuing into the secondary phase for all pupils; the school leaving age was raised to fifteen in 1947. There followed considerable secondary reorganization with the establishment of modern schools. (While the label 'technical' was associated with some modern and grammar schools, there was little distinctly 'technical' provision in Wales.) However the last of the all-age schools did not disappear until the mid 1960s and, even then, many of the modern schools were housed in vacated primary schools, often with staff inherited from the all-age schools and a paucity of specialist teachers trained for the secondary phase. In due course, developing urban areas (for example, Cardiff or Bridgend) and rural areas (for example the counties now forming Powys) were able to secure purpose-built accommodation.

In seeking a favourable status, secondary modern schools sought to emulate the grammar schools — which were particularly well regarded in Wales — and, where possible, sought to prepare pupils for the General Certificate of Education (GCE) Ordinary-level examinations. This policy was adopted especially in the 'selective' modern schools, where provision ('oases of opportunity') was sometimes made for 'grammar' pupils; but the trend was also discernible at other schools where a very small minority of pupils attracted generous treatment in terms of the use of staff.

However, the GCE O-level courses and examinations, geared to the needs of the ablest 20 per cent, were clearly unsuitable for many pupils and schools turned to a range of other schemes. Faith was shown in the certificated public examinations such as those of the Royal Society of Arts, as well as some organized by local education authorities (LEAs). Following the deliberations and recommendations of the Beloe committee, the Certificate of Secondary Education (CSE) was introduced in 1965. To aid its development, the Secondary School Examinations Council (SSEC) published in 1963 its first *Examination Bulletin*, which was largely the work of the Ministry of Education's Curriculum Study Group. This proved a valuable document and a number of local and national courses—usually subject-orientated—were held. The Newsom Report which appeared in the same year was also influential and included a useful description of experiences in various subject areas which motivated pupils. In general, teachers were reasonably well informed and prepared for the first CSE examinations in 1965 and they welcomed its introduction. It attracted support in modern and comprehensive schools but suffered in terms of status and prestige in comparison with the GCE O-level. There is no question but that the new examination secured a major improvement in the provision of the secondary modern schools of Wales, both in terms of their general philosophy and of the nature and content of courses provided. In addition, it proved a useful incentive for pupils and teachers. However, it is an indication of the development in the curriculum and thinking of schools following the introduction of the CSE, that, within a decade, the subject schemes were regarded as dated and somewhat restricted and in need of improvement.

CSE	1965	1966	1967	1968	1969	1970	1971	1972	1973	1974
Candidates	5230	9072	10 157	11 696	12 842	13 926	15 207	16 838	17 635	26 700
Entries	17 884	27 859	35 406	42 014	48 142	52 738	60 443	69 606	71 165	109 724
Subjects	31	34	35	39	44	50	54	71	92	141

(Entries for 1973 and 1974 include those under joint GCE/CSE feasibility study, amounting to 1828, 2163 respectively)

During the early sixties, central government was beginning to show an active interest in the school curriculum, in marked contrast with the previous attitude reflected in the statement by George Tomlinson when Minister of Education, 'Minister knows nowt about curriculum'. This interest found expression in the establishment of the Ministry of Education's Curriculum Study Group led by a team of two — a civil servant and an HMI. However, suspicion of the Ministry's intentions and a desire to limit its influence in the 'secret garden of the curriculum' led to the group's translation to become the basis of the Schools Council for the Curriculum and Examinations. This body, in its membership and soon in its actions, was dominated by teachers but with a powerful LEA influence.

There followed a period of intensive curriculum development. Much of it was linked with the raising of the school-leaving age (RoSLA) to sixteen which, though planned for 1970/1, did not take place until 1973/4. Also the demise of the eleven-plus examination in primary schools following the adoption of comprehensive education brought a major opportunity for curriculum development. The Schools Council made a considerable contribution in the field of public examinations through its oversight of the CSE, through its co-ordinating role across the examination boards, and by its substantial body of research, in particular comparability studies. The

Council's impact on schools came through a number of projects, some of which had a major and lasting influence on the content of courses and the teaching styles adopted. Amongst these, 'Geography for the Young School-leaver', 'Nuffield Secondary Science' and the Welsh-language schemes were especially successful. But in addition to its role in the examination system and participation in specific projects, the Council exercised major influence on schools through the debate it promoted, and the pamphlets it published, and the resulting general climate of thoughtful consideration and reappraisal of traditional approaches which it encouraged. It may be that change was at times initiated for its own sake, but the new thinking which was provoked provided of itself a useful basis for the curriculum reforms following RoSLA, secondary reorganization and the greater freedom accorded primary schools. The considerable school-based discussions and curriculum reviews which were a prominent feature of school organization in the late seventies and early eighties benefited from and were influenced by the knowledge, skills and attitudes developed during this earlier period.

The raising of the school-leaving age brought to fruition the vision of the 1944 Act of a secondary education for all, at least in terms of the involvement of all pupils for the full period eleven to sixteen years old, and the opportunity to sit the sixteen-plus public examinations. Another feature was the provision of additional, usually purpose-built accommodation which in some cases helped LEAs implement their plans for secondary reorganization.

The notion that children should gain positive satisfaction in their education rather than regard it as a benefit to be appreciated later, and the emphasis placed on relevance to the pupil's present situation as well as his future needs, attracted support and attention. A reflection of this mood is seen in the Her Majesty's Inspectorate paper published by the Schools Council Committee for Wales *RSLA: Another Year — To Endure or Enjoy?* (1967) and the Schools Council *Enquiry: Young School Leavers* (HMSO, 1968). Greater emphasis was placed on interest and enjoyment, on pupils gaining better understanding of the subject matter, and on a change of content in an attempt to up-date the teaching and introduce material which appeared more pertinent to the pupils' needs. The enthusiasm of reformers and the challenging nature of the demands on teachers were beneficial influences on teaching and learning in schools. However, the changes were not always well considered and were often adopted uncritically, while some teachers found difficulty in responding effectively. HM Staff Inspector for mathematics in England expressed misgivings in an article on 'Modern Maths Reconsidered' and echoed the concern of many in his comment:

> too many innovations for the ordinary teacher have been introduced and he has been expected to change content at too great a pace. It is better to teach well what one knows and has found to be of value than to fall a victim to 'modernisation' and teach badly what is unfamiliar and of doubtful value.

Curriculum development was not as general nor as radical in Wales as in England, and a more cautious approach was adopted. This conservatism was part of the Welsh educational tradition and related to the high regard for the nation's grammar schools; it was also influenced by the high level of stability of staff, a substantial proportion of whom had spent much of their teaching career in the same school or neighbourhood.

Comprehensive education

A singular feature of secondary education in Wales, and one which had a remarkable effect on primary education through the abolition of the eleven-plus examination, was the rapid growth of comprehensive schools.

Percentage of the 13-year-old age group attending:

SCHOOL	1961	1965	1969	1973	1977	1981	1985
Primary	3.4	1.6	–	–	–	–	–
Modern	60.0	54.3	33.7	9.4	6.4	1.8	0.7
Grammar	25.3	25.3	18.1	4.2	3.6	1.1	0.4
Technical	0.9	0.4	0.2	–	–	–	–
Comprehensive	10.1	15.1	46.3	85.7	89.9	97.0	98.9
Other	0.3	3.3	1.6	0.6	–	–	–
PUPILS (total numbers)	44 622	36 803	35 263	41 592	44 033	43 232	42 759

The earlier schemes were adopted largely on the grounds of

practical necessity, but soon the establishment of comprehensive (or sometimes multilateral) schools was seen by many as a means of extending to all children the benefits felt to be associated with grammar schools. The issue of the Department of Education and Science Circular 10/65 led to a greater urgency in the adoption of reorganization schemes by LEAs. In a number of cases, comprehensive schools were established under less than favourable circumstances, for example in divided premises, sometimes on three or four sites. The commitment to comprehensive education as a principle grew and even schemes which had serious weaknesses were implemented in the belief that the generality of pupils gained much although some might suffer a degree of disadvantage in the short term. Certainly, teachers were under considerable pressure during the first few years following reorganization and worked valiantly under difficult circumstances to ensure success.

Comprehensive schools attracted support in recognition of the additional resources likely to be available in larger schools. In addition there was the desire to give every child the opportunity to excel and a belief that pupils displayed talent at various levels in different fields. To maximize opportunity to individual pupils, some of the earlier schools introduced, wherever they could, extensive setting across each subject in all years. This in fact resulted in fairly stable teaching groups—effectively, streaming—while staffing and timetabling difficulties meant that the lower sets attracted less than satisfactory provision.

Another perceived advantage of the comprehensive school was its capacity to offer a wide range of subjects—including those commonly associated with grammar or with modern schools—to all pupils. This, linked with a desire to cater for the particular needs of pupils and to develop 'relevant' courses led to an increase in the number of subjects on offer, more especially in years IV and V.

Later other ideas came to the fore, in particular a stated adherence to 'mixed ability' classes, although this policy was applied in varying degrees and was rarely pursued rigorously or consistently. Often, the implementation of this policy was seen as an end in itself rather than as an element of a strategy of more general and ambitious goals. Gradually, however, an appreciation that the principal concern of organizational systems was to promote sound standards of teaching and learning became more widespread.

A measure used by many to judge the comprehensive schools was their performance in public examinations and a comparison of these results with those achieved by the former grammar schools. On the whole they passed this test comfortably. The importance of maintaining standards was recognized, and quite naturally there was a tendency to pay particular attention to the more able pupils. The needs of the least able and low-achieving pupils were acknowledged in the allocation of significant staff resources and the creation of small, often excessively small, classes although the quality of the experiences provided was often questionable.

Curriculum and organization

The principle of the equal value of all children was included universally by schools in their statements of aims, although it was not fully or effectively reflected in their practice and general provision. Attempts were increasingly made to provide something approaching a common curriculum in the first two or three years. This was apparent, for example, in the pursuit by all pupils of a number of aesthetic/practical subjects, often on a 'circus' arrangement, and the more general availability of the traditional 'academic' subjects, including a broad and varied range of experiences. The concept of providing a degree of differentiation to reflect ability and aptitude led to opportunities for abler pupils to study a number of languages (although only a small proportion continued into form IV), and also the separate sciences as opposed to a general or combined course (an unfortunate distinction, if only because it radically affected curricular opportunities in years IV and V).

Attempts were made in some schools to offer a more imaginative approach to the curriculum. This development was often linked with a desire to reduce the number of teachers by whom first-year pupils were taught and an attempt to ease the transfer from the class-teacher basis of primary education to that of subject teachers in the secondary school. Integrated or cross-disciplinary courses, for example, embracing history and geography, were introduced. Except for science, which enjoyed the support of national projects, a range of published texts, and wide adoption by schools, these courses attracted only limited success. This reflected the additional demands of some of the ambitious ventures, often outside the previous training and experience of the teachers concerned; it also reflected the fact that interdisciplinary studies were expected to meet the requirements of the separate disciplines which replaced them in the later years of schooling. Indeed, it was a valid criticism of many courses in years I–III that they were seen as a prelude to those to be followed in years IV–V, despite the fact that these experiences might, for many pupils, represent their last contact with certain subjects. Awareness of such weaknesses led to some reconsideration of the material included in the syllabuses followed in the earlier years, and to the encouragement of continued contact into years IV and V. Other factors which became increasingly apparent were the importance of providing stimulating teaching in the early years of secondary education, the need to secure suitably qualified teachers and the necessity of ensuring, by means of in-service education and departmental discussions, a substantial measure of confidence on their part in dealing with the subject matter.

In the attempt to meet the perceived needs of children and to ease the teacher's task, some form of grouping by ability was often adopted and pupils were subjected to an initial test in language and mathematics on entry. However, the unreliability of such tests, and a recognition of this as a most unfortunate introduction for the new pupil, led to their falling into disfavour. Increasing attention was therefore given to the need for the development of closer relations with the feeder primary schools — a cause which had attracted spasmodic attention in the past — if only to secure some agreement with them on teaching objectives on transfer. Such liaison was helpful in the suitable placement of pupils on entry and in encouraging greater continuity and a better-planned response to pupils' learning difficulties and opportunities.

The need for the association of pupils of different abilities, interests and backgrounds and the encouragement of greater social cohesion across the spectrum was acknowledged by schools and many formed registration groups which provided a reasonable cross-section of the intake. This approach was of limited success in its goal of integration for, while it provided some opportunity for contact, the duration of registration periods was brief and of little significance within the schools' overall programmes of activities. More effective, however, were later attempts to extend the registration group's identity, for example by arranging for some subjects to be taught to mixed-ability groups or by providing a pastoral curriculum for the consideration of matters of common interest and concern.

The schools' concern for their social objectives, and the feeling that 'streaming' had regrettable consequences for the achievement of a substantial proportion of pupils, led to a gradual adoption of a greater element of mixed-ability teaching. In many, if not most, cases, inadequate preparation was made for its introduction so that the teaching arrangements were often not entirely effective and the pace of work suffered, while there was a tendency to avoid study in depth. Setting was often allowed in some subjects, notably mathematics and modern languages, at least after the first term or year, although there were examples of the implementation of mixed-ability teaching over the first three years. In general, teaching methods concentrated heavily either on class teaching or on individual (assignment) learning, both of which had obvious limitations, with little use of group work.

While philosophically attracted to the principle of 'mixed-ability' classes, the majority of schools felt unable to adopt it to any significant extent in view of the difficulties associated with teaching such groups. This resulted in a quite extensive use of banding arrangements — usually two, in addition to a 'remedial' form — with setting arranged in some subjects. However, banding had many drawbacks. Thus, although the division between bands took place at a point where considerable error was likely in placement, the expectations of teachers and the perceptions of pupils were heavily influenced by the placement, to the extent that the sixteen-plus examination objectives of classes were often apparent in the first year. Furthermore, teaching content and approaches were often geared to the capacity of the abler groups and diluted to cater for the others.

In time, mixed-ability arrangements were adopted generally, at least in year I, although the extent to which this applied for teaching purposes and into later years varied. The difficulty of catering efficiently and effectively for the range of learning needs remained, although some attempts were made to ease this by the creation of rather smaller teaching groups, although still over twenty-five, and allowing setting in some subjects. In addition, schools moved substantially towards the provision of double periods or hour-long lessons, although this was more especially linked with an effort to reduce the movement of pupils and the time lost between lessons. This provided clear benefits, including that of allowing various class activities, but schools were slow to recognize the need for a review of teaching methods and lesson organization in the light of this change, and again the pace of work suffered.

If a largely common curriculum was the norm in the first two years, with some variation in year III, the pattern in year IV was one of general differentiation but with mathematics, English and sometimes Welsh, along with religious education and physical education, remaining core areas. This change reflected in large measure the demands of public examinations and the need for larger blocks of time to allow a more rigorous and extended study in the various subjects. Choice was also seen as an acknowledgement of the maturity of the pupils and as carrying the advantage of allowing them some influence on their programme of work. New subjects, many of them related to pupils' interests and to vocational opportunities, were introduced. Pupils were seen to lack motivation and achieve only limited success in some areas and have a predilection for others. A special and pleasing development during the late sixties was the provision of some 'out-of-school' experiences, more especially in commerce and industry, although their timetabling gave rise to difficulties and caused pupils who could least afford it to miss other class lessons. Other weaknesses related to the supervision of these activities and their association with main curricular work.

As indicated above, schools developed a number of new courses to cater more especially for those regarded as 'less academic' in their interests and aptitudes. These included studies which were related but had different emphases within subject fields and resulted in titles which users found difficulty in interpreting and doubts about the relative quality of performance which attracted the same grades. It was part of the philosophy of the CSE that the teacher was the most appropriate person to determine the pupil's curricular needs, and examining boards' responsibilities were limited to deciding whether the subject matter was examinable, determining the correct description and setting standards. Many of these courses helped engender interest and commitment amongst pupils and staff and served well in improving motivation. They provided a realistic response to the disenchantment of pupils who had had little success in the earlier years, so that for some pupils the abandonment of particular studies seemed sensible. However, the tendency to allow pupils an unrestricted choice and the growth in the number of courses outside the traditional disciplines, resulted in their opting out of subjects of importance to their future careers, in dropping whole areas such as science or the humanities or the aesthetic-creative, and excluding major fields of human knowledge and experience from their curriculum.

The provision of special packages and grouped options for those of modest or low ability, while ensuring a worthwhile and coherent programme of activities, resulted in a feeling of segregation and a limitation in pupils' career prospects, with shades of 'preparing pupils for their appointed place in society' — an accusation made about many of the RoSLA initiatives.

During the 1970s the writings of curriculum philosophers began to influence educational thinking so that provision for the fourth and fifth years was subjected to critical review by schools. It is interesting to contrast the general attitudes in 1965 and 1985. The former, one of wide choice and variation or provision, and uncertainty concerning balance. The latter, one of greater commonality, with confidence in the identification of the elements of a sound education and the fundamental experiences. Indeed, by 1985, the prevailing pattern was one of open option across the year group, but with a requirement that pupils select from each of a number of specified areas such as science, the humanities, the aesthetic-practical — although such a 'balance' was not always achieved in practice.

It must be acknowledged that the hard realities of greater financial stringency, a more rigorous application of staffing ratios by LEAs and a fall in the number on roll required schools to examine their use of staff more closely. The large number of very small teaching groups could no longer be afforded. At the same time, the excessive size of groups in some of the basic subjects (notably English and mathematics) and the pressure on staff whose programmes consisted almost entirely of large classes, were addressed.

Pastoral care

A significant feature of these decades was the growth of formal pastoral systems in schools. The role of the form teacher as the person who oversaw the punctual and regular attendance of pupils and their progress had, of course, previously been recognized. Secondary reorganization resulted in larger, more complex institutions with new expectations and a wider range of goals. There was a growing recognition of the school's role in influencing a pupil's attitude, personality and general behaviour as well as its responsibility for the care of pupils and the promotion of academic learning. The creation of a discrete and structured pastoral system including the delegation of duties formerly carried by the headteacher was the universal response to this situation.

Most schools in Wales had traditionally organized 'houses', usually four, but had restricted their activities largely to participation in the annual eisteddfod and sports events, although house assemblies might be held to generate a house spirit. A significant minority of schools increased the number of 'houses' in order to create manageable units and extended their role to accommodate the new pastoral responsibilities. Here the year group in each house could be identified as a form (or maybe two) including pupils of all ability levels, and the house activities allowed meaningful interaction between the pupils. This provided potential for a contribution to achieving the school's social goals, although its influence could not match that of the academic structure and, in practice, pupils identified themselves with the group with which they associated in class lessons. An advantage enjoyed by the house system was the continuity of contact, since pupils remained in and were 'cared for' by the same house throughout their time in the main school.

The large majority of schools based their pastoral arrangements on a horizontal system, since this was the basis for their teaching and principal role. This seemed the natural approach and did not conflict with the schools' accommodation or curriculum timetabling arrangements. In essence the system required, in addition to form tutors, year or section (for example, lower and middle schools) heads, or often both, although this proliferation of appointments often gave rise to excessively complicated and hierarchical arrangements. A deputy head was usually designated to carry special responsibility for this area, but this role was generally restricted to one of planning and light general oversight.

A crucial element in a pastoral system, whether vertical or horizontal, is the form tutor. The traditional role was carried in much the same way as ever, but progress beyond this was slow. Part of the difficulty was a lack of time and contact and, in response, schools timetabled pastoral periods and developed a 'pastoral curriculum'. These arrangements encouraged a closer relationship and provided help to pupils in meeting particular demands, such as those of settling into the new school, coping with bullying, dealing with homework, planning revision in year I. Questions remained as to whether the value gained matched the time allocated. A disappointing feature was the reluctance of form tutors to examine pupils' work and progress on a close and regular basis. Many teachers felt, usually without justification, a sense of inadequacy in discussing pupils' work outside their own specialisms and were aware of a danger of interfering with a function belonging to the departmental staff.

The tendency to see the caring system as being concerned with discipline and the general welfare of pupils brought a timely reminder in an HMI paper and the statement: 'In practice care for and teaching the child are so much bound up in each other as to be inseparable. . . The fundamental pastoral purpose is to foster the child's learning.' Schools increasingly saw their pastoral concern as a response to the needs of all pupils and not merely with the extreme difficulties of a few, and recognized that many behavioural problems arose out of failure in and disaffection with school work. Also the clear separation of the pastoral and academic systems was recognized as unfortunate although few went as far as one school which gave responsibility for particular year groups to subject departments or faculties (with mathematics/science/English staff in rotation taking years I/II/III) and deputy heads carrying section roles spanning both pastoral and academic aspects.

Roles of senior staff

The growth of comprehensive schools, often involving amalgamation of grammar and modern schools and housed in divided premises, brought attention to the need for new and more developed organization and management arrangements. A consideration of this was called for by the then Secretary of State, Anthony Crosland, and resulted in courses for heads and senior staff, such as those mounted annually over many years by the Welsh inspectorate.

A major influence on the structures adopted by recently reorganized schools was the desire to give responsibilities to staff who had previously held senior posts in the schools being merged, as well as a recognition of the urgent need to secure a well-ordered and disciplined institution and facilitate the work of class teachers. These considerations led in most cases to over-elaborate systems, a tendency for heads and deputies to take on excessively administrative and disciplinary functions, and an emphasis on the pastoral rather than the academic side. The salary structure imposed by Burnham agreements became a factor in this. It made additional graded posts available and schools found it easier to define new and discrete responsibilities within the pastoral and administrative rather than the academic field.

Most schools had three deputies — one designated academic and having responsibility for timetabling and some curriculum matters, one with oversight of pastoral affairs, and a third often designated 'senior mistress' and carrying miscellaneous duties. The academic arrangements were usually on a subject departmental basis, sometimes overlain with a faculty structure, although this was largely one of administrative convenience and rarely did heads of faculty intervene directly in subject matters. The pastoral arrangements usually involved about six heads of year or house, or three heads of section, or both. The failure of schools adequately to reflect their identified needs in their organization was well illustrated in a school with a major language problem, but where the head of English who had responsibility for dealing with this was seventh in the school's hierarchy — following three deputy heads and heads of section, none of whom played a role in this respect; furthermore the department was allowed only one supporting post carrying a special allowance.

In general, schools allocated about 20 per cent of the staff power to non-teaching time. Heads carried little more than a nominal timetable although some recognized the importance of being directly involved in the schools' prime function, that of teaching pupils. Deputies rarely taught more than half-timetables, while attempts were made to give all teachers one-eighth of their time free (that is, five periods of a forty-period week) with heads of section and a few others (for example, the careers counsellor) carrying substantially lighter teaching programmes. Little scope remained for the provision of additional time for those carrying 'middle-management' duties and as a result limited opportunities existed for them to carry extended roles or even those roles designated in the school's plans. Urgent disciplinary matters tended to go to deputy heads who were more likely to be available to deal with them.

The roles of deputy heads were seen as crucial in the sharing of responsibility with the headteacher. They made a major contribution in securing the smooth running of the school, seeking efficient timetabling of lessons and other activities, in carrying the general administration, and in assisting staff when called upon to do so. They worked closely with the head, in many cases meeting regularly at informal if not formal meetings, and succeeded during the period under discussion in developing clearer lines of communication and consultation with staff. Thus in curriculum matters, while decisions might still be taken by the senior management team, these were based on discussion with a representative body (for example, an academic board) rather than on conversations with individuals. Standing committees (for example, for the curriculum and for pastoral care) and working groups (for example, on homework and assessment) were common features of school organization. However the role of senior staff in the oversight of pupils' work and the monitoring of progress was slow to develop. Regular examination of pupils' work, the early identification of signs of disaffection and urgent response to indications of failure, consideration of whether class activities reflected the school's objectives and whether achievement matched potential and expectation, did not feature at all prominently in their programme. In this respect, schools were persuaded of the crucial role of the class teachers, of the importance of respecting their position and of avoiding any interference with their work.

In time, schools sought a more general influence for deputy heads and some, in an attempt to simplify provision, required one or more to carry appointments as section or perhaps faculty heads. These were pleasing developments, although, in contradiction, arrangements were often complicated when co-ordinating duties and cross-disciplinary roles were allocated to newly created posts instead of being taken by the senior team.

The subject department was seen as the body directing and overseeing pupils' learning. The head of department was nominal leader and provided the scheme of work (often lacking in detail and advice) and undertook all the administration, but this role was underdeveloped and the autonomy of the class teacher remained a powerful tradition. An improvement was, however, discernible over the years, with heads of department granted additional non-teaching time, with departmental meetings becoming much more general although still neglecting pedagogic issues, and with more widespread expectation of greater direction. In addition, other members of departments were given 'allowances' and accepted delegated responsibilities. During this period the provision of suites of subject rooms became common. This encouraged a greater professional association between the teachers, with greater oportunities for informal discussion and the sharing of resources, and the creation of a departmental identity. In some cases, the department undertook its own timetabling arrangements and organized its own disciplinary procedures.

Underachievement

The needs of industry and commerce for a well-prepared and qualified work-force and the concern of parents to secure a good education for their children brought education into public debate and a general recognition of its importance. Great anxiety was expressed regarding undeveloped potential and in particular what was seen as the underachievement of children in Wales, especially as perceived in the sixteen-plus examination results. Discussions were held within schools and LEAs, between HM inspectors and LEA officials and groups of heads, and at a national conference called by the Welsh Office and held at Mold in 1978.

Some change in the academic ethos was to be expected on reorganization. While a concentration on high academic achievement might be seen as normal in the grammar school, a more open situation was created within the comprehensive school by its very nature and its goal of catering for the full ability range. This gave rise to the comment on society's attitude: 'Failure within the grammar school was seen as the pupil's fault; failure in the comprehensive school was regarded as the school's fault.' Not that comprehensive schools neglected the academic needs of their pupils. They sought diligently to cater for them, at least in terms of preparation for public examinations, and the influence of the grammar school was apparent in the curriculum. Furthermore, there is evidence that under-expectation revealed in them was matched by similar tendencies in the former grammar schools.

Another factor which must be taken into account in the attitude and attainment of pupils and schools is the prevailing climate of public opinion. Schools seek to prepare pupils for life and to implant in them the values they cherish, and thereby serve and improve society; at the same time they cannot but in some measure reflect the society in which they exist. Broken homes, tolerance of lower standards of behaviour and the prevailing attitudes of a 'permissive society' themselves unquestionably made the task of schools much harder and greatly affected the pupils' approach to school and their readiness to undertake disciplined study.

The debate concentrated on the achievements of school-leavers and, in particular, the proportion with no certificated qualifications, and the marked difference between the situations in Wales and in England. In this context it should be remembered that the GCE O-level/CSE examinations were intended to cater for 60 per cent of the population, subject by subject, and the complaints referred to the fact that for example in 1975/6 73.5 per cent of the school-leavers in Wales achieved certificates at sixteen-plus as opposed to 83.5 per cent in England. The arrangements for the CSE examination differed in the two countries. The thirteen CSE boards in England had been set up in 1964 for this express purpose while the Welsh board carried responsibility for both examinations and predated the CSE. The Welsh Joint Education Committee prided itself on a concern for the use of sound and proven examination techniques, rigorous standards and high reliability. However, there was a feeling that it was 'unduly authoritarian and rigid in its administration of the system'; it certainly scrutinized Modes II and III proposals thoroughly. The board's officers were very influential in such matters and their expertise respected, but its committees which determined policy were composed largely of teachers. The approaches adopted by the different CSE boards varied considerably and, while much research had been undertaken on comparability of standards at the Grade 1 level, little concern was shown about such comparability at the lower end. This reflected the intention at the establishment of the CSE. Some variation was inevitable and likely to be significant at Grade 5. Indeed the value of a certificated performance at this level might itself be questioned.

A clear difference between Wales and England existed in the use of Modes II and III schemes. The attitude of the Welsh board may well have been a factor here, although schools which had been successful in gaining acceptance of their schemes expressed appreciation of the board's advice and support. Perhaps the conservative attitude of many Welsh teachers (which may have been apparent in the board's responses) also affected the situation. It must be acknowledged that a scheme of high quality made substantial demands on the teachers concerned, including possibly the collaboration of neighbouring schools to secure the necessary range of expertise, an effort hardly justified if the board's syllabus was generally acceptable. Another feature of the WJEC's arrangements was the later timing of the written examinations in the summer term when a number of pupils would already have left school to take up employment.

Whatever the explanation offered for the discrepancy between England and Wales, the need to improve standards and to cater more effectively—more especially for those of modest ability—and to eliminate the unacceptable variation in performance of schools in similar situations and of departments within schools was acknowledged. With the general improvement in achievement and a larger proportion proceeding to higher education, industry and commerce increasingly relied on leavers of lower attainment for their workforces. This added to the call for a further improvement in standards.

Reference has been made to the fundamental philosophical discussions on the curriculum during the late 1970s and 1980s, and concern was frequently expressed at the neglect of the 'basic' subjects and elements (variously described). It is noteworthy that the HMI paper which led the early discussions of underachievement in Wales was entitled *Literacy and Numeracy* and spoke of the common core. This paper emphasized that teachers were as committed as ever to the teaching of the essentials of reading and writing and said that there was no evidence of indifference to arithmetic and computation, but did report underachievement as a disturbingly substantial problem. (The paper covered both primary and secondary phases.)

The tendency of comprehensive schools to adopt banding arrangements for teaching and to pay particular attention to those who were likely to secure good examination results may have been significant. Certainly, concern was expressed at the relative neglect of the academically less able, although this criticism, like many others, was not peculiar to Wales. In this respect, traditional attitudes, cultural influences and the economic pressures and nature of employment opportunities of the past may have led Welsh society to respect high academic achievement but to see little gain in attainment at a lower level.

The later seventies and early eighties saw a concerted effort on the part of schools and LEAs to improve the situation and to devise curricula and teaching arrangements which showed due regard for the middle- and lower-ability groups. This was reflected in, and occurred along with, the strengthening of subject departments and their responsibilities, with increasing regard to qualification and training, and their role in organizing and overseeing teaching, including that of special needs classes. In addition LEAs paid greater attention to the scrutiny and detailed analysis of sixteen-plus examination results in each school and to pursuing cases of concern.

An area of weakness had been the assessment of pupils' work and lack of careful monitoring of their progress from the earliest stages. Much attention was paid to these aspects and a number of local initiatives taken, including quite ambitious schemes, often linked with the development of pupil profiles. Some involved local industry in the provision of criteria for the final year's assessment. One particular project which later attracted wide support across Wales and which catered specifically for the low achiever was the 'Certificate of Education', initially developed by the Mid Glamorgan authority but taken over by the WJEC. The question whether such a scheme should stand outside the GCSE is a matter of debate but this certainly made a substantial contribution in an area of great need.

There is little doubt that the discussion and developments which took place during the decade 1975-85 strengthened the schools in their work and ensured that they were better placed to respond to and even anticipate many of the changes which occurred in the years following. Substantial improvements were made, although some problems were not amenable to solution by schools.

Bilingual education

A remarkable feature of education in Wales during this period was the growth in the demand for schools providing teaching through the medium of Welsh. In most respects, the nature and content of education in Wales has been heavily influenced by events in England. Bilingual schools were a development peculiar to Wales and reflected pressure from parents — not so much educationists and teachers, although these provided influential support. The growth in bilingual education was spectacular, more especially in the Anglicized areas where such provision was seen as the only means of securing an education within a Welsh ethos and of ensuring mastery of Welsh, increasingly difficult under the influence of largely English mass media. Initially, many of the protagonists were Welsh-speakers who wished their children to gain the privilege which had been enjoyed effortlessly by a former generation brought up in a naturally Welsh society. Notable in the developing situation was the interest and support shown by non-Welsh-speakers, including in-migrants from England, so that in some cases as many as 90 per cent of children came from homes where one or both parents were unable to speak Welsh. Especially demanding were situations (mainly in Clwyd) where pupils (in one case representing as many as half the intake) entered bilingual secondary schools without a basis of bilingual primary education.

Designated bilingual secondary schools throughout Wales

	1960	1965	1970	1975	1980	1985	1990
Number	1	5	6	8	11	16	18
Pupils	310	1429	2843	5504	8281	10 332	11 519

Securing suitable provision created difficulties for LEAs, but the major demands fell on teachers who had no previous experience of bilingualism to call on and had to create Welsh-medium resources. The success of bilingual schools owes much to the commitment and enthusiasm, the application and perseverance of teachers.

It is surprising that in general, schools in the Welsh heartland and having a significant proportion of native Welsh-speakers made little Welsh-medium provision, except in religious education and Welsh history, and were slow to follow the lead of designated bilingual schools. However in due course they were caught up in the tide, especially when the threat to the Welsh language became ever more apparent and the advantages of consistent and significant use of Welsh were realized. The early arrangements suffered as a result of the isolation of the teachers involved in the work and of a practice of using both languages in parallel in teaching classes. The active support and encouragement of LEAs and the favourable attitude of the Department of Education and Science and the Welsh Office were all factors in the development.

The language policies of the early schools showed a clear tendency to continue to teach science and mathematics in English, with Welsh adopted for the arts and humanities. As they grew in confidence, teachers realized the artificiality of such an arrangement and the unfortunate inference which could be drawn from it, and the scope of Welsh-medium work was extended. The question of balance in the use of the two languages in the light of the pupils' linguistic backgrounds was the subject of much discussion.

The pioneering spirit of teachers and their commitment to the Welsh language were clear but their task was not easy in view of the paucity of Welsh-medium materials available. In some instances LEAs appointed translators to assist in the creation of 'notes', and soon the WJEC started its Welsh books scheme in recognition of the urgent and substantial demand. The flow of books was considerable, especially after the financial aid of the government's specific grant became available, but the demand always seemed to outstrip supply. The Welsh Office itself played an important part, not only with its financial support but more significantly in establishing a series of initiatives at the University College of Wales, Aberystwyth, for the production of Welsh-medium resources and in helping the education department to establish its own Welsh-medium resources centre which became a major provider in this field. It was fortunate that the WJEC examining board was able to respond confidently to the challenge in its sixteen-plus examinations.

Provision of Welsh-medium examinations by the WJEC Board

	1960	1965	1970	1975	1980	1985	1990
GCE O level							
Subjects	4	6	12	18	31	34	48
Entries	33	145	324	1037	2861	4500	subjects
CSE							with 6917
Subjects		9	13	26	33	37	entries for
Entries		na	na	1239	2047	2299	GCSE
GCE A level							
Subjects	–	–	7	10	19	16	24
Entries			28	164	319	579	903

There can be little doubt that the bilingual schools responded effectively to the wishes of parents and attracted enthusiastic support. They made a major contribution not only in firmly establishing the feasibility of bilingual education but also in helping to promote the use of Welsh in the community and society generally. The sterling work undertaken in these schools must be regarded as the principal and most hopeful development with regard to the Welsh language.

The period under review was one of considerable critical appraisal and was characterized by high ideals and aspirations. The growth in expectations was such that, despite the efforts of schools in their activities—thinking, planning and teaching—complete satisfaction seemed beyond reach. Significant moves were made towards the achievement of a richer learning provision and making this an entitlement for all pupils. Schools' concern for the well-being of their pupils was apparent in all their exertions and these provided a useful basis for later developments.

BIBLIOGRAPHY

Ministry of Education, *Secondary School Examinations Other than the GCE* (HMSO, 1960).
Secondary Schools Examination Council, *The CSE: Some Suggestions for Teachers and Examiners* (HMSO, 1963).
Ministry of Education (Central Advisory Council), *Half Our Future* (HMSO, 1963).
R. C. Lyness, 'Modern Maths reconsidered', *Trends in Education*, 14 (April 1969), 3–8.
HMI, *Pastoral Care in the Comprehensive Schools of Wales* (Welsh Office, 1981).
HMI, *Literacy and Numeracy* (Welsh Office, 1977); *Literacy and Numeracy and Examination Achievements in Wales* (Welsh Office, 1978).
HMI, *Comprehensive Schools of Wales, Years I, II and III* (Welsh Office, 1978).
HMI, *Comprehensive Schools of Wales, Aspects of Organisation and Roles of Senior Staff* (Welsh Office, 1981).
HMI, *Years IV and V in Comprehensive Schools* (Welsh Office, 1981).
HMI, *Welsh-medium Work in Secondary Schools* (Welsh Office, 1981).
HMI, *Public Examinations in Wales, Attainment at 16+* (Welsh Office, 1982).
HMI, *Planning for Progress: A Contribution to the Debate on Achievement in Secondary Schools* (Welsh Office, 1982).
HMI, *Assessment and Monitoring of Progress in Secondary Schools of Wales* (Welsh Office, 1983).
HMI, *Departmental Organisation in Secondary Schools* (Welsh Office, 1984).

Data quoted are taken from Welsh Office Statistics of Education and WJEC Reports on GCE/CSE examinations—both published annually.

'GWREIDDIAU': Prosiect Creu Deunyddiau ar gyfer yr Ysgol Gynradd

INA WILLIAMS

Tîm cymharol fychan o bobl a weithredai fel aelodau pwyllgor llywio'r prosiect cwricwlwm, 'Gwreiddiau'[1] pan sefydlwyd ef gyntaf gan y Swyddfa Gymreig. Er bod y pwyllgor llywio hwn yn dal i weithredu fel uned trwy gyfnod datblygu'r prosiect, casglodd o'i gwmpas amrywiaeth o brofiadau cyfoethog trwy gyfraniad ac arbenigedd tîm ehangach o lawer o bobl, oddi mewn ac oddi allan i ysgolion, dros gyfnod o dair blynedd. Ceisio disgrifio rhai o'r profiadau hynny, a sôn am y fframwaith a dyfodd i'w cynnal yn ystod camau datblygol y prosiect, a wneir yn bennaf yn y bennod hon.

Dros gyfnod o bedwar tymor, rhwng 1988 ac 1990, y treialwyd deunyddiau drafft cynnar y prosiect 'Gwreiddiau' mewn pymtheg o ysgolion ledled Cymru — rhai ohonynt yn ysgolion bach gwledig, eraill mewn ardaloedd poblog, trefol. Pynciau dyniaethol y cwricwlwm sy'n derbyn y prif sylw yn y prosiect hwn. Mae prif amcanion y prosiect yn rhoi pwyslais:

ar hybu trafodaeth a phartneriaeth rhwng plant ac athrawon a rhwng yr ysgol a'r gymuned agos, leol ac â chymunedau pellach i ffwrdd;
ar ddatblygu uwch sgiliau gwybyddol mewn plant, a fydd yn eu galluogi i weithredu'n annibynnol;
ar baratoi deunyddiau a fydd yn gwella'r ddarpariaeth ddysgu ac addysgu a thrwy hynny yn codi safonau'n gyffredinol.

Gellir felly honni fod ei gyfraniad yn ymestyn ymhellach na ffiniau'r meysydd dyniaethol. Gall gynnig syniadau ar gyfer hybu prosesau dysgu a dulliau o weithio sy'n ymroi i ddatblygu'r cwricwlwm cyfan. Diddorol yw nodi arwyddocâd arbennig cyfnod y treialu a'r ffaith iddo gyd-daro â chyfnod sefydlu'r Cwricwlwm Cenedlaethol mewn ysgolion, ynghyd ag ymddangosiad y cyhoeddiadau pynciol statudol ac mai yn y cyd-destun hwn y cytunodd athrawon yr ysgolion treialu i ymgymryd â datblygiad arall eto. Gweithredent fel aelodau o dîm yn datblygu a chreu deunyddiau, a fyddai, nid yn unig yn cyflenwi rhai o anghenion cwricwlwm hanes a daearyddiaeth, ond hefyd yn hybu'r defnydd o'r Gymraeg ar draws y cwricwlwm ac yn cynnig syniadau ar gyfer datblygu meysydd eraill y cwricwlwm yn ogystal.

Mae deunyddiau'r prosiect[2] yn darparu ar gyfer amrywiaeth o wahanol sefyllfaoedd dysgu yn y dosbarth ac yn ymrannu yn:

unedau penodol ar gyfer hanes a daearyddiaeth;
tâp fideo ar ffynonellau hanes;
canllawiau ar gyfer datblygu themâu integredig;
cyhoeddiad sy'n rhestru detholiad o nofelau Cymraeg a Saesneg, gan gynnwys pedair nofel Gymraeg newydd, a fydd yn cadarnhau ac yn ymestyn ymdriniaeth y dosbarth o themâu'r prosiect.

Yr un egwyddorion sylfaenol sy'n cysylltu'r holl ddeunyddiau hyn â'i gilydd, sef pwysleisio gwerth datblygu rôl weithredol y plentyn, a hynny trwy brofiadau a gweithgareddau sy'n rhoi cyfle iddo feithrin sgiliau a'i alluogi i weithredu'n annibynnol.

Teimlid bod yr ysgolion treialu, gwledig a threfol, bach a mawr, fel ei gilydd, mewn sefyllfa fanteisiol i ddatblygu cwricwlwm a fyddai'n seiliedig ar yr egwyddorion uchod. Oherwydd un o'r ffactorau pwysicaf ar gyfer hybu proses sy'n ddibynnol ar bartneriaeth rhwng athrawon a'i gilydd, rhyngddynt a'r plant a rhwng yr ysgol a'r gymuned, yw'r awyrgylch clòs, cartrefol a welwyd yn yr ysgolion hyn. Cyfeiriodd Gittins, fwy nag ugain mlynedd yn ôl, at bwysigrwydd hyn:

> Mae'r ysgol wledig fechan wedi gwneud cyfraniad pwysig i fywyd cefn gwlad ac mae'n dal i wneud hynny o hyd. Fe gafwyd hanes yn ddiweddar am arbrawf addysgol arbennig o ddiddorol a gynhaliwyd mewn ysgol un-athro . . . 'Roedd y gwaith a wneid ynddi yn dangos sut y gall yr ysgol wledig fod fel teulu, gyda chysylltiadau agos a chyfeillgar rhwng y plant a'r athrawon. Os caniateir i'r plant ddysgu trwy weithgareddau mae'n bosibl cyfuno dysgu o fewn amserlen hollol ystwyth.[3]

Nid un o nodweddion ysgol fach yn y cyfnod hwnnw'n unig ydyw'r awyrgylch hwn. Cyfeirir ato eto yn y sylwadau hyn mewn Adroddiad Arolygwyr am un o ysgolion Caerdydd heddiw:

> Y mae'r ysgol wedi llwyddo i greu awyrgylch cynnes, cartrefol a chwaethus lle y gall y disgyblion deimlo'n ddiogel a hyderus . . . Gwelir

pwyslais da ar fagu ysbryd cymunedol a cheir cyd-barch rhwng yr athrawon a'r disgyblion.[4]

Un o oblygiadau mwyaf cydnabod pwysigrwydd rôl weithredol y plentyn, ochr yn ochr â'r egwyddor o gryfhau perthynas yr ysgol â'r gymuned leol ac â'r byd ehangach, yw ychwanegu at y pwysau sydd eisoes ar ysgwyddau athrawon wrth iddynt chwilio am ffyrdd i rannu eu hamser rhwng pawb a phopeth. Mae'r Athro Maurice Galton, cyd-gyfarwyddwr prosiectau ORACLE[5] a PRISMS[6] yn cyfeirio at hyn ac yn pwysleisio mor anodd yw ateb y broblem:

> Such negotiations are not easy. Initially they can lead to high levels of stress, particularly in schools with a large staff, where some colleagues may not understand or may be opposed to such ideas. It is, however, a proud boast of many teachers from small schools that one of the advantages they enjoy is ease of communication between colleagues, and the excellent relationships that are developed with a small group of children.[7]

Bu ymateb athrawon y grŵp treialu i ddeunyddiau drafft 'Gwreiddiau' yn un positif iawn a gwelwyd bod athrawon, yn gyffredinol, yn ymwybodol iawn o'r angen i ddatblygu cwricwlwm perthnasol i gefndir a diddordebau'r plant a'u bod yn chwilio am awgrymiadau ar sut i weithredu. Daeth yn gwbl amlwg o'r trafodaethau a gafwyd ganddynt, o'r nodiadau yn eu dyddiaduron ac ynyr enghreifftiau o waith plant, eu bod, wrth weithredu ar nifer o argymhellion y prosiect, hefyd yn codi pontydd cysylltiol rhyngddynt a'u cydweithwyr, y plant, y rhieni a'r gymuned gyfan. Dywedodd un athro o ysgol lle mae mwyafrif y plant yn dod o gartrefi di-Gymraeg, iddo lwyddo mewn ffordd na wnaeth erioed o'r blaen, i gysylltu cefndir a chartrefi'r plant i gyd â gweithgareddau'r dosbarth, wrth ddatblygu'r thema 'Symudiadau Pobl'. Ar y dechrau esboniodd ei fwriadau i'r plant a'r rhieni gyda'i gilydd. Cafodd pawb gyfle i ymuno yn nhrafodaethau cynllunio'r thema a thrwy gydol y tymor ymatebodd pob teulu'n ddieithriad mewn ffyrdd ymarferol i'r gofynion gwahanol a wnaethpwyd arnynt. Deuent i'r ysgol i sôn am eu cefndiroedd ac am yr ardaloedd yr oeddynt wedi byw ynddynt; cefnogent y plant i chwilio yn eu cartrefi am arteffactau a oedd yn rhan o'r cefndiroedd hynny a'u hannog i fynd â hwy i'r ysgol er mwyn galluogi'r dosbarth cyfan i rannu a chyfnewid profiadau am gefndiroedd gwahanol iawn. Roedd un plentyn wedi byw yn Los Angeles am dair blynedd ac un arall â'i wreiddiau yn ynysoedd gorllewinol yr Alban. Tyfodd yr ysgol o fewn y gymuned i fod yn ganolbwynt bwrlwm a gweithgarwch cwricwlwm. Cysylltwyd plant a theuluoedd â'i gilydd, nid yn unig ar lefel cyfeillgarwch cymdeithasol ond hefyd ar lefel o ymwybyddiaeth ddiwylliannol. Mewn ysgol fach wledig y digwyddodd y profiad hwn ac mae'n cyfateb i'r hyn a ddywed Bell a Sigsworth am sefyllfaoedd gwledig yn gyffredinol:

> Most visibly, there is the openness to the community; this is shown in the encouragement that is given to parents to participate in a variety of ways by the frankness with which the headteacher explains his hopes and his concerns in all his transactions with parents . . . the curriculum does not dominate the interests and knowledge they bring with them to school but endeavours to utilize it.[8]

Nid oedd pob athro yn y grŵp treialu yn fodlon caniatáu trafodaeth a phartneriaeth ar y lefel hon drwy'r amser. Roedd eu rhesymau dros hynny yn weddol amlwg, sef y perygl o golli rheolaeth a chreu cwricwlwm penagored na ellir ymlaen llaw bennu ei ffiniau na rhagdybio disgwyliadau a chyraeddiadau drwyddo. Ond roedd y mwyafrif yn barod i gydnabod fod potensial uwch i gwricwlwm sy'n gyfuniad o ofynion a disgwyliadau athro ar y naill law a dyheadau a gobeithion plant a rhieni ar y llaw arall. Mae creu partneriaeth rhwng athro a phlentyn ac, yn y pen draw, rhwng yr ysgol a'r cartref yn y broses o gynllunio a gweithredu'r cwricwlwm yn golygu ystyried mwy nag un agenda ochr yn ochr â'i gilydd wrth benderfynu ar ddatblygiad y cwricwlwm hwnnw, a bydd yn hanfodol cael trafodaeth cyn y gellir cytuno ar flaenoriaethau a meini prawf i ddisgrifio'r cwricwlwm hwnnw. Cafwyd enghreifftiau amrywiol o hyn yn ystod cyfnod y treialu. Gan un dosbarth, yn ystod cyfnod cynllunio'r thema 'Datblygu Cymuned' trefnwyd noson goffi i rieni a soniwyd wrthynt am y bwriadau, gan wahodd awgrymiadau ganddynt a chynigion am help ymarferol yn ystod cyfnod gweithredu'r thema. Mae trafodaeth fel hon nid yn unig yn gyfrwng effeithiol i gadarnhau gwir bartneriaeth ar lefelau addysgol a chymdeithasol rhwng yr ysgol a'r gymuned y mae'n rhan ohoni, ond mae hefyd yn mynd i sicrhau cwricwlwm perthnasol ac ystyrlon i'r plant.

Tystiolaeth yr athrawon y buwyd yn cydweithio â hwy oedd bod y drafodaeth hon rhwng athrawon y plant ac eraill yn elfen y mae angen ei meithrin yn ofalus. Nid rhywbeth sy'n digwydd yn hollol naturiol a chyfrifol ydyw ac mae gan yr athrawon rôl bwysig mewn sicrhau y bydd yr elfen hon yn un gwbl ddiffuant ac yn cyfrannu at yr addysg a gynigir yn y dosbarth. Wrth gwrs, mae gan rieni ddiddordeb mewn addysg yn gyffredinol, ond ar lefel benodol y mae eu diddordeb yn ei amlygu ei hunan, mewn perthynas â'u plant eu hunain neu'r grŵp y mae'r plentyn hwnnw'n perthyn iddo. Rhaid i'r athrawon sicrhau cyfle cyfartal i'r holl blant dan eu gofal. Eto, pan fo'r plant eu hunain yn cyfrannu mewn trafodaeth gwyddom fod llawer o ffactorau, rhai'n gadarnhaol a rhai'n negyddol, sy'n lliwio'r cyfraniad hwnnw. Mae nodweddion cynhenid mewn plant o'r oed hwn, megis chwilfrydedd, dyfalbarhad a bywiogrwydd, yn hybu unrhyw broses addysgol tra bod elfennau eraill megis swildod, hunanoldeb, diogi a difaterwch yn llesteirio unrhyw ddatblygiad. Gwelodd athrawon y grŵp yr angen i arsylwi er mwyn cofnodi pa elfennau a oedd yn rheoli ar unrhyw adeg. Rhoddwyd arnynt ofynion gwahanol, sef ffrwyno, hybu neu dderbyn y gwahanol elfennau yn ôl y galw.

> Yr agwedd bwysicaf ar unrhyw gwricwlwm yw'r cydadwaith rhwng athro a disgybl . . . bydd athrawon yn addysgu orau a disgyblion yn dysgu orau mewn cydadwaith bywiog lle mae'r disgybl yn gweithio ar dasgau priodol ac yn gyfranogwr gweithgar ynddynt, a lle gall yr athro, drwy ymyrryd yn sensitif, gyfoethogi addysg y disgyblion a chanfod cryfderau a gwendidau'r addysgu.[9]

Wrth weithredu fel hyn roedd yr athrawon yn dangos i'r plant eu bod yn barod i wrando a derbyn awgrymiadau ond bod disgwyl i'r plant ddeall fod ganddynt gyfrifoldeb i weithredu ar sail eu cynigion. Wrth ddatblygu thema 'Yr Ysgol' gwelwyd ei bod yn ofynnol i blentyn a gynigiodd fynd allan i holi nifer o'r henoed yn y gymuned am fywyd ysgol pan oeddynt hwy yn blant, gyflawni'r dasg hon gyda hygrededd trwy baratoi holiadur priodol, trefnu amser, dangos cwrteisi, adrodd yn ôl ac ati. Os na wneir hyn, yna mae pawb yn colli hyder yn y plentyn a'i syniadau. Os rhennir y drafodaeth, yna hefyd fe rennir y cyfrifoldeb. Lle nad oes trafodaeth, yr unig ddisgwyliadau sydd gan blentyn yw ei fod yn ufuddhau i orchmynion gan eraill, yr athro gan amlaf. Yn yr un modd, os yw rhieni'n awgrymu y byddai ymweld â rhyw le hanesyddol o fudd i'r plant ac yna'n amharod i helpu gyda'r trefniadau, i ddangos diddordeb yn y profiad ac i'w ymestyn trwy fynd â'u plant y tu allan i amser ysgol ar ymweliadau cyffelyb, bydd gan yr athrawon le i amau cymhelliad y rhieni dros gynnig awgrym o'r fath.

Wrth ddatblygu agweddau ar thema'r prosiect 'Cadwraeth Ynni' mewn un ysgol, bodlonodd y rhieni droi eu cartrefi'n ganolfannau ymchwil am dridiau er mwyn galluogi'r plant i weithredu'r damcaniaethau a oedd ganddynt ar sut y gallai pob teulu, trwy ymdrechion penodol, gwtogi ar ei ddefnydd o drydan, nwy ac olew.

Gwelwyd sefydlu amryw arferion cynilo da gan y plant eu hunain, a barhaodd o'r cyfnod byr hwn i gyfnodau hwy a chafodd rhieni fantais ariannol o'r arbrawf. Ond datgelwyd yn ddiweddarach fod yr arian a gynilwyd yn achos rhai cartrefi wedi cael ei ychwanegu at lwfans arian poced y plant!

Mae athrawon yn gyffredinol wedi arfer gweithredu trwy arwain y plant i ystyried pwy fydd 'y gynulleidfa' wrth iddynt baratoi darnau o waith neu ymgymryd â thasgau penodol. Mae meddwl fel hyn yn rhoi ffocws pendant i'r holl gamau cynllunio a datblygu. Sylweddolwyd gymaint yw gwerth diffinio'r 'gynulleidfa' wrth weithredu'r ddwy thema 'Y Pentref' a 'Chyfnewid Ysgolion'.[10] Yn y gyntaf, mae'r prif weithgarwch yn canolbwyntio ar baratoi arolwg o fywyd y pentref ar sail ymweliadau, arsylwadau, casglu ffynonellau a phwyso ar dystiolaeth lafar er mwyn casglu data, ac yna eu coladu a'u cofnodi. Fel hyn rhoddir ar gof a chadw hanes cyfnod ym mywyd y gymuned leol, ond nid dyma ddiwedd y gwaith na holl bwrpas y gwaith. Wedi cyflawni'r dasg hon mae modd symud ymlaen yn naturiol i weithgarwch ehangach, sy'n cynnig profiadau cydlynus a datblygol, trwy weithredu'r thema 'Cyfnewid Ysgolion'. Byddai'r ysgol gyfnewid hithau wedi gwneud astudiaeth ar 'Y Pentref' a dyma felly ffocws i'r broses o gyfnewid profiadau wrth efeillio. Wrth efeillio, cafodd ysgolion y grŵp treialu gyfle i gyfnewid llyfrau gwybodaeth, dogfennau, lluniau, arteffactau ac yn y blaen a baratowyd ac a gasglwyd ynghyd gan blant y ddwy ysgol. Symudent yn naturiol i wneud astudiaeth gymharol o'r ddwy sefyllfa gan sylwi ar yr hyn oedd yn gyffredin ac yn wahanol ynddynt. Cawsant gyfle i gyfathrebu trwy lythyru, trwy raglenni cyfrifiadur, manteisio ar rwydwaith y rhaglen radio i ysgolion, sef 'Digwydd', a hyn i gyd cyn, yn ystod a rhwng cyfnewid ymweliadau â'i gilydd.

Dyma un enghraifft, o blith nifer o rai eraill a awgrymir yn themâu'r prosiect, o ysgolion yn ymwneud â themâu sy'n galluogi plant i ymdeimlo â'u gwreiddiau ac sydd yr un pryd yn creu ynddynt ymwybyddiaeth a dealltwriaeth am gymunedau eraill, a hynny ar sail profiadau real, uniongyrchol. Cyn cychwyn ar y gwaith uchod gwahoddwyd y plant i lunio datganiadau am eu cymuned hwy a'r gymuned yr oedd yr ysgol efeillio'n rhan ohoni. Sylweddolwyd o'r datganiadau mai'r duedd oedd cymryd yn ganiataol y gwelid elfennau tebyg mewn cymunedau a phentrefi cyfagos i'w gilydd. Cawsant gyfle drostynt eu hunain i sylweddoli nad yw hyn o anghenraid yn wir ac y gall pentrefi sydd wedi eu gwahanu gan bellter daearyddol fod yn berchen ar lawer o ffactorau cyffredin yn ogystal â rhai gwahaniaethol.

Arhosir gyda'r ddwy uned hon er mwyn tynnu sylw at y cyfle a geir o fewn deunyddiau'r prosiect i ymgymryd mewn dyfnder ag astudiaethau. Teimlai athrawon fod angen gwneud hyn ar adegau a hynny o bosibl gyda grwpiau o blant hŷn neu aeddfetach o ran eu cyraeddiadau, eu sgiliau a'u profiadau. Mewn dosbarth lle mae plant o ddau neu dri grŵp oedran mae'n rhaid darparu ar gyfer galluoedd ac anghenion gwahanol. Yn ystod cyfnod gweithredu'r themâu integredig, roedd angen cyfle i neilltuo grŵp neu grwpiau o blant er mwyn eu cyfarwyddo i ymgymryd â thasgau llai arwynebol eu natur. Mae'r unedau hanes a daearyddiaeth wedi eu darparu i ateb y gofynion gwahaniaethol hyn ac unedau megis 'Sgwâr y Pentref' neu 'Yr Ysgol' yn gwau'n naturiol i'r cyd-destun ehangach a ddisgrifiwyd uchod. Cynigir yn yr unedau hyn arweiniad pendant ar gyfer ymgymryd ag astudiaethau manwl trwy ffocysu ar agweddau penodol o fywyd y sgwâr megis yr adeiladau, masnach, pobl a digwyddiadau. Mae'r broses addysgol ynddynt yn pwysleisio'r angen, nid yn unig i ddefnyddio ffynonellau cysefin o bob math, ond hefyd i wahodd plant i holi ynglŷn â dilysrwydd ffynhonnell wrth iddynt symud o'r presennol yn ôl at y gorffennol ac ymlaen at y dyfodol yn hanes a datblygiad 'Y Sgwâr' leol a sgwariau eraill.

Hyd yma soniwyd am rai o'r gweithgareddau, y profiadau, y sgiliau a'r cysyniadau sy'n gynwysedig yn holl ddeunyddiau'r prosiect. Camgymeriad o'r mwyaf fyddai i unrhyw brosiect cwricwlwm o'r tu allan geisio diffinio'n benodol feysydd gwybodaeth a chynnwys y gwaith thematig ar gyfer ysgolion yn gyffredinol. Byddai hon yn ffordd o ymwrthod â rhai o brif amcanion ac egwyddorion sylfaenol ymgymryd â gwaith thematig yn y lle cyntaf trwy anwybyddu'r cyfle a geir ynddo i gwricwlwm ddatblygu ar sail profiadau sy'n berthnasol ac ystyrlon i gefndir a diddordebau'r plant a chyddestun cymdeithasol, daearyddol pob ysgol yn unigol. Nid yw hyn yn gyfystyr â dweud y gellir osgoi pob cyfrifoldeb am drafod y cynnwys. Mae deunyddiau'r prosiect, wrth bwysleisio'r prosesau dysgu, yn cynnig fframwaith y gellir, o'i gwmpas, adeiladu mwy nag un cynnwys neu gorff o wybodaeth. Gosodir y cyfrifoldeb am wneud hyn ar ysgwyddau ysgolion unigol er mwyn iddynt sicrhau cwricwlwm perthnasol ac ystyrlon, ond cynigir rhai canllawiau i'w galluogi i ddod i benderfyniad am y cynnwys mewn modd a all sicrhau datblygiad a chydlyniant i'r cwricwlwm. Cymhellir ar y cychwyn gynnal nifer o sesiynau trafod rhydd yn y dosbarth pan gaiff pob un gyfle i wneud awgrymiadau ynglŷn â'r hyn y carai ei ddarganfod mewn perthynas â phob thema. Y cam nesaf yw gosod trefn arnynt trwy eu dosbarthu a'u cysylltu er mwyn gallu ffurfio nifer o gwestiynau allweddol i'w gofyn mewn perthynas â phob thema. Y cwestiynau hyn wedyn sy'n rhoi ffocws i'r gweithgareddau, y profiadau a'r ffynonellau sy'n rheoli'r prosesau darganfod, archwilio, arbrofi ac ymholi ar ran y plant eu hunain.

Mae'r patrwm hwn ychydig yn wahanol i'r arfer a geir yn gyffredinol o fewn ysgolion unigol neu glystyrau o ysgolion pan ddaw athrawon ynghyd i drafod y cwricwlwm integredig, thematig mewn cyfarfodydd addysg mewn swydd. Gan amlaf, gwelir awydd yn y cyfarfodydd trafod a chynllunio hyn i ganolbwyntio ar y cynnwys o'r cychwyn un trwy ddod â nifer o elfennau ynghyd megis pynciau'r cwricwlwm, cyfraniad, arbenigedd a diddordebau athrawon, a'r posibilrwydd o rannu adnoddau a pharatoi deunyddiau ar y cyd.[11] Yn aml defnyddir y we dopig neu'r siart llif wrth gynllunio'r gwaith gan osod teitl y thema yn y canol ac, mewn bocsys o gwmpas, nodir pynciau'r cwricwlwm a manylir ar y targedau a'r datganiadau cyrhaeddiad yn ogystal. Gall hyn arwain at yr arfer o ddibynnu'n ormodol ar adnoddau printiedig a ffynonellau ail-law gan anwybyddu'r angen i ystyried defnyddio amrywiaeth eang o ffynonellau gwybodaeth.

Gweithredai athrawon y grŵp treialu ychydig yn wahanol i'r arfer hwn. Wrth agor y drws i gwricwlwm sy'n seiliedig ar brofiadau uniongyrchol rhaid oedd dibynnu ar ddefnyddio ffynonellau y tu hwnt i ffiniau cyfeirlyfrau, cardiau gwaith ac adnoddau tebyg i'r rhai sydd ar gael yn y mwyafrif o ysgolion ar hyn o bryd. Gwelwyd bod nifer o ysgolion y grŵp yn berchen ar amrywiaeth o ffynonellau amlgyfrwng. Dros y blynyddoedd, roeddynt wedi casglu ynghyd doreth o luniau, ffotograffau, mapiau, dogfennau, copïau o lawysgrifau, cyfrifiadau, cyfarwyddiaduron, ac arteffactau ac roeddynt yn cynnal cysylltiad clòs a byw â llyfrgelloedd ac amgueddfeydd lleol a chenedlaethol. Roedd y rhieni a'r plant wedi cyfrannu at y casgliadau hyn ac ar silffoedd y llyfrgell roedd llyfrau, siartiau, graffiau, tablau ac ati a baratowyd gan y plant eu hunain, yn cofnodi agweddau ar eu gwaith thema mewn perthynas â'r gymuned leol a rhannau eraill o'r byd. Byddai'r plant, wrth ymwneud â'u themâu, yn defnyddio'r holl adnoddau hyn ac yn troi'n naturiol at yr offer clyweled o bob math oedd yn yr ysgol—camerâu, peiriant fideo, recordydd tâp, cyfrifiadur, clipfyrddau, cwmpawd, ffeiliau ac ati. Defnyddiai'r plant yr adnoddau a'r cyfarpar hwn yn gwbl naturiol a hyderus i'w helpu i holi a ffurfio cwestiynau yn ogystal ag i'w hateb.

Mewn awyrgylch o'r fath roedd y broses ymchwiliol yn datblygu'n ddiymdrech ac yn rhoi pleser a boddhad i bob plentyn yn y dosbarth am ei bod yn bosibl gweithio ar wahanol lefelau yn ôl gallu a chyrhaeddiad yr unigolyn. Wrth ddefnyddio'r ffynonellau a'r adnoddau i ddatblygu themâu'r prosiect, roedd yn amlwg fod y plant yn profi ymdeimlad o berchenogaeth unigryw drostynt. Diddorol nodi yma fod hyn yn amrywio o thema i thema a bod y lleiaf cyfarwydd o themâu'r prosiect megis 'Cadwraeth', 'Symudiadau'r Teulu' a 'Datblygu Cymuned', am eu bod wedi eu cychwyn o ddim fel petai yn yr ysgolion, wedi rhoi i'r plant a'r athrawon ymdeimlad o berchenogaeth lwyr drostynt.

Mae deunyddiau 'Gwreiddiau' yn rhoi pwyslais mawr ar gyddestun cymdeithasol y dysgu ac yn gwahodd athrawon mewn trafodaethau â'r plant i ystyried pwy fydd yn ymgymryd â gwahanol agweddau ar y gwaith: a fyddant yn gweithio'n unigol, yn barau, yn grwpiau o dri neu chwech o bosibl, neu'n ddosbarth cyfan. Roedd hyn yn ffordd eto o hybu sgiliau cyfathrebu ac o osod cyfrifoldeb ar y plant. Ond yn fwy na dim, roedd angen rhoi sylw i arbrofi gyda gwahanol ddulliau o gyfathrebu wrth i'r grwpiau adrodd yn ôl. Byddai angen gwybod o'r cychwyn pwy fyddai'r gynulleidfa bob tro, ac arbrofi gydag amrywiaeth o ddulliau cofnodi gwaith ar eu cyfer. O ganlyniad cafwyd amrywiaeth o esiamplau o waith yn ffeiliau'r plant—nid o anghenraid rhwng plentyn a phlentyn ond rhwng plant y gwahanol grwpiau a'i gilydd. Gwelwyd y dyfeisgarwch creadigol y soniwyd amdano eisoes yng nghyd-destun trafod a chynllunio ymlaen llaw, trwy gamau'r gweithredu, yn ei amlygu ei hunan eto ar lefel cofnodi a chyfathrebu. Mewn un dosbarth gwelwyd grŵp yn cofnodi'r gwaith ar 'Yr Ysgol' trwy baratoi sgript a chyflwyno rhaglen radio, grŵp arall yn cyflwyno gwybodaeth trwy gyfres o luniau, ffotograffau a thestun, a grŵp arall yn trosglwyddo gwybodaeth ffeithiol yn gêm taith antur neu'n helfa drysor go iawn ar gyfer y grwpiau eraill. Fel hyn roedd cyfle i bob grŵp gyflawni astudiaeth mewn dyfnder tra eto'n elwa, ar lefel lai dwys a mwy goddefol, o astudiaethau grwpiau eraill. Gwelwyd bod amrywiaeth fel hwn yn cynnal diddordeb ac yn hybu chwilfrydedd. Mae penderfynu ar gyd-destun cymdeithasol y dysgu, trefniadaeth y dosbarth a chydweddu tasg â gallu a chyrhaeddiad y plentyn unigol yn dibynnu'n llwyr ar arweiniad, ac o bosibl ar adegau, ymyrraeth yr athro. Yr un mor bwysig yw sicrhau gosod plentyn mewn sefyllfa lle mae'r dasg yn heriol ac yn ei ymestyn ar adegau priodol. Mae'n llai tebygol o fethu cyrraedd y nod a digalonni ar y ffordd os yw ef ei hunan wedi bod yn allweddol yn cynnig syniadau ac awgrymiadau ar sut y gellir datblygu rhyw agwedd benodol ar y thema dan sylw.

Agwedd arall a gafodd ystyriaeth gan y grŵp treialu oedd yr angen i chwilio am ddulliau o gofnodi datblygiad plant ar y naill law ac o werthuso'r profiadau, y gweithgareddau a'r deunyddiau ar y llaw arall. Teimlid bod tuedd yn y gorffennol i roi pwyslais gormodol ar farcio gwaith ysgrifenedig gan anwybyddu gwerth yr ymdrechion eraill, a gadael y marcio tan y diwedd pan oedd y thema wedi ei chwblhau ac nad oedd cyfle i newid cyfeiriad neu bwyslais nac i blentyn ddwysáu ei ymdrechion. Teimlai'r athrawon fod cofnodi o'r fath yn annigonol a bod angen arbrofi gyda dulliau eraill, a hynny'n bennaf er mwyn rhoi credyd i'r plant am yr holl weithgareddau yr oeddynt yn ymwneud â hwy wrth ddatblygu thema, megis cynnig syniadau, cydweithio â phlentyn arall neu â phlant eraill mewn grŵp; cyfrannu deunyddiau crai megis arteffactau, dogfennau ac ati; dangos dyfalbarhad; sylweddoli'r angen i weithredu'n gyfrifol, ac yn y blaen.

Bu'r arbrofi'n ddiddorol a llwyddiannus fel y gellir dangos trwy nodi un enghraifft syml yn unig mewn perthynas â'r thema 'Cadwraeth Natur'. Gofynnwyd i bob grŵp baratoi paragraff syml yn crynhoi'r hyn a wyddent am y 'Fforestydd Glaw', a chawsant fwy nag un cyfle i baratoi datganiadau o'r fath, yn nyddiau cynnar datblygu'r thema, ac ar gyfnodau rheolaidd yn ystod y gweithredu. Gofynnwyd iddynt hefyd nodi ble a sut y daethant o hyd i'r wybodaeth newydd. Fel hyn roedd modd mesur datblygiad mewn dealltwriaeth yn ogystal â gwybodaeth, gallu'r plant i ddatblygu'n gysyniadol a'u parodrwydd i ymchwilio mewn nifer o ffynonellau er mwyn casglu tystiolaeth i gadarnhau, addasu neu o bosibl newid yn gyfan gwbl eu syniadau cynnar.[12] Byddai'r athro wrth gofnodi yn rhoi credyd iddynt am yr holl sgiliau perthnasol wrth iddynt chwilio am ffynonellau, casglu'r ffeithiau angenrheidiol ynddynt a'u gosod mewn trefn er mwyn dod i benderfyniad ac yna gofnodi'n ysgrifenedig, neu fel arall, trwy gyfrwng tablau, graffiau, neu ddarluniau.

Gellir dweud bod cyfoeth o brofiadau tîm eang o gyfranogwyr yn cynnwys athrawon a phlant mewn ysgolion, aelodau o gymunedau lleol yr ysgolion hynny, ymgynghorwyr, arolygwyr, darlithwyr ac awduron, wedi chwarae rhan allweddol mewn datblygu deunyddiau'r prosiect 'Gwreiddiau'. Wrth i athrawon weithredu'r deunyddiau drafft cynnar, y gobaith oedd derbyn ganddynt syniadau ymarferol ar gyfer gwella'r deunyddiau crai hynny. Fe gafwyd hyn, a llawer mwy ganddynt, ar sail eu profiadau'n gweithredu'r canllawiau cynnar ochr yn ochr â'u hymgais i ymateb i anghenion plant ac i gwrdd â gofynion y cwricwlwm mewn amrywiaeth eang o sefyllfaoedd ledled Cymru.

Gwelwyd ei bod hi'n bosibl cynnig i'r holl ysgolion, ar lefel eang, gyffredinol, fframwaith ar gyfer datblygu themâu pynciol ac integredig. Ynddo canolbwyntir ar ddisgrifio proses neu ddull o weithio a chaniateir rhyddid i athrawon benderfynu yn unigol ar y cynnwys. Profiad ysgolion yn gyffredinol oedd ei bod yn fanteisiol penderfynu ar y cynnwys hwnnw o fwy nag un cyfeiriad trwy roi cyfle i blant, rhieni, athrawon eraill ac aelodau o'r gymuned leol i ddod ynghyd i drafod posibiliadau yn ystod camau cynllunio, gweithredu a gwerthuso'r themâu. O wneud hyn, gellir datblygu cwricwlwm sy'n seiliedig ar brofiadau a gweithgareddau sy'n tyfu yn ddaearyddol ac amseryddol o'r gymuned leol. Ar yr un pryd ymestynnir y cyfle i ddatblygu sgiliau addysgol o bob math, gan gynnwys yn fwyaf arbennig, amrywiaeth eang o sgiliau cyfathrebu. Mae dysgu trwy brofiadau yn mynd i olygu dysgu ar sail defnyddio amrywiaeth o ffynonellau, nifer mawr ohonynt i'w cael yn y cartref a'r gymuned leol, a gall hyn gryfhau'r cysylltiadau rhwng yr ysgol a'r gymuned, y dosbarth a'r cartref ar lefel gweithgarwch datblygu cwricwlwm yn ogystal ag ar lefel cydweithrediad cymdeithasol.

Mae'n ofynnol hefyd drafod cyd-destun cymdeithasol y dysgu; cytuno pwy fydd y gynulleidfa ac ai cyfrifoldeb unigolion, grwpiau, parau neu ddosbarth cyfan fydd cyflawni tasgau penodol ar eu cyfer. Oblegid gall strategaeth drefniadol dosbarth lesteirio neu hyrwyddo'r prosesau addysgol sydd wrth wraidd unrhyw brosiect cwricwlwm.

Gall y profiadau a gafwyd wrth ddatblygu prosiect cwricwlwm 'Gwreiddiau' fod yn sylfaen i adeiladu arnynt i'r dyfodol. Yn y bennod hon disgrifiwyd y math o fframwaith y gellir ei ddefnyddio ar gyfer dod â thîm neu grwpiau o bobl ynghyd i ddatblygu prosiect cwricwlwm ar y cyd. Cyflwynwyd yma rai o'r egwyddorion sylfaenol hynny y gellir eu trafod wrth ystyried athroniaeth unrhyw brosiect cwricwlwm. Cyfeiriwyd hefyd at beth o ffrwyth y cydweithio a fu rhwng aelodau'r tîm wrth iddynt benderfynu ar y math o ddeunyddiau ac adnoddau i'w darparu ar gyfer ysgolion. Y gobaith yw y bydd y deunyddiau hyn yn gwella'r ddarpariaeth ddysgu ac addysgu yn y dosbarth a thrwy hynny yn codi safonau'n gyffredinol. Pwysleisiwyd droeon fod y ddarpariaeth hon yn benodol ar gyfer cynnal athrawon yn eu hymdrechion i feithrin mewn plant sgiliau addysgol a fydd yn eu galluogi i weithredu'n annibynnol, i ddatgan barn a chael llais mewn gwneud penderfyniadau am y cwricwlwm. Cafwyd tystiolaeth hefyd i brofi bod yr ysgolion cyfrwng Cymraeg hynny a ddefnyddiwyd ar gyfer y treialu yn manteisio ar eu sefyllfa unigryw. Llwyddent i greu awyrgylch cartrefol yn y dosbarth a pherthynas glòs rhyngddynt a'r plant, eu teuluoedd a'r gymuned gyfan. Roedd hyn yn eu galluogi i ddatblygu cwricwlwm a oedd yn gosod y plentyn yn gadarn yn y canol wrth benderfynu beth fyddai ei anghenion ar gyfer y dyfodol yn ogystal ag ymateb iddynt yn y presennol.

CYFEIRIADAU

1. 'Gwreiddiau': Prosiect y Swyddfa Gymreig, 1987-90 (Cyfarwyddwr: Ina Williams; Canolfan Astudiaethau Addysg, Yr Adran Addysg, Coleg Prifysgol Cymru, Aberystwyth).
2. Ina Williams, 'Datblygu prosiect cwricwlwm yn y dyniaethau', *Welsh Historian* (Gwanwyn 1990), 29–33.
3. Adroddiad Pwyllgor Gittins, *Addysg Gynradd Cymru* (Gwasg Ei Mawrhydi, Llundain, 1967), 118.
4. *Adroddiad gan Arolygwyr Ei Mawrhydi ar Ysgol y Wern, Llanishen, De Morgannwg*, (Y Swyddfa Gymreig, 1989), 31.
5. Maurice Galton et al., *Progress and Performance in the Primary Classroom* (Llundain, 1980), 200–12.
6. Maurice Galton et al., *Curriculum Provision in the Small Primary School* (Llundain, 1990).
7. Ibid., 181.
8. A. Bell and A. Sigsworth, *The Small Rural Primary School* (Llundain, 1987), 177.
9. *Fframwaith ar Gyfer y Cwricwlwm Cyflawn 5-16 yng Nghymru* (Cyngor Cwricwlwm Cymru, 1989), 11.
10. John Harris et al., *A Guide to the English Language in the National Curriculum* (Cheltenham, 1990), 112–13.

11. Michael Bonnett, 'Self expression and structure in project work', yn *Topic and Thematic Work in the Primary and Middle Years*, gol. Colin Conner (Cambridge Institute of Education, 1988), 62.
12. Elizabeth Clough, 'Evaluation of learning in topic work: some implications for INSET', yn Conner, op. cit., 81.

Addysg Uwchradd Ddwyieithog

JANEM JONES

Fel disgybl a gafodd ei haddysg uwchradd ym mhumdegau'r ganrif trwy gyfrwng ei hail iaith sef y Saesneg, hoffwn edrych mor wrthrychol â phosibl ar y cyfnewidiadau a ddigwyddodd ym myd addysg ddwyieithog uwchradd yn y deugain mlynedd a aeth heibio ers hynny. Yn ail, ceisir dadansoddi'r cyfnewidiadau a'u gosod yng nghyd-destun ymchwil gymdeithasegol ac ieithyddol y cyfnod yng Nghymru. Yn drydydd, ceisir deall y datblygiad. Credir bod gwahaniaeth sylfaenol rhwng cyfnewidiadau a datblygiadau. Nid yw pob cyfnewid yn ddatblygiad ac y mae'n rhaid dadansoddi cyn deall beth sy'n ddatblygiad.

Y cyfnewidiadau

Ym 1951 roedd 28.9 y cant o boblogaeth Cymru yn ôl y cyfrifiad yn siarad Cymraeg. Ym 1981 y canran oedd 18.7—gostyngiad o 10.2 y cant. Yn y sir lle cefais i fy addysg roedd 31.6 y cant o'r boblogaeth ym 1951 yn siarad Cymraeg. Erbyn 1981, y ffigwr oedd 16.4 y cant: gostyngiad o 15.2 y cant.[1] Amrwd yw ffigurau cyfrifiad gan na cheir ynddynt ddarlun o amlder defnydd person o iaith. Yn gwbl arwynebol, darlun trist a geir yn y ffigurau o safbwynt dyfodol y Gymraeg. Er hyn, erbyn 1969 byddai disgybl a fynychai yr un ysgol uwchradd â mi yn derbyn y canran helaethaf o'i addysg trwy gyfrwng y Gymraeg mewn ysgol uwchradd benodedig ddwyieithog. Y mae nifer mawr o'm cyfoedion o ardaloedd eraill yng Nghymru a fedrai ddweud yr un peth:

> The implication is that were that small child of the 1950s a small child today, then her options might be very different: she would

certainly be exposed to choices about the language of her education
to an extent inconceivable in the 1950s . . . there has been a profound
change in the provision of Welsh medium education and perhaps more
importantly in the perceptions of the value of Welsh and Welsh medium
education.[2]

Ym mhumdegau'r ganrif hon pwnc digon dibwys, os bodolai o
gwbl, oedd y Gymraeg ar gwricwlwm yr ysgol uwchradd. Yn fynych
anogid disgybl i adael y Gymraeg gan awgrymu fod ieithoedd eraill
yn llawer elwach i'w hastudio. Er bod eithriadau i hyn, gellir dweud
mai bach iawn oedd y diddordeb a oedd gan nifer o awdurdodau
addysg lleol yn y Gymraeg fel pwnc nac fel cyfrwng dysgu yn yr ysgol
uwchradd yn y cyfnod hwn. Ers Deddf Addysg 1988, y mae'r
Cwricwlwm Cenedlaethol yn sicrhau lle i'r Gymraeg fel pwnc craidd
neu bwnc sylfaen ym mhob ysgol uwchradd. Erbyn Medi 1989, 10.8
y cant o ysgolion uwchradd Cymru a oedd heb fod â'r Gymraeg ar
gwricwlwm yr ysgol.[3] Diffinnir ysgolion uwchradd Cymraeg ers
Deddf Addysg 1988 fel ysgolion lle y mae mwy na hanner y pynciau
canlynol, sef addysg grefyddol a'r pynciau sylfaen ar wahân i'r
Gymraeg a'r Saesneg, yn cael eu dysgu trwy gyfrwng y Gymraeg.
Dengys y ffigurau diweddaraf (Medi 1989) felly fod 42 o ysgolion
uwchradd Cymru yn ysgolion Cymraeg yn ôl diffiniad Deddf
Addysg 1988 a bod 26,058 o ddisgyblion yn eu mynychu.[4] Pan rennir
y 42 ysgol yn ysgolion penodedig dwyieithog ac ysgolion traddodiadol
dwyieithog ceir bod 18 o'r 42 ysgol yn rhai penodedig dwyieithog. Y
mae'r 24 ysgol draddodiadol ddwyieithog yn Nyfed (4), Gwynedd
(17) a Phowys (3) a hynny mewn ardaloedd gwledig. Dengys ffigurau
Cyd-bwyllgor Addysg Cymru fod 48 o bynciau Tystysgrif Gyffredinol Addysg Uwchradd (TGAU) ar gael trwy gyfrwng y Gymraeg ar
gyfer 8,917 o ddisgyblion a 24 o bynciau safon A ar gael ar gyfer 903
o ddisgyblion, trwy gyfrwng y Gymraeg ym Mehefin 1990.[5] Digon
gwahanol oedd y darlun yn y 1950au. Ym 1956, y mae'n wir i
Bwyllgor Addysg Sir y Fflint trwy ymdrechion y Cyfarwyddwr
Addysg benderfynu sefydlu ysgol uwchradd benodedig ddwyieithog
ac i hynny greu'r cynsail a'r brwdfrydedd ar gyfer addysg ddwyieithog uwchradd o hynny ymlaen. Ond addysg gyfrwng Saesneg a geid
bron yn ddiwahân yn ysgolion uwchradd Cymru yn y pumdegau. Y
neges gudd a gyflwynid i ddisgybl y pumdegau yn yr ysgol uwchradd
oedd mai Saesneg oedd 'iaith dod ymlaen yn y byd'. Safbwynt
goddrychol yw honni inni ddioddef yn addysgol gan inni gael ein
dysgu trwy gyfrwng y Saesneg a oedd heb amheuaeth yn ail iaith

inni. Addysgid ni hefyd ochr yn ochr â rhai disgyblion yr oedd y Saesneg yn famiaith ac yn unig iaith iddynt. Rhyfedd erbyn heddiw yw sylweddoli inni a'n rhieni dderbyn yr addysg hon yn ddigwestiwn.

Awgrymwyd bod twf addysg ddwyieithog yng Nghymru yn un o wyrthiau bychain Ewrop gyfoes.[6] Y mae perygl i wyrth. Anodd ei dadansoddi ond dyma y mae'n rhaid ceisio ei wneud os am ddeall y datblygiad. Wrth ddadansoddi y daw dealltwriaeth.

Dadansoddi'r cyfnewidiadau

> The establishment and consolidation of Welsh-medium secondary education in the post-war years has been a considerable success story. It has certainly owed much to parental demand and local authority response, but it has been sanctioned, even encouraged, by the Welsh educational arm of central government, itself responding to a variety of political and cultural pressures, particularly a resurgent Welsh nationalism. The reason why Wales has been allowed to be distinctive in such a fundamental way is that the distinctiveness has in no measure threatened the essential structure or organization of the school system.[7]

Y mae'r geiriau uchod yn ddadleuol, yn ddadlennol ac yn ogleisiol. Yn gyntaf a yw addysg uwchradd ddwyieithog yn llwyddiant a beth yw mesur y llwyddiant hwnnw? A fu yn effeithiol ac a yw yn effeithiol wrth warchod a datblygu'r Gymraeg? A yw disgyblion sy'n derbyn eu haddysg uwchradd trwy gyfrwng y Gymraeg yn gallu trafod pob maes profiad yn foddhaol trwy gyfrwng y Gymraeg a'r Saesneg? A yw addysg uwchradd trwy gyfrwng y Gymraeg yn gwneud yr un tegwch â'r disgybl o gartref Cymraeg ac o gartref di-Gymraeg? Sut y mae polisïau iaith yr awdurdodau addysg lleol erbyn heddiw yn effeithio ar y cyfle a roddir i bob disgybl dderbyn addysg uwchradd ddwyieithog? Beth yn union a olygir yng Nghymru wrth addysg uwchradd ddwyieithog? Onid yr un peth a olygir wrth addysg gyfrwng Cymraeg neu ganran o gwricwlwm trwy gyfrwng y Gymraeg? Yn ail, y mae'r dyfyniad yn ddadlennol: pwysau o du rhieni ac ymateb llywodraeth leol a llywodraeth ganol yn sicr sydd wedi sicrhau ysgolion penodedig dwyieithog. Y mae twf ysgolion traddodiadol dwyieithog i'w priodoli i ffactorau mwy cymhleth. Yn drydydd, y mae'r dyfyniad yn ogleisiol pan awgryma nad yw dwyieithrwydd na Chymreictod wedi effeithio ar na strwythur na threfniadaeth ysgolion uwchradd yng Nghymru. Yr un mor ogleisiol yw teitl darlith Williams ym 1988: 'Addysg Ddwyieithog yng Nghymru ynte Addysg ar gyfer Cymru Ddwyieithog'.[8]

I ddadansoddi felly. A yw addysg ddwyieithog uwchradd yn llwyddiant o safbwynt gwarchod, datblygu a hyrwyddo'r Gymraeg? Credir yn gyffredinol heddiw mai'r system addysg yw'r asiant unigol cryfaf i gadarnhau'r Gymraeg. Ond dengys ymchwil i berfformiad ieithyddol disgyblion sy'n derbyn eu haddysg uwchradd trwy gyfrwng y Gymraeg mai'r gymuned ieithyddol o bosibl a gaiff yr effaith fwyaf cadarnhaol ar Gymraeg y disgyblion. Awgryma'r ymchwil dri pheth ar sail y canlyniadau. Yn gyntaf, dylai'r ysgol gymryd rhan weithredol mewn gweithgareddau cymunedol allgyrsiol lle bo cymuned Gymraeg yn bod: y mae'n bwysig gwarchod yr hyn sydd ar gael. Yn ail, dylai plant o gartrefi ac o gymunedau Cymraeg eu hiaith dderbyn llawer mwy o'u haddysg trwy gyfrwng y Gymraeg. Dengys yr ymchwil yn glir fod Cymraeg y disgyblion hyn yn gwella po fwyaf o'r cwricwlwm a gynigir iddynt trwy gyfrwng y Gymraeg. Yn drydydd, awgrymir y dylai yr holl ysgolion uwchradd penodedig dwyieithog mewn ardaloedd di-Gymraeg roi cyfle i'w disgyblion gyfrannu o gymuned ieithyddol Gymraeg. Dylai'r ysgolion hyn roi pwyslais arbennig ar weithgareddau allgyrsiol trwy gyfrwng y Gymraeg a cheisio creu eu cymuned Gymraeg eu hunain y tu allan i oriau'r ysgol o thu allan i gampws yr ysgol.[9] Ym 1981 fe drafodwyd y syniad o greu canolfannau lleol a fyddai'n ganolfannau adnoddau i gymunedau a phenodwyd swyddogion cyswllt mewn rhai ardaloedd Seisnigedig i hyrwyddo'r defnydd o'r Gymraeg yn y gymuned.

> yn union fel yr ydym wedi ceisio sefydliadu addysg ddwyieithog fel elfen 'normal' yn natblygiad academaidd plentyn, felly'n union y dylem yn awr feddwl am sefydliadu canolfannau adnoddau diwylliannol fel elfen 'normal' yn natblygiad cymdeithasol y gymuned.[10]

Go brin fod yr ymchwil i ddatblygiad iaith disgyblion mewn ysgolion dwyieithog yn profi llwyddiant yr ysgolion o safbwynt gwarchod a datblygu iaith. Yn sicr, y mae angen ymchwil bellach ar raddfa lawer ehangach i iaith plant mewn ysgolion uwchradd dwyieithog yng Nghymru.

A yw'r ysgolion uwchradd dwyieithog yn llwyddiant o safbwynt cynnydd academaidd? Dengys Roberts fod llwyddiant yr ysgolion uwchradd dwyieithog a astudir ganddi yn ddigamsyniol o safbwynt arholiadau cyhoeddus. Esbonia nad cefndir dosbarth canol sy'n gyfrifol am hyn ond yn hytrach lefel uchel o ymroddiad i'r iaith

Gymraeg ac i addysg ddwyieithog ymhlith athrawon yn yr ysgolion uwchradd penodedig dwyieithog ynghyd ag agwedd ffafriol ymhlith y disgyblion tuag at yr iaith a'r diwylliant Cymreig. Y mae'r ymroddiad a'r agweddau positif hyn yn ôl Roberts yn gyfrifol am lwyddiant yr ysgolion hyn mewn arholiadau cyhoeddus.

> The findings intimate that the school's role as an agency of minority cultural reproduction predisposes a favourable attitude towards the language and culture, which in turn may predispose teaching and learning commitment and the success of the bilingual school.[11]

Prin felly yw'r ymchwil i effeithiolrwydd ysgolion uwchradd dwyieithog yng Nghymru. Dengys Baker[12] fod yng Nghymru draddodiad o ddadansoddi data ar gyraeddiadau dwyieithog: gwaith Saer (1922), Smith (1923), Barke a Parry-Williams (1938), W. R. Jones (1933) a gwaith diweddarach W. R. Jones yn y cyfnod wedi'r Ail Ryfel Byd hyd at arolwg cenedlaethol y Sefydliad Cenedlaethol er hyrwyddo Ymchwil a Chyd-Bwyllgor Addysg Cymru ym 1960, yr arolwg i ymagweddiad plant at y Gymraeg a'r Saesneg gan Sharp *et al* ym 1973 a chynllun dwyieithog y Cyngor Ysgolion (Dodson 1978, 1985). Ond yn sicr, y mae'n bryd cael ymchwil dymor hir i effeithiolrwydd addysg gyfrwng Cymraeg. Dyma'r angen bellach.

> Byddwn yn croesawu dadansoddiadau o ddatblygiad carfanau o blant dros gyfnod o amser, y naill garfan yn dilyn rhaglen addysg ddwyieithog a'r llall un uniaith . . . Mae'n amlwg y byddai raid iddynt oll gychwyn ar eu haddysg yr un pryd ac y byddid yn cychwyn yr astudiaethau hydredol mewn sawl cyd-destun gwahanol gan amrywio'r lleoliadau, y cefndir ieithyddol, math o ysgol, dulliau dysgu, cynnal yr iaith (neu i'r newid a fu yn eu natur) . . .[13]

Y math yma o ymchwil a allai ateb cwestiynau rhieni, athrawon a llunwyr polisïau.

Byddai'n deg, o ddadansoddi, gytuno fod yr awdurdodau addysg lleol yn ymateb o safbwynt addysg ddwyieithog uwchradd i bwysau o du rhieni a charfanau eraill. Ond onid oes arnynt hefyd ddyletswydd i gynnig arweiniad? Y mae dadansoddi'r polisïau iaith yn help i ddeall datblygiad addysg ddwyieithog. Amcan polisi iaith Clwyd yw:

> sicrhau fod disgyblion yn derbyn y symbyliad addysgol a rydd dysgu ail iaith a dod yn weddol rugl yn y ddwy iaith fel proses sy'n parhau i'r ysgol uwchradd . . . Darperir addysg uwchradd ar gyfer yr holl blant yn bennaf drwy gyfrwng y Saesneg neu'r Gymraeg *yn ôl dymuniad y rhieni* . . .[14]

Y mae pedair ysgol uwchradd benodedig ddwyieithog yng Nghlwyd a daw'r mwyafrif o'r disgyblion i'r ysgolion hynny o gartrefi di-Gymraeg. Gall y disgyblion astudio'r cwricwlwm cyfan yn yr ysgolion hyn trwy gyfrwng y Gymraeg.

Y mae polisi iaith Gymraeg Dyfed yn fwy cymhleth. Hwyrach y byddai'n decach dweud fod y polisi yn cynnig arweiniad yn ogystal ag yn ymateb i bwysau o du rhieni. 'Mae Awdurdod Addysg Dyfed yn credu yn y gwerth addysgol o feddu ar ddwy iaith ac yn datgan yn bendant o blaid polisi dwyieithog yn ei ysgolion cynradd.'[15]

Fe osodir yr ysgolion mewn categori A a chategori B yn ôl penderfyniad llywodraethwyr yr ysgol ac o safbwynt 'amrywiaethau diwylliannol a ieithyddol'. Y mae ysgolion categori A yn ysgolion cyfrwng Cymraeg. Ceir hefyd ysgolion trefol lle ceir ysgol benodedig Gymraeg ac ysgol Saesneg neu ffrwd benodedig Gymraeg a ffrwd Saesneg. Y mae'r polisi yn datgan yn glir y dylai pob ysgol gynradd ddysgu a defnyddio'r Gymraeg i raddau o fewn y cwricwlwm.

Os cynnig arweiniad a wneir yn yr ysgolion cynradd o safbwynt polisi iaith Dyfed, ymateb i bwysau o du rhieni a charfanau eraill a wna'r polisi o safbwynt sefydlu ysgolion penodedig dwyieithog. Y mae yn y sir bum ysgol benodedig ddwyieithog, un yn yr arfaeth a phedair ysgol draddodiadol ddwyieithog. Fel rhan o bolisi'r sir ac fel rhan o strategaeth marchnata addysg ddwyieithog, fe addysgir mathemateg a'r gwyddorau trwy gyfrwng y Saesneg a gweddill y cwricwlwm trwy gyfrwng y Gymraeg. Mewn un o'r ysgolion penodedig dwyieithog, fe gafwyd pwysau o du rhieni i gynnig mathemateg a'r gwyddorau trwy gyfrwng y Gymraeg a bellach yn yr ysgol honno ceir ffrwd Saesneg a ffrwd Gymraeg yn y meysydd hynny. Nid oes polisi pendant felly yn perthyn i'r ysgolion traddodiadol uwchradd dwyieithog a cheir bod polisi iaith yr ysgolion hynny yn dibynnu ar y prifathro ac ar yr adnoddau staff sydd ar gael. Ar adegau dysgir trwy gyfrwng y Saesneg a'r Gymraeg yn gyfochrog ac o ganlyniad mewn ambell ysgol draddodiadol uwchradd ddwyieithog yn Nyfed, cynigir mwy o bynciau trwy gyfrwng y Gymraeg nag y gwneir yn yr ysgolion uwchradd penodedig dwyieithog. Fe all hyn osod cryn straen ar adnoddau staffio ysgol fach gan ei bod yn ofynnol i'r pwnc gael ei gynnig trwy gyfrwng dwy iaith.

Yn sicr, cynnig arweiniad a wna polisi iaith Gwynedd:[16]

> Nid disgrifiad o sefyllfa sy'n bodoli eisoes yw polisi. Datganiad o fwriadau neu o dargedau i'w cyrraedd ydyw polisi ond gorau oll os

yw'n dangos pa gamau i'w cymryd i gyrraedd y targedau hynny, gwell fyth os yw'n cynnig canllawiau ar sut i weithredu yn ogystal.[17]

Y mae'r ddogfen yn un fanwl o safbwynt polisïau iaith ysgolion cynradd, uwchradd a cholegau addysg bellach. Yn yr ysgol gynradd, y mae'n datgan fod gan bob plentyn o Gymro yr hawl i addysg trwy gyfrwng y Gymraeg a bod cyfrifoldeb ar yr awdurdod i ddysgu ac addysgu pob plentyn fel y gall dyfu yn ddwyieithog.

> Mae gan y plant sy'n arddel hunaniaeth Gymreig hawl foesol i addysg sy'n dyrchafu'r Gymraeg a'r etifeddiaeth draddodiadol Gymreig . . . Ar y llaw arall yr un yw'r ddyletswydd i gyflwyno manteision yr etifeddiaeth hon i blant nad ydynt efallai'n gynhenid Gymraeg ond sy'n rhan annatod o gymdeithas yr ysgol a'r gymuned . . .[18]

Er mwyn hyrwyddo'r polisi yn y sector uwchradd ystyrir bod pob ysgol yn ysgol draddodiadol ddwyieithog ond nid yn unffurf ddwyieithog.

> Oherwydd y gwahaniaethau sylweddol yn natur eu cefndir ieithyddol a'u maint, rhaid wrth drefniadau gwahanol i gyrraedd nodau'r polisi . . .

Y mae'r drefniadaeth bum model A, B(I), B(II), C(I), C(II), Ch yn gwbl glir. Ceir ysgolion model A sy'n cynnig y cyfran helaethaf o'r cwricwlwm trwy gyfrwng y Gymraeg ond yn diogelu hyfedredd y disgyblion mewn dwy iaith. Dyma'r ysgolion penodedig dwyieithog. Mae ysgolion model B(I) mewn ardaloedd Cymraeg ac maent yn ysgolion dros chwe chant mewn rhif. Yn yr ysgolion hyn ceir rhwng 20 y cant a 70 y cant o'r cwricwlwm trwy gyfrwng y Gymraeg yn ôl hyfedredd y disgyblion yn yr iaith. Gwneir trefniadau arbennig ar gyfer hwyrddyfodiaid. Ar adegau yn ysgolion y categori hwn, ceir dysgu pynciau yn gyfochrog yn y Gymraeg a'r Saesneg. Eto ysgolion dros chwe chant mewn rhif yw ysgolion model B(II) a cheir hwy mewn ardaloedd a fu yn ardaloedd Cymraeg eu hiaith ond a Seisnigeiddiwyd bellach. Eto ceir 20 y cant i 70 y cant o'r cwricwlwm trwy gyfrwng y Gymraeg yn ôl hyfedredd y disgyblion yn yr iaith. Yn y model hwn hefyd ceir dysgu cyfochrog yn y ddwy iaith. Cynigir canllawiau pendant o ran trefniadaeth i ysgolion modelau B(I) a B(II) ac awgrymir ym mlynyddoedd I i III y dylid mabwysiadu tair lefel ieithyddol. Wrth ddysgu cyfochrog, pwysleisir y dylid darparu defnyddiau ymlaen llaw yn y ddwy iaith ac y dylid mabwysiadu dulliau grŵp o ddysgu.

Y mae ysgolion model C(I) mewn ardaloedd Cymraeg. Ysgolion cymharol fach ydynt o dan chwe chant mewn rhif. Caiff y disgyblion

Cymraeg eu hiaith sy'n eu mynychu 70 y cant o'u cwricwlwm trwy gyfrwng y Gymraeg a chynigir trefniant dwyieithog arbennig ar gyfer dysgwyr. Trefnir darpariaeth frys yn ystod blynyddoedd I a II er mwyn canolbwyntio ar feistrolaeth o'r Gymraeg fel y gall y dysgwyr astudio nifer sylweddol o bynciau trwy gyfrwng y Gymraeg erbyn blwyddyn III. Canolir hwyrddyfodiaid mewn ysgol gyfagos. Ardaloedd ieithyddol gymysg sef ardaloedd sydd wedi eu Seisnigeiddio ers amser yw dalgylchoedd ysgolion model C(II). Y mae'r ysgolion hyn hefyd fel y rhai ym model C(I) yn rhai cymharol fach o dan chwe chant o ran rhif. Cynigir rhwng 30 y cant a 70 y cant o'r cwricwlwm trwy gyfrwng y Gymraeg yn ôl hyfedredd y disgyblion yn y Gymraeg. Yn ystod blynyddoedd I–III gwneir darpariaeth ar dair lefel ieithyddol a gwneir datganiad pellach wrth drafod y model hwn, sef y bydd angen i'r awdurdod addysg wneud rhai darpariaethau o ran adnoddau i alluogi unrhyw ysgol yn y model hwn i gynnal dilyniant i'r addysg ddwyieithog ar ôl blwyddyn III. Pwysleisir mor bwysig y mae dilyniant ieithyddol.[20] Ysgolion mawr lle nad oes fawr ddim Cymry cynhenid yw ysgolion categori Ch. Yn hanesyddol yr ysgolion cyfrwng Saesneg oedd y rhain a rannai yr un dalgylch â'r ysgolion penodedig dwyieithog. Yn ôl polisi presennol yr awdurdod, dylai holl ddisgyblion yr ysgolion hyn gael cyswllt â'r Gymraeg am tua 20 i 30 y cant o'r cwricwlwm ym mlynyddoedd I–III. Yn ystod blynyddoedd IV–V, pwysleisir y dylai'r disgyblion ddal i gyflawni rhai gweithgareddau trwy gyfrwng y Gymraeg trwy ddulliau modiwlar neu drwy ddilyn rhai pynciau yn ddwyieithog. Y mae'r polisi yn bendant fod 'yn rhaid i'r ysgolion yn y model hwn adlewyrchu Cymreictod yn eu gweinyddiad a'u trefniadau'.[21]

Er mwyn hwyluso'r polisi iaith uwchradd sefydlir pwyllgor cyswllt rhwng yr ysgolion cynradd ac uwchradd a fydd yn trafod polisïau iaith ysgolion y dalgylch ac yn trafod dilyniant mewn perthynas â'r defnydd o iaith ar draws y cwricwlwm. Yn ogystal, fe fydd gan bob ysgol uwchradd gydgysylltwr addysg ddwyieithog a fydd â chyfrifoldeb am arfarnu polisi iaith yr ysgol ac asesu beth yw anghenion yr ysgol mewn cyd-destun dwyieithog.[22]

Lluniwyd polisi iaith Awdurdod Addysg Powys ym 1965 a chyflwynwyd atodiad iddo ym 1987. Adlewyrchu natur ieithyddol yr hen siroedd a wnâi polisi 1976.

> Siaredir Cymraeg yn bennaf mewn dwy ardal yn hanner gogledd-orllewinol y sir a'r rhan de-orllewinol . . . yn yr ardaloedd hyn y

Gymraeg yw'r brif iaith bob dydd ac adlewyrchir y sefyllfa yma yn yr ysgolion.[23]

Yn llawlyfr Powys—*Gwybodaeth i Rieni 1990/1*—ceir gwybodaeth debyg ond sydd bellach yn adlewyrchu deddf addysg 1988 ac oblygiadau y Cwricwlwm Cenedlaethol.

> Yn y sector uwchradd, dysgir y Gymraeg fel pwnc ym mhob ysgol uwchradd ac mewn nifer o ysgolion fe'i defnyddir fel cyfrwng i ddysgu pynciau eraill. Mae maint yr addysg a gynigir drwy gyfrwng y Gymraeg yn amrywio yn ôl yr ysgol . . .[24]

Yn y llawlyfr ceir rhestr o ysgolion uwchradd sy'n cynnig peth addysg trwy gyfrwng y Gymraeg sef chwe ysgol. Yn ystadegau'r Swyddfa Gymreig ar gyfer 1989/90, nodir tair ysgol uwchradd ym Mhowys fel ysgolion Cymraeg yn ôl diffiniad Deddf Addysg 1988.[25]

Nid oes gan Awdurdod Addysg Gorllewin Morgannwg ddogfen bolisi iaith. Ceir y datganiad o bolisi yn rhan o'r llawlyfr sy'n wybodaeth i rieni.

> Ceisir sicrhau drwy bolisi'r Awdurdod ynglŷn â'r Gymraeg fod pob plentyn ym mhob ysgol gynradd yn cael y cyfle i ddysgu'r Gymraeg yn iaith gyntaf neu'n ail iaith. Yn naturiol yn yr ysgolion Cymraeg eu cyfrwng, addysgir Cymraeg yn iaith gyntaf, ac yn ail iaith yn yr ysgolion Saesneg eu cyfrwng. Yn ystod y blynyddoedd nesaf, fe gyflwynir y Gymraeg yn raddol fel rhan o'r cwricwlwm cenedlaethol i'r holl ddisgyblion yn ysgolion Gorllewin Morgannwg.[26]

Rhestrir pedwar math o drefniadaeth cynradd sef ysgolion Saesneg eu cyfrwng, Cymraeg eu cyfrwng, Cymraeg traddodiadol ac un ysgol gynradd ddwyieithog. O safbwynt y sector uwchradd nodir dwy ysgol benodedig ddwyieithog, un yn darparu addysg ar gyfer disgyblion 11–18 a'r llall yn darparu addysg ar gyfer disgyblion 11–16. Nodir bod yr ysgol sy'n darparu addysg 11–18 yn cyflwyno mathemateg a'r gwyddorau trwy gyfrwng y Saesneg. Nid yw'r llawlyfr yn nodi maint y ddarpariaeth Gymraeg ei chyfrwng yn yr ysgol 11–16 ond gwyddys fod mathemateg a'r gwyddorau yn cael eu cynnig trwy gyfrwng y Gymraeg a'r Saesneg yn yr ysgol honno. Ymateb a wna polisi iaith Awdurdod Addysg Gorllewin Morgannwg i bwysau o du rhieni a charfanau eraill am addysg gyfrwng Cymraeg.

Fel Awdurdod Addysg Gorllewin Morgannwg ceir datganiad o bolisi iaith Awdurdod Addysg Morgannwg Ganol yn rhan o'i lawlyfr gwybodaeth i rieni. Methwyd â chael gafael ar gopi Cymraeg o'i lawlyfr.

> The Authority's policy is that subject to resources available, every child

should have the opportunity to learn and to use the Welsh language effectively . . . Bilingual education is available at Welsh medium primary schools . . . Welsh medium schools or units will be established according to the resources available, to meet the wishes of parents for bilingual education . . . Children may continue their bilingual education at the secondary level in Welsh medium comprehensive schools. . .[27]

Y mae tair ysgol ddwyieithog yn y sir (pedair os ystyrir ysgol sy'n dal yn rhan o drefniadaeth ysgol gyfrwng Saesneg ond a fydd yn datblygu yn ysgol ddwyieithog benodedig lawn). Yn yr ysgolion uwchradd penodedig hyn darperir y cwricwlwm i gyd trwy gyfrwng y Gymraeg a daw canran helaeth sef 96 y cant i 99 y cant o'r disgyblion o gartrefi di-Gymraeg. Yn sicr, fe ymatebodd Awdurdod Addysg Morgannwg Ganol i bwysau cynyddol o du rhieni a charfanau eraill am addysg trwy gyfrwng y Gymraeg. Dyma'r sir lle y ceir yr adfywiad mwyaf o safbwynt yr iaith Gymraeg ymhlith ieuenctid.

Ceir polisi iaith Awdurdod Addysg De Morgannwg mewn llyfryn sy'n rhoi gwybodaeth i rieni. Yn yr ysgolion cynradd, nodir mai Saesneg yw'r cyfrwng dysgu ar wahân i'r hyn a geir mewn ysgolion Cymraeg neu unedau dwyieithog. Ceir wyth ysgol gynradd Gymraeg a chwe uned ddwyieithog yn y sir yn ôl y llawlyfr. Nodir na ellir trosglwyddo disgybl o ysgol gynradd gyfrwng Saesneg i ysgol gynradd Gymraeg ar ôl ei flwyddyn gyntaf yn yr ysgol gynradd. Ceir un ysgol uwchradd Gymraeg yn y sir ac ynddi dysgir pob pwnc trwy gyfrwng y Gymraeg. Y mae'n angenrheidiol felly fod y disgyblion a dderbynnir[28] yn medru siarad, darllen ac ysgrifennu Cymraeg yn rhugl.

Neilltuir lle yn yr ysgol uwchradd Gymraeg i'r disgyblion a fynychodd yr ysgolion cynradd Cymraeg a'r unedau dwyieithog. Ni rwystrir disgyblion o ysgolion eraill rhag mynychu'r ysgol uwchradd Gymraeg ond: 'Bydd yn ofynnol i'r Awdurdod sicrhau bod y disgyblion hyn yn ddigon rhugl yn y Gymraeg i ymdopi ag addysg uwchradd drwy gyfrwng y Gymraeg.'[29] Rhoddir pwyslais arbennig ar ddilyniant addysg gyfrwng Cymraeg yn y sir hon. Yn sicr, fe fu ymateb i'r galw am addysg Gymraeg.

Methwyd â chael gafael ar unrhyw ddogfen a gyfeiriai at bolisi iaith Gymraeg Awdurdod Addysg Gwent. Deellir bod gan yr Awdurdod bellach ymgynghorydd sydd â chyfrifoldeb arbennig am y Gymraeg. Ceir chwe ysgol gynradd Gymraeg yn y sir yn ôl ystadegau'r Swyddfa Gymreig ac un ysgol uwchradd benodedig ddwyieithog[30] sydd heb eto gyrraedd ei llawn dwf. Daw 99 y cant o'r disgyblion sy'n mynychu'r ysgol benodedig ddwyieithog o gartrefi di-Gymraeg a dysgir pob pwnc yn yr ysgol trwy gyfrwng y Gymraeg. Y mae galw cynyddol yng Ngwent am addysg Gymraeg ac y mae'r Awdurdod Addysg yn ymateb i raddau helaeth i'r galw hwnnw.

O ddadansoddi'r cyfnewidiadau ym mholisïau'r awdurdodau addysg lleol, teg fyddai datgan mai un awdurdod yn unig sy'n cynnig arweiniad. Ymateb i raddau mwy neu lai a wna'r awdurdodau eraill i bwysau o du rhieni a charfanau eraill am addysg Gymraeg.

> The reason why Wales has ben allowed to be distinctive . . . is that the distinctiveness has in no measure threatened the essential structure or organization of the school system.[31]

Cyfyd y cwestiwn pa mor wahanol yw'r addysg uwchradd a gyfrennir ym mhumdegau'r ganrif hon i'r hyn a gyfrennir heddiw o ran ei strwythur a'i threfniadaeth. Y mae'n ddigon gwahanol yn sicr o safbwynt strwythur cyfun ac o safbwynt ei hagwedd at y Gymraeg. Ond pa mor wahanol yw ysgolion uwchradd dwyieithog Cymru o ran ei strwythur a'u trefniadaeth i ysgolion Lloegr? Gellir cytuno â Jones nad yw'r hyn sy'n wahanol yn ysgolion Cymru wedi bygwth strwythurau hanfodol na threfniadaeth y system addysg. Ond y mae trefniadaeth yr ysgolion dwyieithog yn wahanol; y mae pwnc craidd neu sylfaen ychwanegol yng Nghwricwlwm Cenedlaethol holl ysgolion Cymru; y mae agweddau rhieni a disgyblion at y gwahanol fathau o ysgolion yn fwy cymhleth ac yn sicr y mae'r Gymraeg a'r diwylliant Cymreig bellach yn treiddio trwy holl drefniadaeth ysgolion uwchradd ac yn effeithio ar y drefniadaeth honno. Y mae llywodraeth leol a chanol yn ymwybodol iawn o'r ffactor wahanol hon.

Deall y datblygiadau

Nid yw'n hawdd deall gwyrth. Meiddir anghytuno â Williams[32] pan sonia am dwf addysg ddwyieithog yng Nghymru fel gwyrth. Yr hyn a geir yw cyfuniad o gyfnewidiadau hanesyddol a chymdeithasegol wedi dod ynghyd mewn dull digon *ad hoc.*

Awgrymodd un adroddiad gan Arolygwyr Ei Mawrhydi (AEM) ym 1981 fod awyrgylch ysgolion uwchradd modern Cymru yn llawer mwy Cymreig a Chymraeg nag awyrgylch yr ysgolion gramadeg. Y mae yma awgrym i ddeall datblygiad addysg uwchradd ddwyieithog. Ym 1990 caeodd yr ysgol ramadeg olaf ei drysau ac o bosibl dyma ddiwedd ar gyfnod y math o addysg a gyflwynai hyd yn oed yn ardaloedd Cymreiciaf Cymru y neges mai Saesneg oedd iaith dod ymlaen yn y byd. Y mae'r un adroddiad gan AEM ym 1981 yn sôn na chlywid y Gymraeg mewn ysgol ramadeg yn un o ardaloedd Cymreiciaf Cymru y tu allan i'r gwasanaeth boreol, y wers Gymraeg ac ambell gyngerdd Gŵyl Ddewi.[33] Ceir tystiolaeth debyg o sawl ysgol ramadeg arall. Diddorol yn y cyswllt hwn yw nodi mai o ganlyniad i ad-drefnu cyfun y daeth 14 o'r 18 ysgol benodedig ddwyieithog i fod. Awgrymir felly mai un ffactor yn nhwf addysg ddwyieithog oedd datblygiad ysgolion cyfun.

O ddadansoddi'r cyfnewidiadau ym maes addysg ddwyieithog, fe sylweddolir bod y datblygiad yn llawer iawn mwy dramatig yn yr ardaloedd diwydiannol, trefol a dinesig a Seisnigeiddiwyd bron yn llwyr. Fel y dengys Roberts,[34] bu llwyddiant academaidd yr ysgolion uwchradd dwyieithog penodedig yn yr ardaloedd hyn yn fodd i esgor ar gynnydd pendant. Y mae'r rhesymau dros y cynnydd yn gymhleth: awydd rhieni i roi i'w plant y dreftadaeth Gymreig nas trosglwyddwyd iddynt hwy a'r teimlad fod yr ysgolion dwyieithog penodedig yn ysgolion dosbarth canol. O gyfweld sawl rhiant di-Gymraeg yn yr ardaloedd hyn, awgrymwyd yn gyson mai un o'r rhesymau pwysicaf yn eu dewis o ysgol oedd fod gan yr ysgol enw da. Esgorodd addysg ddwyieithog yn yr ardaloedd hyn ar ymwybyddiaeth o werth y diwylliant Cymreig ymhlith cymdeithas yr ysgol. Arwydd o'r datblygiad yw'r twf mewn dosbarthiadau dysgu Cymraeg i oedolion yn ogystal â dosbarthiadau i rieni i ddysgu Cymraeg yn ystod oriau ysgol eu plant. Y rheswm am y datblygiad yw'r ymdeimlad o falchder a enynnwyd gan yr ysgolion dwyieithog.

Gwnaethpwyd ymbil emosiynol mewn araith gan un o lywyddion y dydd yn Eisteddfod Genedlaethol Hwlffordd ym 1972 dros sefydlu ysgolion uwchradd penodedig dwyieithog yn yr ardaloedd Cymraeg. Lled-awgrymwyd y gallai fod mwy o Gymraeg yng Ngwent ar ddiwedd y ganrif nag yn ardaloedd Cymraeg gwledig Dyfed oni fyddid yn gwneud rhywbeth ar frys. Bum mlynedd cyn hynny ym 1967 fe rybuddiodd Adroddiad y Cyngor Canol ar Addysg fod miloedd yn cael eu colli o safbwynt y Gymraeg yn yr ardaloedd Cymraeg ac y dylid symud ar frys i ddarparu addysg trwy gyfrwng y Gymraeg yn yr ardaloedd hynny. Gochelir yn yr adroddiad rhag gorlawenhau yn llwyddiant dysgwyr Cymraeg yn yr ardaloedd Seisnigedig gan anghofio gwarchod yr iaith yn yr ardaloedd cymysg ieithyddol oherwydd fod y Gymraeg yn dal i gael ei siarad yn y gymuned.

Hyd yn oed mewn rhai ardaloedd lle mae'r Gymraeg yn gadarn, fe all newid yn y patrwm ieithyddol olygu bod lleiafrif sylweddol o'r plant yn ddi-Gymraeg . . . Soniwyd hefyd am ddifaterwch rhieni a hyd yn oed am elyniaeth rhai i'r Gymraeg mewn ardaloedd Cymraeg neu rai cymysg eu hiaith.[35]

Ffactorau economaidd, demograffig a chymdeithasol a fu'n gyfrifol am y newid ym mhatrwm ieithyddol rhannau o Ddyfed, Gwynedd a Phowys; y mewnlifiad cyson o boblogaeth di-Gymraeg a brynai gartrefi am lawer llai o arian yng Nghymru nag a gawsant o werthu eu cartrefi yn rhai ardaloedd yn Lloegr. Fe gychwynnodd y mewnlifiad yn y 1960au gan ddwysau trwy'r saithdegau a'r wythdegau. Cafodd effaith drawiadol ar iaith ysgolion cynradd ac uwchradd yr ardaloedd gwledig. Mewn ymateb i'r argyfwng ieithyddol hwn y cafwyd polisïau iaith mwy cadarn megis polisi iaith Gwynedd ym 1975, cynlluniau athrawon bro, sefydlu canolfannau iaith i hwyrddyfodiaid, a'r pwysau cynyddol i sefydlu ysgolion penodedig dwyieithog. Y mae'r rhesymau dros y datblygiad eto yn rhai sydd yn ymwneud ag ymwybyddiaeth o golli treftadaeth ac iaith ac ymateb mewn argyfwng i hynny.

Awgrymwyd yn ddiweddar gan rai rhieni, athrawon a charfanau sy'n pwyso am ysgol uwchradd benodedig ddwyieithog yng nghanolbarth Ceredigion nad oes y fath beth yn bod ag ysgol uwchradd draddodiadol ddwyieithog. Dadleuant fod yr argyfwng ieithyddol yng nghanolbarth Ceredigion wedi dwysáu i'r fath raddau fel ei bod yn amhosibl cynnal addysg gyfrwng Cymraeg heb sefydlu un neu ddwy ysgol uwchradd sy'n benodedig ddwyieithog. Datganodd Pwyllgor Addysg Dyfed ym Mawrth 1991 na ddylid sefydlu ysgol benodedig ddwyieithog yng Nghanolbarth Ceredigion ond yn hytrach cadw a datblygu'r tair ysgol bresennol yn rhai traddodiadol dwyieithog. Dadl y Pwyllgor Addysg yw y byddai sefydlu ysgol benodedig ddwyieithog yn seisnigeiddio un ysgol ac yn gwanhau yr ysgol leiaf o'r tair fel na ellid ei chynnal fel ysgol uwchradd. Y mae'r dadleuon yn rhai cryf o'r ddwy ochr. Gwendid dadl y Pwyllgor Addysg ar hyn o bryd yw nad oes ganddo ddiffiniad o'r hyn a olygir o safbwynt ysgol uwchradd draddodiadol ddwyieithog ac o ganlyniad anodd diffinio polisi iaith ysgol felly oni dderbynnir polisi Awdurdod Addysg Gwynedd o fodelau.[36]

Bu'r pwyso gan wahanol garfanau ieithyddol a gwleidyddol am gorff i ddatblygu addysg Gymraeg yn ddigon cryf i Ysgrifennydd Gwladol Cymru ym 1986 wahodd Cyd-bwyllgor Addysg Cymru i sefydlu Pwyllgor Datblygu Addysg Gymraeg gan addo darparu adnoddau angenrheidiol i gynnal y pwyllgor. Prif elfennau swyddogaeth y pwyllgor fyddai:

Bod yn fforwm a fyddai'n gallu cynghori llywodraeth ganol a lleol ar bolisi iaith;
gwella cydlynu ymhlith asiantaethau sy'n cyfrannu at addysg yn yr iaith Gymraeg;
dynodi anghenion datblygiad a blaenoriaethau oddi mewn i'r anghenion hynny ac i fod yn gyfrwng i'w hateb;
dosbarthu gwybodaeth;
dynodi anghenion ymchwil.

Amlinellwyd strategaeth i gyflawni'r swyddogaethau.[37] Erbyn 1990 sylweddolodd y pwyllgor fod ei faes:

> ... yn ymrannu'n ddwy sef archwilio polisïau addysg llywodraeth ganol a lleol sy'n ymwneud ag addysg Gymraeg ac estyn cyngor lle bo hynny'n briodol a nodi anghenion addysgol ar gyfer ysgolion a cholegau.[38]

Anniddig ac anfodlon o hyd yw'r carfanau sy'n pwyso am fwy o addysg Gymraeg: anfodlon am mai is-bwyllgor o Gyd-bwyllgor Addysg Cymru yw'r pwyllgor yn hytrach na phwyllgor annibynnol: anniddig am na roddwyd i'r pwyllgor, yn eu barn hwy, ddigon o gyllid i gyflawni y pum swyddogaeth. Fe fu'r pwyllgor yn sicr yn fforwm i gynghori llywodraeth ganol ar fater y Gymraeg yn y Cwricwlwm Cenedlaethol; bu'n cydlynu gweithgareddau y tair canolfan adnoddau cenedlaethol yng Nghymru; bu'n dynodi anghenion datblygiad a blaenoriaethau trwy gynghori llywodraeth ganol ynglŷn â cheisiadau am grant Cymraeg (Adran 21) y Swyddfa Gymreig ac fe luniodd strategaeth ar gyfer ymchwil. Yn sicr, fe ymatebodd i'r sefyllfa ieithyddol ond amser a ddengys sut y gall gydlynu, datblygu ac arfarnu addysg Gymraeg.

Sefyllfa argyfyngus yr iaith Gymraeg a phwysau carfanau gwleidyddol ac ieithyddol a barodd i'r llywodraeth ganol o dan Ddeddf Addysg 1980 sefydlu grantiau addysg Gymraeg, Adran 21. Ym 1980/1 roedd cyfanswm y grant yn £501,775: ym 1990/1 roedd yn £3,303,000. Dyrennir y grant i awdurdodau addysg lleol i ddatblygu addysg Gymraeg ac yn arbennig i ddatblygu cynlluniau athrawon bro a chanolfannau iaith i hwyrddyfodiaid; i ganolfannau adnoddau yn Nhrefforest, Aberystwyth a Bangor er mwyn datblygu defnyddiau dysgu cyfrwng Cymraeg; i ddatblygu cyrsiau Cymraeg i oedolion mewn gwahanol ardaloed a sefydliadau yng Nghymru; i ddatblygu cyrsiau Cymraeg hyfforddiant cychwynnol i athrawon ac ar gyfer theatr mewn addysg. Yn ychwanegol dyrennir grantiau hefyd i gyrff megis Mudiad Ysgolion Meithrin, Cyngor Cwricwlwm Cymru a Rhieni dros Addysg Gymraeg. Clustnodwyd £160,000 mewn perthynas â'r grant cynnal addysg i ddarparu gwasanaeth hyfforddiant mewn swydd ar gyfer y Gymraeg yn y Cwricwlwm Cenedlaethol a £223,000 ar gyfer grantiau hyfforddi'r awdurdodau addysg lleol i helpu athrawon sy'n trosglwyddo o'r cyfrwng Saesneg i'r cyfrwng Cymraeg ac i athrawon yn y sectorau cynradd ac uwchradd i wella'u sgiliau ieithyddol. Rhoddir ers tair blynedd £1,200 i fyfyrwyr i hyfforddi i ddysgu trwy gyfrwng y Gymraeg yn y sector uwchradd (hyd at 50 y flwyddyn), ers blwyddyn £800 i fyfyrwyr i hyfforddi ar gyfer y sector cynradd, £1,200 dros gyfnod o bedair blynedd i fyfyrwyr sy'n dilyn cyrsiau B.Add cyfrwng Cymraeg fel atodiadau cymhelliad i wella a datblygu eu sgiliau ieithyddol. Rhoddir grant bonws o £1,500 ers blwyddyn fel rhan o grantiau bonws y Weinyddiaeth Addysg i fyfyrwyr sy'n hyfforddi i ddysgu Cymraeg fel pwnc yn yr ysgol uwchradd.

Heb amheuaeth, ceir datblygiad pendant o safbwynt cefnogaeth ariannol llywodraeth ganol. Ymteb i bwysau carfanau ieithyddol a gwleidyddol ac ymwybyddiaeth o argyfwng ieithyddol Cymru sydd yma.

Diweddglo

Bu'r cyfnewidiadau yn fawr, bu'r datblygiad yn syfrdanol, bu'r ymateb i bwysau ac i argyfwng ieithyddol yn bendant os yn ddigynllun. Y mae prinder dybryd o athrawon Cymraeg ac athrawon cyfrwng Cymraeg i weithredu'r datblygiadau a hebddynt hwy anodd os nad amhosibl fydd gweithredu.[39]

Medd amcaniadau o ddisgyblion/athrawon (sail 1989):

> Of the subjects suffering deficits/languages are expected to experience the greatest shortfalls with Welsh having the largest mismatch of all subjects ...[40]

Yn ôl yr arolwg ar gyfer yr amcaniadau, fe fydd angen 370

o athrawon Cymraeg ychwanegol i weithredu'r Cwricwlwm Cenedlaethol erbyn y flwyddyn 2000. Y mae angen gweithredu ar frys a hwyrach y gellir dysgu o batrwm hyfforddiant athrawon ar gyfer dysgu'r Fasgeg yng ngwlad y Basg.[41]

Nid ydym yn glir wrth lunio polisïau beth a olygwn wrth addysg ddwyieithog. Ai addysg ddwyieithog ynteu addysg Gymraeg a olygir. Y mae'r ffactorau sy'n effeithio ar y Gymraeg yn y cartref a'r gymuned yn greiddiol i gynlluniau addysg ac y mae'n bwysig cofio nad oes bellach yng Nghymru un ysgol gynradd nac uwchradd lle y daw'r disgyblion i gyd o gartrefi Cymraeg. Y mae angen yn awr am ymchwil eang, gydlynus a thymor hir i bolisïau addysg ddwyieithog yng Nghymru yng ngoleuni ymchwil i gwricwlwm a threfniadaeth a datblygiad iaith plant yn yr ysgolion Cymraeg a dwyieithog; y mae angen dysgu o brofiad gwledydd eraill sydd ag ieithoedd lleiafrifol ond gan gydnabod y gwahaniaethau; y mae angen gweithredu yn bendant ond nid yn unffurf trwy Gymru ar sail yr ymchwil gan gydnabod y gwahaniaethau sylfaenol ieithyddol rhwng gwahanol gymunedau. Medd adroddiad y Cyngor Canol ym 1961 wrth drafod y lleihad yn nifer y siaradwyr Cymraeg:

> Bu dirywiad amlwg yng nghyfartaledd y plant â'r Gymraeg yn iaith gyntaf iddyn nhw, ond ar raddfa fechan y bu cynnydd yn y Gymraeg ymhlith plant â'r Saesneg yn iaith gyntaf ac nid oedd hynny'n cydbwyso'r dirywiad . . .[42]

a chan sôn am arolygon iaith yn y 1950au ac arolwg iaith y Cyngor Canol ei hun

> pe gostyngai'r cyfartaledd yn llinell syth ar graff cymaint â nawfed rhan o'r rhif gwreiddiol bob saith mlynedd, yna fe ostyngai'r cyfartaledd presennol o siaradwyr Cymraeg hyd y traean ymhen 40 mlynedd. Golyga hyn y byddai'r 26 y cant o siaradwyr Cymraeg ym 1961 wedi gostwng hyd at rhwng 13 a 9 y cant erbyn y flwyddyn 2,000 . . .
> . . . Awgryma'n harolwg ninnau fod y dirywiad yn parhau. Mae'r rhesymau'n niferus a chymhleth . . .[43]

Tybed a ddengys cyfrifiad 1991 ffrwyth datblygiadau'r degawd olaf?

CYFEIRIADAU

1. *Cyfrifiad 1981*: Yr iaith Gymraeg yng Nghymru, t. 50, tabl 4.
2. C. Roberts, 'Teaching and learning commitment in bilingual schools' (Traethawd Ph.D. Prifysgol Cymru, 1985), 1–2.
3. Y Swyddfa Gymreig, *Ystadegau Addysg yng Nghymru*, Rhif 4 (1990), t. 77, tabl 7.13.

4. Ibid., t. 76, tabl 7.09.
5. Ibid., t. 79, tabl 7.18.
6. C. Williams, *Addysg Ddwyieithog yng Nghymru ynteu addysg ar gyfer Cymru Ddwyieithog*, Rhif 1 (Canolfan Astudiaethau Iaith, Bangor, 1988), 5.
7. G. E. Jones, *Which Nation's Schools* (Cardiff, 1990), 195.
8. C. Williams, op. cit.
9. B. M. Jones a J. Jones, *Datblygiad Iaith Disgyblion mewn Ysgolion Uwchradd Dwyieithog* (Canolfan Astudiaethau Addysg, Aberystwyth, 1991).
10. C. Williams, op. cit., 13.
11. C. Roberts, op. cit., abstract.
12. C. Baker, *Key Issues in Bilingualism and Bilingual Education, Multilingual Matters*, 35 (1987).
13. C. Williams, op. cit., 10, 13.
14. K. Evans, *Polisi Iaith Gymraeg Ysgolion Clwyd* (Adran Addysg, Cyngor Sir Clwyd — dim dyddiad ond y ddogfen sy'n weithredol ar hyn o bryd).
15. Pwyllgor Addysg Dyfed, 'Datganiad polisi yr Awdurdod', teipysgrif (Gorffennaf 1990).
16. Adran Addysg, Cyngor Sir Gwynedd, *Dogfen Polisi Iaith Gwynedd* (dim dyddiad ond dyma'r polisi diweddaraf cyfredol).
17. Ibid., t. 1.
18. Ibid., t. 4.
19. Adran Addysg, Cyngor Sir Gwynedd, 'Modelau addysg ddwyieithog ysgolion uwchradd' (vii).
20. Ibid.
21. Ibid., ii a iii.
22. Ibid.
23. Adran Addysg, Cyngor Sir Powys, *Yr Iaith Gymraeg mewn Addysg* (Llandrindod 1976), 1, a *Lle'r Gymraeg fel pwnc a chyfrwng yn y cwrs addysg*, Atodiad i Bolisi Iaith yr Awdurdod (Llandrindod 1987), 2.
24. Pwyllgor Addysg, Powys, *Ysgolion a Threfniadau Mynediad* (Llandrindod 1990/1), 13.
25. Y Swyddfa Gymreig, op. cit., 76.
26. Cyngor Sir Gorllewin Morgannwg, *Gwybodaeth i Rieni* (Tachwedd 1988), 9–11.
27. Mid Glamorgan County Council Education Department, *General Information about Policy and Arrangements for Primary, Secondary and Special Education* (December 1988).
28. County of South Glamorgan, *Information for Parents*. Admission to Infant and Junior Schools (undated).
29. Ibid., *Secondary Schools and Admission Arrangements*, 5.
30. Y Swyddfa Gymreig, op. cit., 76.
31. G. E. Jones, op. cit.
32. C. Williams, op. cit., 5.
33. AEM (Cymru) *Gwaith Cyfrwng Cymraeg mewn ysgolion uwchradd*, Arolwg Addysg 9 (HMSO 1981), 42.
34. C. Roberts, op. cit.

35. Adroddiad y Cyngor Canol ar Addysg, *Addysg Gynradd Cymru* (HMSO, Llundain, 1967), 216.
36. Adran Addysg, Cyngor Sir Gwynedd, op. cit. (vii).
37. Pwyllgor Datblygu Addysg Gymraeg: *Adroddiad Blynyddol* (Gorffennaf 1990), 5.
38. Ibid., 2.
39. Y Swyddfa Gymreig, *Bwletin Ystadegau Addysg Cymru*, Rhif 10, *Amcaniadau Disgyblion/Athrawon (sail 1989)*, 21.
40. Ibid., 23, tabl 4.3.
41. Basque Government, Education, University and Research Department *Irale: Literacy Training and Basquisation of the Teaching Staff* (Central Publications Office, Basque Government, January 1986).
42. Adroddiad y Cyngor Canol ar Addysg, 1961, op. cit. 232-3.
43. Ibid., 239.

Methodology in In-Service Education

HYWEL I. EVANS

More than thirty years have passed since I was appointed Faculty Officer of the Collegiate Faculty of Education at the University College of North Wales, Bangor. Apart from my direct responsibility for method classes in religious education for students following the teacher-training course (now the Post-Graduate Certificate of Education), I was charged with the development of in-service education for teachers and youth leaders throughout the then six counties of north Wales. The Collegiate Faculty corresponded in general terms with what in England were the university institutes of education. The involvement of the Collegiate Faculty at Bangor in in-service work, at the time of my appointment, was threefold. There were residential courses for teachers to be run at Easter in 1962, already well advanced in their preparations — in physics for teachers of A-level, in history, and in speech education. There was a major residential course for local education authority and voluntary organization youth officers to be run in September 1962 as a follow-up to a pioneering course — The Challenge of Youth Today — which had made a national impact in the previous year. Finally, breaking very new ground, and in anticipation of the publication of the Bessey Report,[1] there was a two-year part-time course to be run as twelve weekend meetings for part-time youth leaders from the six counties.

I served as Faculty Officer for twelve years and during that time saw in-service work develop very dramatically, not only in north Wales but throughout England and Wales. That development can be measured not only in the number and scope of 'courses' provided and the numbers of teachers who chose to attend, but in the increasing sophistication, if that is not too pretentious a word, of the methodological approaches that were adopted.

The basic methodology of the three Easter courses provided in 1962 was relevant then and remains appropriate for many such activities today. The physics course included laboratory work, both demonstration and 'hands-on' experience related to topics that were then new in A-level syllabuses. Detailed notes on the activities had been prepared by the university physics department staff and so teachers returned to their schools at the end of the course with a body of thoroughly up-to-date teaching material which they had themselves trialled. For the history course, visits to the historical sites conducted by specialist historians were the central element. Speech education was a course which brought together a more mixed clientele for a diet of lectures with discussion immediately following each one. That, too, was the basic recipe of the September course for youth officers with the significant addition of a team of four group leaders, who had jointly planned the course and who led a series of seminar-group discussions throughout it, structured so as to facilitate the pooling of experience by the members of the groups. Because the September course lecturers included figures of national or even international status, such as Dr Kurt Hahn, Sir John Hunt, Huw Wheldon, Jack Longland, Jim Hogan and Revd Dr Edward Patey, a large number of non-resident course members were attracted to attend those lectures but the more substantial and lasting work of the course was that undertaken in the group seminars. The published report of the course[2] included transcripts of the principal lectures and a summary of the seminar group conclusions. Residential courses made up of lectures and discussions continue to abound but the absolute need to provide structure and purpose to such discussion is all too frequently neglected.

Following the recommendations of the Bessey Report courses to train part-time youth leaders were established in every LEA in Wales. Some authorities, like Carmarthen, Pembroke and Cardigan, chose to establish joint courses, as of course the Collegiate Faculty had already done in north Wales. In view of the existence of this activity in every one of the seventeen Welsh authorities, the Welsh Joint Education Committee asked its Further Education Officer, B.J. Griffiths, to set up co-ordinating machinery. The result of this was the establishment at Llandrindod of a two-year part-time course for tutors of part-time youth leader courses, with Dr Leslie Button of the Department of Education at University College, Swansea, as course director and four, later five, of us as group tutors working under his leadership. The rationale for these courses is set out in detail in Dr Button's published works[3] and I need only testify here to its success in achieving the whole-hearted commitment of course members and tutors. The emphasis at every stage was upon the actual experience of the course members themselves in working with the part-time youth leaders or students for whom they were responsible. Each meeting ended with a specific agenda of tasks to be undertaken by every one of us with our students before the next meeting and that next meeting was based upon the responses we had faced. The role of the tutor, and of the course director, was to help course members recognize and apply the general principles of developmental group work in and to the real situations that had arisen from the tasks attempted. In that such an approach to learning concentrated upon reality the course members' and tutors' failures were as valid and important topics for course discussion as their successes, and learning to cope with emotional turmoil and conflict was one of the course outcomes which I still most value.

The Llandrindod course had a beneficial effect on the content and methodology of the Faculty's course for the part-time leaders of the six north Wales counties. At first that had been the epitome of everything that a course should not be — guest lecturers, each one an expert in his own field, developmental psychology, drama, physical education, delinquency, adolescent leisure pursuits or whatever, but not one of them with experience of running nor even visiting a part-time youth club. By 1964, with direct co-operation from the six county youth officers and some regional officers of the voluntary youth organizations the course had settled to a one-year pattern of six weekend meetings held between September and March in different locations throughout north Wales. The involvement of the youth officers gave the course a practical focus which it had previously lacked and the participation of five or six of us from north Wales in the Llandrindod course helped us to amend the teaching approach so as to take proper account of the course members' experience. The course continued to develop long after youth leadership ceased to be a government or LEA priority and the courses for part-time youth leaders run today each year by Gwynedd/Powys and by Clwyd owe their origin and something of their philosophy to the organizational and methodological innovations of the Collegiate Faculty's work.

The first course for primary-school staff organized by the

Collegiate Faculty took place at the Cartrefle College of Education, Wrexham, at Easter 1963. The Principal of the college, Mary Taylor, had previously been primary adviser for Bolton, and had a commitment to the classroom relevance of all college courses. She had also a concern for in-service education that was very unusual among colleges of education at that time. At her suggestion the use of structural apparatus in the teaching of mathematics in the primary school was the main focus of that first course and the time was largely devoted to workshop sessions using Dienes, Stern and Cuisenaire apparatus. I suspect that the content and methodology of that course owed much to Edith Biggs, HMI, and certainly much of the very considerable amount of activity which the Faculty sponsored throughout the six counties in the years that followed were modelled upon Edith Biggs's work.[4] Miss Biggs herself only visited the Faculty area once, to the best of my recollection, and on that occasion I ventured into one of the workshop sessions that was in progress. When challenged by Miss Biggs, I explained that I wished to observe the course at work. 'Certainly not', she replied, 'Either join in or go away.' I joined in and found great frustration in multibase work, being quite at home in working out the calculations on paper but wholly unable to carry them out with Dienes blocks! It was the careful programming of the activities so as to ensure the total involvement of course members that seemed to me one of the secrets of the success of that course.

It was in 1966 that the limitations of short courses led the Collegiate Faculty to propose a more sustained and structured pattern of activity. Each of the six authorities was invited to establish six groups of teachers, each with a named leader who would be appointed as leader by the Faculty and paid a modest honorarium. Each group would be expected to meet five or six times between October and Easter and to submit a report on the curriculum development work which they had undertaken. A modest sum of money was made available to each group to be spent at their discretion, for example on the purchase of materials for trial or evaluation. An initial three-day residential course for the thirty-six group leaders was held at Bangor. The outcome of the whole project was to be a publication, based on the reports of each group.

This pattern of working proved an outstanding success and in subsequent years language, mathematics, religious education, music and other curricular areas were explored. In 1972–4 it was decided to look at the whole curriculum of the primary school, making use of the same basic structure of thirty-six groups but inviting each to nominate a chairperson rather than work under a leader. Each group then nominated one of its number to attend the initial course at Bangor, another to participate in a two-day visit to the West Riding, and yet others in the following terms to take part in visits to Oxfordshire and to ILEA. The published reports[5] of that project were well received.

In retrospect, however, I consider it to have been a mistake to have aimed at a written report as the outcome of a curriculum project. While the reports of the 'Whole Curriculum' project and that of the 'Language' project[6] proved worthwhile documents, much of their value derived from the specialist input of the individual project co-ordinators rather than from the work of the groups themselves. For the group members I am quite certain that it was the process of curriculum discussion and evaluation that had lasting worth, rather than the document which they submitted to the Faculty.

The methodological value of the whole curriculum project, in obvious contrast with the traditional short course, was its collegiate nature. Although every group meeting elected its chairman and scribe all members in turn were called upon to represent the group and to report back to the group on the visit or activity in which they had participated. It is interesting to note that the Curriculum Council for Wales, through its pattern of teacher support groups, is currently making use of a somewhat similar strategy to facilitate the implementation of the National Curriculum subjects and cross-curricular themes.

In 1970 DES/ATO Letter 2/70 opened a new chapter in the organization and methodology of Faculty work in north Wales. In essence the Letter proposed to make earmarked grants for the provision of in-service courses to area training organizations provided they established a structure of consultative machinery which involved their constituent authorities, their teacher-training institutions and teachers themselves. Such an organization, the Collegiate Faculty Conference on In-Service Training, was already in existence in north Wales, having grown naturally from a meeting of the county primary advisers with staff from the colleges in December 1966. At the outset this conference had been chaired by a senior officer of one of the authorities but he was succeeded in due course by a primary headteacher. Although the machinery to implement 2/70 was already in place in north Wales the definition of in-service work in the DES/ATO letter did not lie easily beside the kinds of activity which were being found relevant by teachers and authorities in the area. Even twenty years ago we had come to realize that to equate in-service education with the provision of 'courses' was simplistic and inadequate.

Thanks to vigorous support from the Inspectorate, we were given permission to use the DES/ATO money for curriculum projects, based on the pattern outlined above. Two of these projects proved notably successful and each continued for several years. The one, of course, was preparation for the raising of the school-leaving age (RoSLA), and the other, preparation for the transfer from health authorities to local education authorities of the responsibility for the education of children classed as severely sub-normal (SSN).

The success of both projects derived from factors which have continuing value. The RoSLA project began traditionally enough, bringing together from every secondary school in the six counties the member of staff who had been appointed school co-ordinator of RoSLA planning. Weekend courses focused on issues then perceived as of current concern—many of which have been explored more recently by the Technical and Vocational Education Initiative (TVEI)—outdoor education, residential experience, the Swindon project on records of personal achievement. Almost from the outset, however, the school co-ordinators began to emphasize that the task of preparing for the raising of the school-leaving age was a whole school task—and not one for them alone. Courses after that first year were therefore broadened to attract other staff to attend side by side with the RoSLA co-ordinators, and then to involve the heads, the LEA advisory staff and ultimately county council members and other school governors. This acknowledgement of the extent of the impact of a major curricular development was, to the best of my knowledge, unique in the early seventies and remains rare today, though there are many aspects of National Curriculum and of local management of schools that could be more effectively and economically addressed if the training of heads, of other staff, and of governors was tackled in an integrated manner rather than separately.

The other project, on the transfer of responsibility for what were then called SSN children from health authorities to LEAs, also addressed the task of whole school planning, but in a more direct manner. The 'Training Centres', which were to become schools, were staffed by people with a wide range of qualifications — very few of which carried with them qualified teacher status — and LEAs were given some degree of discretion in deciding which of these people should be granted qualified teacher status on account of their experience. While the division between qualified teachers and others was of profound importance to the individuals involved it did not affect the need for in-service support for all staff, and the decision was therefore taken, with the approval of the Inspectorate, to address the project to all staff in the training centres and hospital schools of the six authorities, making no distinction between those designated as teachers and the others. Such an approach proved itself wholly justified in the exceptional situation that prevailed in that sector of education at that time. It could well be timely now to reconsider the appropriateness of the rigid division that is still made these days betwen teachers and other staff. Local management of schools has led to senior teaching and administrative staff sitting side by side to master the technicalities of SIMS, and it is surely imperative that ancillary and support staff helping pupils and teachers in science or technology classes should be familiar with the National Curriculum and assessment requirements in those subjects.

One feature of great potential value to in-service education which developed in the late sixties owed nothing to the intiative of the Collegiate Faculty — the establishment of teachers' centres. Each LEA in north Wales set up teachers' centres but no two authorities went about it in the same way and so the end-products were markedly different. By far the most effective approach seemed to be that of the authority which earmarked a school which would become available in a year or two for use as the centre and then invited teachers to form a steering committee to plan the accommodation, furniture and above all the activities that would be based there. This elaborate planning function fully justified itself and by the time the building became available there were in existence a whole gamut of valuable in-service activities throughout the county which made it at once a real centre of teacher professional interest. One of the more rural authorities also developed an approach which proved to have such value that it has continued up to the present day — which was to define the function of the teachers' centre leader in terms of facilitating in-service activity within individual schools, or clusters of schools, throughout a wide area — providing for him in due course an actual base with a range of imaginative resources available but making no attempt to persuade groups of teachers to meet at that base if some other meeting-place seemed to them more convenient. In both these authorities teachers seemed to feel a sense of ownership of the centre's activities in a way that was not apparent in those authorities which had started by choosing a building because of its immediate availability and geographical location, filling that building with a range of apparatus that could not be provided within every school and then at once appointing a 'Warden' or 'Leader'.

One development which was to become of great interest to teachers was the decision in 1967 of the University of Wales to allow graduates of other universities access to its Master of Education degree by part-time study. The collegiate faculties at Cardiff and Swansea, being in major urban centres, were in a position to provide tuition for the M.Ed. degree on an evening basis. No similar arrangement in north Wales had any hope of meeting the needs of the teachers of the area. We decided therefore to use the structure of weekend courses at different locations which was continuing to prove its worth for part-time youth leader training. Having decided on the course structure we were faced with the more difficult decision of defining criteria for acceptance of teachers to the course, since it was reasonable to expect the M.Ed. to be much oversubscribed within a year or two. It was our new head of department, Professor J. Roger Webster, who guided us to the constructive decision to select each year a group of teachers with a focus of common professional interest. Thus the first group, who began their studies in 1968, were all teachers of the humanities, the 1969 group were mathematicians and scientists and their successors in 1970 were all teachers of language. One-quarter of the taught course consisted of curriculum studies, concentrating obviously on the area of their immediate interest though within a whole curriculum context.

It was our intention, at the outset, that we would encourage each group, at the conclusion of the taught course, to seek out a set of related topics for their final dissertations, which might then provide the basis for a faculty publication on current curricular issues in the teaching of the humanities, science or language. We were less attracted by the idea of this final publication than by the vision of what might be achieved in terms of curriculum development and evaluation through the professional collaboration within these groups, each of about a dozen experienced practitioners, at the conclusion of a demanding taught course. The University regulations which required that work submitted by a candidate should be identifiably his own and that all contributions by others should be acknowledged made this vision of collaboration in M.Ed. dissertation work inappropriate. I have to confess, however, that I and my colleagues were more than slightly taken aback by the lack of enthusiasm, amounting indeed to a degree of hostility, to the idea of collaboration in degree work shown by the M.Ed. students themselves. We attributed this, as we came to see that it was a characteristic of every M.Ed. group in its turn, to the emphasis that is laid at virtually every stage of schooling on the dishonesty and undesirability of 'copying' another child's or student's work. Today, of course, the aims and objectives of virtually every college, school, course of study or cross-curricular dimension lay stress upon the need for students to learn to co-operate with others in group activity. This may prove to be wholly consistent with the National Curriculum requirement to assess and report on the attainment level of the individual child, at 7, 11, 14 and 16, but on the other hand it may not. We saw our M.Ed. experience as an example of the assessment tail wagging the curriculum dog — and readers of this essay will have no difficulty in adding more such experiences of their own.

The world we inhabit now is very different from that of the late sixties, in terms of in-service education as much as in every other way. My aim in outlining at such length my own experiences in that period is not to seek to portray some vanished golden age but to argue that the need for systematic planning of the methodology, as well as the content, of in-service education is essential.

One major change that has taken place is the provision of earmarked funding. Such funding first appeared on a large scale through the TVEI initiative, as TVEI-related in-service training (TRIST). In rapid succession it changed its name to grant-related in-service training (GRIST), then to the Local Education Authorities Training Grant Scheme (LEATGS), and now to Grants for Education Support and Training (GEST). It has been the responsibility of the LEAs to administer these grants and they have therefore been required very rapidly to develop expertise in the planning and conduct of in-service activities. Such expertise is having to be developed also, of course, within schools themselves.

A second principal difference between the activities for which I was responsible in the Collegiate Faculty and those which face organizers of in-service work today is that the Faculty worked only with teachers who chose to participate. By now teachers are required to undertake in-service work on the five 'Baker' days and also in school time. This has caused less difficulty than I would have anticipated. The fact that teachers have a critical attitude to the in-service activities provided and that they are frequently loud in their condemnation of work that seems to them a waste of time is predictable and wholly proper, as long as their condemnation is conveyed to the people who planned and provided that activity.

One frequent complaint applies particularly to courses that consist of lectures. A lecture, by its very nature, can hardly meet the need of the members of the audience for differentiated guidance or stimulus, and may be as inappropriate as traditional whole class lessons would be for mixed-ability groups. Where there is wholly new material to be presented a lecture, with supporting documentation, has its place but, if teaching approaches are to be considered, structured seminars and workshops that require staff from different schools to pool their expertise are far more worthwhile, though much more difficult to plan, to lead and to follow through. The combined expertise and insight of a professional audience is usually greater and of more worth than that of any single expert lecturer. The starting point of much in-service work should therefore be to elicit the relevant elements of that expertise from the course participants in such a way that all are enriched and so as to facilitate the assimilation within their expertise of the new insights, or new contexts, which are the topic of the course.

I have referred already to in-service work initiated by the Collegiate Faculty in the early seventies where the nature of the task called for such sharing of professional experience. During such activity the boundary between course tutor and course member became sometimes very thin, since the tutor's experience, no less than that of the course member, was open to challenge. The pedagogical skill of the tutor, however, was manifest in the quality of the planning undertaken beforehand and in the sensitivity and purposefulness with which the actual course session was led.

There is of course a place in in-service education for lectures and presentations which provide updated subject knowledge and for discussion that seeks to clarify aspects of such lectures. The advent of the National Curriculum, with its new language of attainment targets, programmes of study, statements of attainment and standard assessment tasks, makes such authoritative exposition a necessity. But the essence of the in-service need is not new information nor even new jargon but more considered opportunities for teachers to come together and to explore ways of maintaining and articulating the best of existing professional practice within these new structures, to the benefit of their pupils.

In-service activity during school time almost necessarily implies discontinuity in pupils' learning experiences and inconvenience and additional work for the teachers who participate. It follows that the attitude of the participants is ambivalent — pleased at the opportunity to meet with colleagues from other schools but still aware of the responsibilities and concerns that will await them on their return to school. The quality of the preparation of the in-service activity is therefore of the utmost importance. Attempts to justify the common failure to send out adequate background information and preliminary reading before a course are sometimes based on the frivolous ground that 'most teachers would not find the time to read it before coming'. One consequence of this attitude by course organizers is that the time of the conscientious teacher, who has actually sought out preliminary material on the topic, is almost wholly wasted. Criticism of the cascade method of training, which was adopted for the introduction of the GCSE examination, often included justified resentment at the series of courses which contented themselves with 'awareness raising', that is, going through the published handbooks with the teachers as if they were unable to read them for themselves.

Not only should preparation for an in-service activity be made possible for teachers who are invited to participate but follow-up work in their own schools should also be expected. There will, of course, be teachers who are unable to complete such preliminary or follow-up work but to plan on the basis that preliminary and follow-up work are impossible is to insult the professionalism of all the teachers. It may also reflect the awareness of the course planner that the content of the course has all too little relevance to the present classroom duties of the course participants.

More attention needs to be paid to acknowledging the readiness of teachers to commit themselves to in-service activity. The establishment of the part-time M.Ed. and the later availability in Wales of the B.Ed. for serving teachers transformed the in-service scene in the seventies and eighties. It must be a matter of concern that so many of the award-bearing courses have become, or are rapidly becoming, non-viable as LEAs claim, with some degree of justification, that they have devolved so much of their in-service budgets to schools that they can no longer support teachers for part-time degree or diploma courses. Within individual schools the sum involved in supporting a teacher for such a course may well seem prohibitive; the more so since the commitment could extend over two, three or even more years.

One reason frequently adduced to justify LEA failure to support award-bearing courses seems to me quite specious. It is claimed that a distinction can be drawn between in-service work that benefits the institution and other in-service activity that benefits principally the individual participant, especially in terms of his or her professional advancement. The argument is put forward even by some heads, advisers and inspectors whose own careers have owed at least something to their pursuance of a part-time M.Ed. or similar course in the days when funding for such courses came from the 'pool'. Unless it is to be argued that the desire for professional advancement is itself in some way dishonourable I would maintain that the distinction between the needs of the teacher and the needs of the school is false.

If we are to encourage those many teachers who are prepared to put their fullest efforts into in-service work and also to motivate those fewer who are reluctant participants, we must find mechanisms for the accreditation of such work, presumably on a unit basis, and a way of aggregating such credits into professional qualifications such as certificates of further professional study, diplomas and degrees. The positive attitude of the University of Wales towards such developments is greatly to be welcomed.

The task of providing a structure of in-service support which is adequate for the delivery of the National Curriculum, as presently conceived, is monumental. It is being tackled by the Department of Education and Science and the other bodies charged with the responsibility of facilitating the implementation of the National Curriculum and its associated assessment requirements. The strategy adopted seems to rest upon the assumption that it will be adequate to provide training for each National Curriculum subject in succession, and on the assumption that every primary school will have a subject curriculum leader and every secondary school a head of subject department. The provision of funding, on a year-by-year basis, for the appointment of an army of advisory teachers is therefore seen as the key to success.

The entire structure rests on the belief that teachers who have subject knowledge or expertise will be able and willing to pass that on to their colleagues. The experience of the last few years shows that that willingness does indeed exist. It is the skill of teaching colleagues that cannot be taken for granted. Outstanding classroom teachers do not necessarily prove a success in conveying their know-how and enthusiasm to colleagues and it is unreasonable to expect them to be able to do so within a matter of days of their appointment as 'advisory teachers'. In the early days of the introduction of the National Curriculum, some months before the appearance of the statutory orders for one of the core subjects, an advertisement appeared in Wales for 'expert trainers' to carry national responsibility for planning and providing the in-service support for the National Curriculum in that core subject. The advertisement attracted excellent candidates and the appointments made have proved a distinguished success but the naïvety that coined such a title, the simplistic thinking that decided that a person could be dubbed an instant 'expert' to train others is at the heart of my misgivings about current in-service education.

Merely gathering teachers together and leaving them to discuss matters of common concern is no guarantee of profitable dialogue and outcome. The skill of planning and leading such activities is a skill that has to be learned, like every other professional skill, and the lack of any structure to address this need — the need for 'training the in-service provider' — is a fundamental weakness in present and planned provision. My whole professional and personal background leads me to welcome the increased role of in-service work in the profession today. I find it, however, a matter of concern that the value, and even the cost-effectiveness, of much that is provided is undermined by the failure to pay adequate attention to the methodology of its delivery.

REFERENCES

1. *The Training of Part-time Youth Leaders and Assistants* (London, HMSO, 1962).
2. *The Challenge of Youth Today — Bangor, September 1961* (Collegiate Faculty of Education, UCNW, Bangor, 1963).

3. L. Button, *Discovery and Experience* (Oxford, 1971); L. Button, *Developmental Group Work with Adolescents* (London, 1975).
4. *Mathematics in Primary Schools*, Curriculum Bulletin No 1 (Schools Council, 1966).
5. J. Rogers, *Primary School Project — Report 1* (1975), and *Primary School Project — Report 2* (1976) (Collegiate Faculty of Education, UCNW, Bangor).
6. J. Edwards, *Language Project — Final Report* (Collegiate Faculty of Education, UCNW, Bangor, 1969).

University and Training College —an Unlikely Marriage?

D. GERWYN LEWIS

> I hope to live to see a closer approximation of our training college system with the liberal culture of the universities so that all that is best and highest in modern education may be brought within the reach of those to whom the teaching of the great mass of the children of this and coming generations will be entrusted.[1]

Such was the aspiration expressed by a Canon Walburton to the Cross Commission in the 1880s. Walburton was, in fact, long dead before that vision began to assume a degree of reality. University involvement with the training college system did not commence until the publication of the Burnham Report in 1925.[2] Thus began the involvement of the federal University of Wales in the field of teacher training and education. This was the first major landmark, later to be followed by three other significant landmarks, which dictated to a large extent the pattern of teacher education in the Principality of Wales. These were the McNair Report of 1944,[3] the Robbins Report of 1963[4] and finally, the James Report of 1972.[5] The form and nature of the links between university and training institutions in Wales have inevitably been dictated by these reports. They represent in varying degrees pinnacles, plateaux and troughs in the history of teacher training within the Principality.

The Burnham Report, 1925

Prior to the publication of the Burnham Report the work of examining students at all training colleges, including those in Wales, had been the responsibility of the Board of Education (the predecessor of the present Department of Education and Science). However, by the late 1910s and early 1920s there existed a considerable educational lobby which urged the establishment of direct links between the universities and the training colleges. Shakoor notes that 'after the Act of 1918 the question of University participation in the training of teachers became an important topic of discussion in educational circles'.[6] Even the Board of Education was pushing for links to be established. In 1919, the President of that Board speaking to the British Association stated that 'the quality of the education which is given to the rising generation will depend upon the extent to which the Universities are enabled to print their impress upon the teachers in our schools'.[7] The National Union of Teachers urged the training colleges 'to work under University direction'[8] for the award of a university diploma. As a result, the Burnham Report in May 1925 included the major recommendation that the universities should take over from the Board of Education the examination for the Teacher's Certificate by creating joint examining boards. With some alacrity, not normally associated with governmental bodies, the Board of Education in December 1925 accepted the main conclusions of the report.

In Wales, the federal University itself, under the powers conferred upon it by charter, was requested to establish a Training College Delegacy. Not for the last time, there occurred within the University a debate as to whether there should be established a single delegacy based on the federal University (favoured by the University Council) or three or four delegacies based on the individual university colleges (favoured by the Academic Board). The wishes of the training colleges themselves prevailed — they were more interested in establishing links with the central University than with the local constituents. Two factors were important, one idealistic and the other pragmatic. At the first level the appeal was to be associated with a national institution which at the time still enjoyed a degree of popular appeal. At the second level, the controlling bodies of the training colleges — the local authorities or Church associations — wished to retain their effective administrative and fiscal control over the colleges, and they were of the view that the federal University was much less likely to be a challenge than a strong and potent local university college. Thus, in 1929 there was established in Wales a University Board for Training Colleges which reigned supreme until the publication in 1944 of the McNair Report.

The Joint Board scheme was not an overwhelming success either in the United Kingdom or more specifically in Wales. The new boards inherited an overcrowded curriculum, and by the time of their demise that curriculum was essentially unaltered. What the system did was to ensure the effective continuance of an established order, with the University merely replacing the Board of Education as the examining authority. It still operated very much under the aegis of that Board itself and, even when major cut-backs in teacher training were occurring in the 1930s, its failure to comment, other than in narrow fiscal terms, was symbolic perhaps of its lack of maturity, authority or will. On the other hand, in mitigation it must be remembered that the Joint Boards were born in difficult times. They came into being just as the world economic depression was rising to a peak, and 'they inherited the consequences of the Labour Government's failure to raise the school leaving age in 1931 . . . the period 1931–36 was one of acute anxiety in the Colleges (several nearly closed) and unemployment among newly trained teachers was exacerbated by a falling birth rate'.[9] Furthermore, their terms of reference were very limited and very little attention was given to the possibilities of wider co-operation between the universities and the training colleges. In Wales, this situation was compounded by the fact that the training colleges were linked to the national, federal University which perhaps militated against the establishment of active co-operation with any of the local university colleges. By the mid 1940s the system was ripe for change.

The McNair Report, 1944

The whole education system was in a state of turmoil with preparations, under the leadership of R. A. Butler, well in hand for the publication of what was to become a beacon in a dark world, the Education Act of 1944. Inevitably, alongside this was the necessity of reforming the teacher-training system. It was in May 1944 that the McNair Report was published. Its recommendations were many and diverse, but suffice it here to state that the most significant of these as far as the future development of the system was concerned was the one relating to the establishment of Area Training Organizations (ATOs) which would consist of an organic federation of approved training institutions with universities playing a central role by assuming responsibility for the training and assessment of all students seeking recognition as qualified teachers. Wales merited a special chapter and there was complete unanimity that the University of Wales was the proper body to assume responsibility for the education and professional training of teachers. Choices were available as to how the system should be developed in Wales, again revolving around the question of whether it should be based on the central University or its constituent members. The decision was to establish a single central School of Education operating through two major bodies, the University Education Board, and the University Faculty of Education. Considerable powers were vested in the Board which was required to 'survey the general educational needs of Wales' in the context of teacher training, and furthermore 'to formulate . . . a comprehensive system of teacher training in Wales and Monmouthshire'.[10] The University Faculty of Education would be the academic authority of the School charged with exercising academic control over the curriculum of the training colleges including developing schemes and syllabuses of study, regulations and research for example. In order to ensure the involvement of the constituent colleges, Collegiate Faculties of Education were established with specific responsibilities for the organization of school practice, the provision of in-service courses and the promotion of research.

On such a basis was laid the aspirations and hopes of all interested parties for the development of an enhanced and forward-looking system for educating potential teachers ready and capable of dealing with the changing demands of a post-war society.

The School of Education in Wales remained in existence until 1975 and operated during the period 1948–75 with a mixed degree of success and failure. Perhaps its major success was in acting as a buffer against what the McNair Report itself had described as 'the encroachments of centralisation'.[11] It saw itself very much as a broadly-based body representative of all the major agencies concerned with teacher training within the Principality. It was linked to the national, federal University. It felt capable of flexing its muscles when necessary and it did so to some effect on a number of occasions, in what increasingly became a clash with the Ministry of Education over the control of teacher education in Wales. In the 1950s it took up cudgels on behalf of the then newly established Cardiff Training College and the fledgeling, temporary college based at Wrexham, in terms of the role of one and the proposed permanence of the other. The basis of its complaint was that whatever advice was being tendered to the Ministry of Education was being either ignored or rejected. This was merely a prelude to the major conflict which occurred in the early 1960s over the issue of the expansion of the training colleges in Wales. The School was suspicious that the Ministry was seeking to establish two major centres of teacher training in Wales, one in Cardiff, the other in Bangor, with the inevitable consequences of a much diminished role for other centres in Wales. The strongest possible representations were made by the School to the Ministry, and, in a sense, its action proved to be a sensible one in that very soon it became a matter of dire necessity for all colleges to expand to their utmost capacities in order to deal with the needs of a rapidly expanding school population.

Another area of success was in revising a curriculum which had not undergone any major changes for well over a quarter of a century. It changed an overloaded and fragmentary curriculum into one which had greater coherence and depth than had hitherto been the case. The number of subjects to be studied was reduced and the concept of a study in depth of a single subject was given considerable prominence. The 'theory of education' courses were given the necessary degree of flexibility to meet the needs of schools adapting to the impact of the 1944 Education Act. In 1960, the length of the Teacher's Certificate course was expanded from two to three years, and an even greater emphasis was given to the main course, which resulted in the training-college curriculum showing a marked similarity, in terms of structure and content, to patterns already on offer within the University itself. Ironically, it was this emphasis on the academic aspects of the course and on the personal education of the student which was to lead directly to the criticisms of the system in the late 1960s and early 1970s. It first found official voice in the Gittins Report which challenged the relevance of the academic nature of many courses for potential infant and primary teachers. The same theme was to be reiterated, in very strong terms, in the James Report of 1971. What appeared at first to be a much-to-be-desired solution was later seen as a concrete example of the University imposing its own patterns and attitudes on a compliant and subservient teacher-training sector. It was a development which contained the seeds of its own destruction. Yet, the irony of the situation is that in the early 1990s there seems to be a resurgence of belief in the value of encouraging the personal development of the student at the expense of what are seen as the more arid aspects of the study of theories of education. The pendulum continues to swing.

The other important facet of the work of the School was its attempt to cope with its peculiarly Welsh role. Not only was the School expected to produce teachers in the same way as all the other ATOs, but it was also required to produce particular categories of teachers capable of meeting the distinctive linguistic needs of the schools of Wales. Teachers capable of teaching Welsh as a subject needed to be provided, as did teachers trained in such a manner as to be able to provide general tuition in a variety of disciplines through the medium of that language. It proved itself sensitive to these demands. It ensured that all training colleges offered courses of high standing in Welsh language and literature. By the end of the 1960s it was encouraging colleges to provide equally demanding courses geared to the needs of students with only a minimal knowledge of Welsh. It designated two of its colleges, the Normal College, Bangor and Trinity College, Carmarthen, as bilingual colleges, thus concentrating, in a sensible way, scarce resources in two strategically situated centres. Research was conducted into the problems of bilingual teaching and education. The School's contribution was not insignificant in that it realized the extent of the problem in Wales, responded positively and sought to ensure that those special categories of teachers it produced were at least aware of the position and armed with a limited body of knowledge and basic techniques to deal with the demands of a bilingual situation.

Yet the basic flaw in the School of Education was one which was later to characterize the very nature of the University of Wales itself — its basic inability to act as an independent body capable of looking objectively at the needs of Wales as a whole. When confronted with major issues which required an independent and objective assessment, the committees of the School had revealed themselves not as University bodies but in the main as a collection of individuals representing vested interests. The dominant, and permanent, voice within the School had been that of the principals of the colleges and they found it impossible to adopt non-partisan attitudes with the result that issues were seen in the context of the likely effect on individual colleges rather than in terms of Wales as a whole. This can perhaps be exemplified by the struggle of the Cardiff and Wrexham Training Colleges to establish themselves in the early 1950s. The attitude of the School was equivocal to say the least. It failed to see the potential enhancement of the system in Wales as a whole by the establishment of a major teacher training centre in the largest, and what was to become the capital, city of Wales. Similarly, it failed to highlight the lack of higher education provision in north-east Wales, and constantly sought the closure of the Wrexham College. This lack of foresight had its origin in the wish of the existing centres to avoid the challenge which new colleges posed, especially in terms of the recruitment of students. As far as other developments were concerned, the view was taken that all colleges should participate in *all* developments. In the early 1960s all colleges had to be co-educational. When the Bachelor of Education (B.Ed.) degree was introduced in the late 1960s, again all colleges sought to offer the entire range of subjects with the result that student numbers in certain disciplines at many colleges were small, inadequate and a strain on the resources of the colleges concerned. This failure to operate as an independent, University-based body, prepared to take rational, objective and, at times, unpopular decisions gave added power to the Ministry of Education. When confronted with this unwillingness to plan, the Ministry had little alternative other than to take action itself. This was to contribute in a not insignificant manner to the demise of the School in the mid 1970s. Yet, before that was to occur, the links between University and colleges were to be further strengthened in the mid 1960s by the establishment of the B.Ed. degree.

The Robbins Report, 1963

> The innovation which went furthest to give the colleges a position more akin to the universities was a result of a recommendation of the Robbins Report on Higher Education in 1963. This was the introduction of a first degree course in education, the Bachelor of Education (B.Ed.) . . .[12]

In the same way as the McNair Report had built on the foundations of the Burnham Report so the Robbins Report sought to extend even further the relationship of the training colleges with the universities. For the first time colleges were to teach to degree level. Yet, to a large extent it was a case of an opportunity lost. Rather than seeking to create a unique degree with a large measure of professional relevance for intending teachers, what emerged in Wales was a highly conservative scheme, reflecting the kind of structure which was familiar to the University, that is a three-subject course, reducing to a two-subject course in the fourth and final year, a pattern similar to either pass degrees or general honours schemes offered by university colleges at the time. It was a scheme for only a small number of students with many in-built and difficult hurdles to be overcome *en route*. It was suitable for potential secondary-school teachers with its emphasis on the study of two main subjects, mainly of a conventional nature, but its relevance for potential primary-school teachers was suspect in the extreme. The concept of awarding honours was opposed; there was to be no element of school practice in the final year. In short, the package offered by the University was not a generous one. On the other hand, it has to be understood that the University for the very first time was being requested to allow institutions, other than its own constituents, to teach one of its degrees and, in spite of the Burnham and McNair links, many University academics regarded the training colleges, or colleges of education as they were now to be known, as highly peripheral institutions. It is not proposed to discuss here the amendments made over the years — suffice it to state that concessions were granted but only after much pressure by the colleges and much heart-searching by the Academic Board of the University. It was not really until the 1980s that a fully professionally relevant, classified honours B.Ed. degree became widely available at the colleges of education.

However, there was one notable success achieved by the School of Education as far as the B.Ed. was concerned, and that was the devising of a highly specialized in-service B.Ed. degree for teachers. There was an urgent need to create opportunities for existing teachers to further their careers by gaining a B.Ed. degree, and there was certainly an awareness of this within the School. At the same time, it was recognized that the largely academic offering available to college of education students was highly unsuitable for experienced schoolteachers. The gauntlet was picked up by the more progressive elements within the School. Professor J. R. Webster, then Professor of Education at Bangor, was the main initiator of the new scheme, and in this he was very ably supported by the not insignificant voice of Mary Taylor, the dynamic and thrusting principal of the Cartrefle College of Education in Wrexham. They sought to exclude the emphasis on the subject-based disciplines so as to allow experienced teachers the opportunity to capitalize on their own hard-gained expertise in the actual classroom. The core of the course was to be the pursuance of a study in depth of a particular problem encountered by the teacher in a professional context. This would be supplemented by relevant curriculum studies and other aspects of the ancillary disciplines of education. Oddly enough, opposition came not from the so-called dyed-in-the-wool academics of the constituent colleges. In fact, the Academic Board welcomed the establishment of a degree scheme that was totally different in both nomenclature and kind from its own traditional offerings. Teachers themselves and their professional organizations welcomed it. The opposition came mainly from the colleges of education, especially from the subject specialists at those colleges who saw it as part of an encroaching tide of professionalization of the curriculum which threatened to make the study of traditional academic subjects subsidiary to education and the potential needs of teachers in the classroom. Webster and his committee, however, stuck to their guns and ultimately carried the day. This victory represented a watershed in the relationship between the University and the colleges of education. From this point onwards, the University was to show a greater amount of sympathy and understanding for those colleges and their aspirations than had hitherto been the case, based on the knowledge that no disastrous lowering of standards either had occurred or was likely to occur by the offering of suitable degree courses at the colleges.

The James Report, 1972

The whole thrust of the Burnham, McNair and Robbins Reports had been in the direction of developing and strengthening links between universities and colleges. In 1972, however, a report was published which totally reversed that trend — the James Report. From the mid 1960s onwards there had been considerable sniping at the system — and it was largely connected with what many saw as the 'over-academicism' of the teacher-training curriculum. This view first found official voice in the Gittins and Plowden Reports, which were highly critical of the non-suitability of key element courses for potential infant and primary-school teachers. The same criticisms were made in a letter issued in 1970 by Edward Short, then Secretary of State for Education, which asked all Area Training Organizations to review the manner in which they were fulfilling their statutory obligations. Before these reviews were completed there was a change of government and a change of policy which resulted in the establishment of the James Committee of Inquiry and ultimately to the publication in January 1972 of its radical proposals, including the recommendation that ATOs should be abolished. Its criticisms of the university link were strident.

> Placing undue emphasis on the present link with Universities has its own attendant dangers. The most obvious of these is that some colleges have been encouraged to strive for the wrong kind of excellence. Their courses have in many cases become too academic . . . In an attempt to make the College courses academically 'respectable' students are sometimes fed with a diet of theoretical speculation . . . too often the desire to imitate the university . . . has led to a distortion of syllabuses.[13]

James was not content merely to castigate courses. He went much further:

> There is another, and more insidious, danger of the University connection in its present form. What are the practical and psychological effects of recognizing another body of higher status . . . as a guardian of one's standards. Our visits to Colleges have pointed to a possible answer. In a number of cases the atmosphere encountered could only be described as one of competent acquiescence . . . It seems clear that the effect of the University control can, at its worst, be one of enervation.[14]

Much of what was wrong was being laid at the door of the universities. Local authorities and the Department of Education and Science were largely exonerated.

> In our visits to Colleges very little evidence was found that principals or members of their staff felt their freedom to innovate . . . threatened either by local education authorities or by the DES.[15]

As for validation of courses the Report spoke of the 'CNAA's (Council for National Academic Awards) sympathetic attitude to innovation . . . most of us hope that the academic functions will be discharged by that body'.[16] In short, what was being advocated was the abolition of the ATO system and a much diminished role for universities in the education and training of teachers.

One member of the committee was Professor J. R. Webster and he fought a sterling battle not only to retain the strong university link, but within the Welsh context actually to enhance the role of the University. He wanted to see being created in Wales a Wales College Council.

> It is important that the education and training of teachers in Wales should be under the aegis of one national body, as is University education in that country. The appropriate method of achieving this would be the creation of a Wales College Council composed of the University, the Colleges of Education, the one existing Polytechnic and the local authorities with the University providing the secretariat and the administration.[17]

In the ensuing negotiations he was not to get his way. He was faced wtih the opposition of both the Department of Education and Science and the Welsh Joint Education Committee, both anxious to extend their own influence over the teacher-education system. Throughout the early 1970s an acrimonious battle carried on, involving the University, supported by teachers' organizations and the colleges themselves on the one hand and the WJEC on the other. Webster's concern all along was the fear 'that we are losing the University control and gaining LEA control'.[18] Taylor, the Dean of Education at Cardiff, was even more explicit:

> Possibly the saddest aspect of the Report is the scrapping of the relationship of the Colleges with the University to satisfy the power needs of local authorities and central government.[19]

By the late 1970s a regional committee was in the process of being established, under the auspices of the WJEC, which later in the 1980s was to be superseded by the setting up of the Welsh Advisory Board, with an independent secretariat, but working very closely in association with the Education Department of the Welsh Office.

Yet, in spite of losing the administrative battle, other aspects of the University's role were safeguarded and, in fact, enhanced. Whilst in England many colleges transferred their allegiances from their local universities to the CNAA, in Wales all colleges, with the exception of the Glamorgan College of Education which became part of the Polytechnic of Wales (later to be closed as a teacher-training centre), sought to retain their validating link with the University of Wales. By the early 1990s that University has a greater involvement than any other British university in the validation of a wide variety of courses in many disciplines. That situation would not have occurred had it not been for the stand taken on behalf of universities, and the University of Wales in particular, by Webster as a member of the James Committee. Later in the 1980s, as chairman of a reconstituted University Faculty of Education, he was to be a prominent advocate for identifying a new role for that Faculty in the field of educational research. Clearly he was the dominating figure in the Welsh teacher-training system for almost a quarter of a century; his three main contributions at University level can be identified as:

(1) the pioneering work of establishing a unique degree for teachers which remains in existence in the early 1990s;
(2) securing in the early 1970s the continued involvement of the University of Wales as a potent force in public-sector education and particularly teacher education; and
(3) identifying the need for the University to develop an all-Wales research policy for education.

The impact of change is as yet too difficult to assess so soon after the 1980s. What is interesting is to see central government re-establishing its full control over the system. In the 1920s the Board of Education sought to cede many of its powers to the universities; McNair accelerated the process; Robbins pushed it even further. James put a brake on that involvement, and gave the central authority the opportunity fifty years later to regain control. With the introduction of a national curriculum and through such mechanisms as the Council for the Accreditation of Teacher Education (CATE), central government has virtually retrieved the powers which it had held in the 1920s, thereby being the major voice in the control of the teacher-training system. Universities, together with the CNAA, can validate courses but only within the strict parameters laid down by CATE. Her Majesty's Inspectorate, through the same mechanism, can now insist on being invited to inspect university departments of education. In Wales, strange decisions have been taken, notably the decision to cease initial training at the University of Wales College of Cardiff, and to allocate Cardiff student numbers to what until that time had been the ailing Department of Education at Swansea. We see a system with so many masters with fingers in the pot that it is surprising that the colleges find any time, freedom or scope actually to undertake their primary task of training and educating the nation's teachers. They are answerable to the Welsh Office, Her Majesty's Inspectorate, CATE, LEAs, and the University of Wales. Even at this moment (April 1991) there are renewed rumblings that in the event of another Conservative administration, the system will once more be radically changed by abolishing the B.Ed. and the PGCE in their present form because, it is claimed, of the over-emphasis on the theoretical aspects of training.

It has all been seen and heard before, and one wonders what new cycle will commence in the 1990s and to what extent that new cycle will do little more than mirror many of the events which have already occurred during the past three-quarters of a century. All that can be said for the present is that Walburton's dream of the pervading 'liberal culture of the universities' has once more been superseded by McNair's fear of the 'encroachments of centralisation'.

REFERENCES

1. D. G. Lewis, *The University and the Colleges of Education in Wales, 1925–78* (Cardiff, 1980) 25.
2. Board of Education, *The Training of Teachers for Public Elementary Schools* (London, 1925) (Burnham Report).
3. Board of Education, *Teachers and Youth Leaders* (London, 1944) (McNair Report).
4. Committee on Higher Education appointed by the Prime Minister, *Higher Education* (London, 1963) (Robbins Report).
5. Department of Education and Science, *Teacher Education and Training* (London, 1972) (James Report).
6. A. Shakoor, *The Training of Teachers in England and Wales, 1900–39* (University of Leicester Ph.D. thesis, 1964), 318.
7. Ibid., 332.
8. Ibid., 332–41 *passim*.
9. H. C. Dent, 'An historical perspective', in S. Hewitt (ed.), *The Training of Teachers* (London, s.a.), 20.
10. Statute XLV I of the University Education Board, Section 2a.
11. McNair Report, p. 50.
12. P. W. Musgrove, *Society and Education in England since 1800* (London, 1988), 118.
13. James Report, p. 53.
14. Ibid.
15. Ibid., 54.
16. Ibid., 55.
17. Ibid., 66.
18. 'Since James — interviews with Lord James, Roger Webster and James Porter', *British Journal of Teacher Education*, 1 No.1 (January 1975), 6.
19. University Faculty of Education and University Education Board, Minutes of 9 February 1972, Minutes of Joint Meeting, p. 2.

Thirty Years On—Non-University Teacher Education in Wales

M. I. HARRIS

In a commemorative booklet in 1964, the then Principal of Caerleon Training College, G.P. Ambrose, wrote:

> When the students at the opening of the 1962 session maintained in the dining hall a moment of solemn silence to commemorate the end of an era, their instinct was sound.

The 'solemn silence' was held to mark the entry of the first female students into the College — but it in effect recognized that the nature of public-sector teacher training was changing drastically throughout the Principality.

After 1948 when, as a result of the McNair Report, the University of Wales School of Education was established, the training colleges had settled into a well-recognized and accepted pattern. There was some expansion of student numbers to meet the anticipated increased demand for teachers, there was an increase in the number of colleges as a result of the designation of Cardiff and Wrexham Training Colleges, and there were also moves towards the development of co-educational teacher-training institutions.

In general, however, these changes did not disrupt the accepted model of a teacher-training system under the administrative control of local authorities or voluntary bodies and under the academic supervision of the University School of Education. The fact that the university education departments were academically responsible to their Senates and not to the School of Education was not a matter of great concern to the colleges, which accepted their subsidiary status as providers of certificated primary-school teachers in contrast to the postgraduate, secondary-school teacher output from the university departments.

The training colleges were generally small, single-sex institutions receiving their resources through county councils or voluntary bodies. They produced only teachers, generally for the primary stage, by means of a two-year certificate, entry for which did not require matriculation. The colleges were largely residential; fees for tuition and accommodation were received from the students' home authorities, and the principals acted *in loco parentis* with the operation of benign but precise disciplinary codes. Within these clearly delineated limits, staff and students developed a strong collegiate and social life-style that had many attractions – so that today many look back nostalgically to what they regard as 'the golden age'.

This tradition was effectively under threat from the early years of the 1960s onwards because of national and international concerns as to the nature and quality of teacher education. Any cosiness which may have existed in the training colleges was largely removed by the avalanche of changes required from the start of the decade.

The selective secondary-school pattern introduced by the 1944 Education Act was coming under severe re-examination at a national, political level. For a combination of political and financial reasons, comprehensive school education became widespread. This had immediate effects upon the colleges in that an increasing number of their teacher output now started to seek posts in junior comprehensive schools, though their training was for a lower age range. Even more significant was the fact that, with the removal of the eleven-plus examination as the selective system reduced, many primary schools were seeking major changes in curriculum and teaching methods — demands to which the colleges had to respond in their training.

Parallel developments were also occurring in the reassessment of the nature and organization of learning by academic and professional staff. The increasing awareness of the work of Piaget and Bruner and the initial shock for many of Bloom's *Taxonomy of Educational Objectives* were causing many staff, urged on in some instances by an influx of new colleagues, to reassess the nature and relevance of their courses. This re-examination was aided by the involvement of staff in a variety of curriculum development projects undertaken by the School's Council. Reassessment of the nature of quality of science and mathematics curricula in Britain and the United States of America had been greatly assisted by the political concerns which followed the launch of the first sputnik by the USSR. Major curriculum projects were launched in the USA, to be followed shortly in Britain by Nuffield-sponsored research into the state and possible development of science and mathematics teaching in British schools. With the establishment of the Schools Council, together with its Welsh Committee, a wide range of projects involving colleges, schools and local authority education departments were initiated — projects which influenced the training courses as well as directly affecting the curriculum in schools.

This increasing ferment of professional interest and involvement by staff was enhanced by the entry into the colleges of a large number of newly appointed staff to meet the needs of the growth in student numbers required to provide teachers for the national increase in the child population. The student places in Wales increased from 1,360 in 1958 to 6,135 in 1968 — with appropriate staff increases to maintain a staff student ratio of about 1:10. Unfortunately there were relatively few graduates available in the primary-school sector to fill these new vacancies, with the result that the main influx of staff consisted of subject specialists from the grammar schools which were in many cases giving way to comprehensive schools. These new staff, generally young and well-qualified in their specialist subjects, brought a new dimension into the colleges very much in line with the stated developments of the three-year course which had been developing for some years.

The need to expand the two-year certificate had been advocated in the McNair Report, but it was not until 1960 that this development finally took place. Even then, its introduction at about the same time as the Department of Education and Science decided to alter the balance of training raised doubt as to the wisdom of the change. The findings of the Robbins Report in 1963, and the strength of the support of the professional associations for a move to an all-graduate profession, ensured the introduction of a longer, more academically based teaching qualification.

Life in the training colleges, or colleges of education as they were known after the Robbins Report, was one of constant change, so that an attitude of infinite adaptability became a requisite for staff and managements throughout most of the last three decades. The curricula in primary and secondary schools were undergoing great changes, with resultant effects on college course curricula. The college courses themselves were also undergoing major structural changes — first to establish the three-year certificate course and then the Bachelor of Education degree; student intakes, now universally co-educational, were rising rapidly with resultant large-scale capital projects being undertaken; and there were large intakes of staff who, though generally well qualified in their subjects, had little experience of teacher training in a wider context. As if such major changes were not sufficient, there were, as a result of the Weaver Report, significant and time-consuming developments in the mechanisms for the new relationships between colleges and their providing bodies. The final element of change was the required involvement of the colleges in the attempts in the 1970s to modularize courses that had but recently been developed on a linear model.

The opportunities for development that these changes presented were grasped by the colleges in various ways and to varying extents. In many instances the changes were seen as an opportunity for academic staff, often clearly differentiated from 'education' staff inside the colleges, to deepen the academic content and understanding by their students of their special subject studies — as urged by the introduction of main courses, especially as the B.Ed. degree was developed. Some staffs, aided by the removal by the School of Education of boards of study in favour of infrequent colloquia, used the opportunity to re-examine the quality of college courses in the light of school requirements. Such movements were, however, limited in their scope and general acceptance by the colleges.

It was not surprising that, in this confused situation, criticisms of the effectiveness of the teacher-training institutions became increasingly strong and persistent. Dissatisfaction with the quality and relevance of newly trained teachers was expressed in a variety of reports, including Plowden and Gittins, by the national teacher unions and finally by the Government itself which set up a Committee of Inquiry under the chairmanship of Lord James of Rusholme in the autumn of 1970.

The report and the associated White Paper *A Framework for Expansion*, both published in 1972, were received in the colleges with a mixture of satisfaction, dismay and trepidation. For some staff, the stated proposals by the Government provided a real opportunity to establish a worthy public-sector, teacher-training system linking pre-service, induction and in-service. Also, although it had not been emphasized in the White Paper, it was appreciated that here was an opportunity for colleges of education to diversify into areas other than education through the introduction of the Diploma of Higher

Education (Dip.H.E.). This would increase the legitimacy of the colleges to a real place in higher education. At the same time, the development of academic boards after Weaver, the removal of the ATO system and the growing awareness of other validating bodies were seen as providing opportunities for greater freedom and responsibility for the colleges and institutes.

Other staff saw the situation very differently. Some had already seen the abandonment of the boards of studies as a weakening of their association with the University and, to them, the removal of the ATO was interpreted as a further move from the wished-for paternalism. Many believed that the new courses introduced for the three-year certificate and the B.Ed. degree could provide for the necessary level of academic attainment and professional relevance if given a chance to develop. To abandon what had recently been achieved for an untried new qualification was seen as completely unnecessary. Similarly many staff were convinced that the advantages of a student intake progressing to a polytechnic-type range of courses were illusory.

Within Wales the introduction and formulation of the Dip. H.E. required much effort and debate between the colleges and the University. For many involved in the development, Wales appeared to enjoy some advantages arising from earlier opportunities for the development of alternative curricula urged by the ATO, together with the experience gained in the HMI-inspired exercises in modularization applied to teacher-training courses. These factors, together with the close discussions on related courses which some of the colleges were then having with local technical and art colleges, especially after DES Circular 7/73, gave the Dip. H.E. a real attraction as a significant mechanism for the diversified development of colleges.

The prospects of enhancing the role of the colleges of education by deepening and broadening the nature of the courses on offer were to prove exciting to the colleges themselves. After long discussion of the relative merits of the traditional university 'consecutive' model of teacher training as contrasted with the 'concurrent' mode of the two- and three-year certificate and B.Ed. degree, most of the colleges opted for the consecutive model. The Dip. H.E. stood as a qualification in its own right but was also considered as Part 1 of the B.Ed. degree and other possible degrees which were to be developed. The

Dip. H.E. was structured as a two-year, four-semester modular course with a wide range of student choice built in to its provision.

Disillusion and despondency were not long in coming to the colleges. The bright hopes for a new form of teacher provision linking colleges, schools and the advisory/inspectorial services of the providing local authorities soon faded as it became clear that the resources for induction and in-service as planned by James were not to be available. The model of a two-year academic course followed by a lengthy introduction to the teaching profession through the combined and interrelated use of colleges and schools was not implemented. As a result, the rump of the system, consisting of a 'two-plus-two' consecutive college course was rapidly modified. Increasingly the academic and pedagogical elements of the scheme were interchanged so that, in the long term, the Dip. H.E. experiment was abandoned.

The resulting disillusionment and frustration were intensified when it became apparent that promises that greater diversification of courses would be encouraged and permitted were not going to be kept.

After DES Circular 7/73 which forecast a great reduction in full-time teacher-training student numbers, there were major structural changes in the whole of the higher education provision in Wales outside the University. The resultant mergers between the Polytechnic, colleges of education, art and technical colleges resulted, with the exception of Bangor Normal College and Trinity College, Carmarthen, in the establishment of much larger institutions. One major element in the discussions that took place preparatory to mergers was that, in addition to bringing together the courses in the separate colleges, further diversification would be encouraged to take up the slack in the system as a result of the savage reduction of teacher-training places in Wales. The initial reduction proposed was from 6,300 to 4,800 places but this was later reduced to 2,900. Such diversification was permitted in a large number of colleges in England, but in Wales, for reasons that are cloudy, some years elapsed before the colleges, through the Regional Advisory Council (RAC), were allowed to develop a general studies degree, in most cases based upon the Dip. H.E. (In the one college which tried to develop this degree without a Dip. H.E. base, the authority to offer it as a free-standing degree was withdrawn within a few years.) This failure to permit colleges to diversify at the very time that teacher-training numbers were being severely reduced made the removal of the Dip. H.E. inevitable on logistic if on no other grounds.

Within the teacher-training faculties of the newly established institutions there was an element of *déjà vu* in this change of course structures. Many of the staff had participated in the development of the three-year certificate and of the B.Ed. degree which, by necessity, meant that for three or four years there was overlap between the traditional and new schemes within each college. Then, with the introduction of the Dip. H.E., there was a further period of overlap of courses for three or four years — whilst before this was over there were already indications of a need to develop yet another degree structure with consequent overlap with the existing provision. In such circumstances it was not surprising that senior staff had much concern with maintaining the morale and reducing the cynicism of staff who were required to continue to provide courses in constantly changing conditions.

One ever-present element of change that was of concern to the colleges was the prospect of closure. At the mergers in 1975 one non-university college had disappeared through movement into the University (St Mary's College, Bangor). As student numbers were progressively reduced whilst diversification possibilities were restricted, it became increasingly obvious that the teacher-training faculties and colleges were too small to be economically or academically viable. The prospects of closure were imminent and no colleges considered themselves immune. In the event, in 1977, only the teacher-training faculty at the Polytechnic of Wales, which had itself been transferred from Barry, was closed, though other colleges felt the cold breath of possible extinction. Though relieved at escaping closure, colleges realized that the problem of too many small teaching units existing in Wales continued to prove a constant threat to continued existence — a threat which has not yet been removed.

Although the continual demands for changes and the ever-present fear of closure were undermining the confidence and morale of teacher-training staffs, there were other factors after 1975 which helped to counterbalance the feelings of inadequacy which the constant criticism was developing.

The college merger developments as a result of Circular 7/73 resulted in the larger part of teacher training being located in bigger institutions with greatly enhanced higher-education course provision. The management problems of welding into a corporate institution a number of colleges with different traditions, student clienteles, courses with different subjects, structures, attendance and teaching modes were very considerable and took years to bring to a reasonably satisfactory state. Yet during this process, the experiences, often painful and ever-demanding, developed in most lecturers a confidence in their own abilities and an appreciation of the demands of higher education which had hitherto been only partially perceived. The confidence gained and the support experienced through the combined strength of the new institutions were significant in developing a more independent and enterprising attitude amongst the staff. Over the years this has resulted in the production of courses, clearly identified by high-quality documentation, that have satisfied not only the University, as an increasingly stringent validating body, but also other agencies including the Council for the Accreditation of Teacher Education, the Inspectorate — on frequent full inspections — and even a joint Wales Advisory Body/University Grants Committee national survey of public-sector and University teacher training. In this survey the public sector did not suffer in comparison with the University provision.

Of particular value to the merged institutions was their close association with the CNAA, with its stringent standards in relation to course structure, resource requirements, staffing and evaluation. Though at times appearing over-demanding, intrusive and bureaucratic, CNAA played an important part in the growth in confidence of teacher-training personnel who had experienced the rigours of CNAA institutional visits and observed the nature of the course review visits with which colleagues in other disciplines within the new institutions had to contend.

The growth in confidence in the colleges was also based upon their experiences with the Wales Advisory Body (WAB). This national body, with responsibility for developing the higher education public sector in Wales, demanded from the colleges a range of systematized information and planning which required a great effort of adjustment from management and staff involved. Analyses of student intakes, cohort progressions, ratios, unit costs, planning cycles involving monitoring evaluation and delivery, and cost of courses were required on a regular basis. Many staff found such demands a time-wasting imposition but for the colleges as a whole it brought a degree of academic and managerial professionalism greater than any previously required. Involvement in these activities and the degree of success achieved in producing integrated and comprehended systems within the colleges brought with them an increasing confidence in their ability to manage their own affairs.

Another reason for growth of confidence lay in the increasingly close and interrelated activities between the colleges, local education authorities and the staffs of schools. A feature of the newly merged colleges was the establishment of advisory boards on the model long established in technical colleges. These boards, operating through governing bodies, were established to ensure that college courses maintained their relevance in the vocational areas for which their students were preparing or already engaged. The impact on teacher training was particularly valuable as the advisory board formed a channel between colleges and schools. A considerable change in the relationship between schools and their local colleges has taken place through the growth of joint college/school ventures in in-service training, joint research projects, the involvement of school staffs in college course development, interviews of prospective students and joint school-practice activities such as IT/INSET (Initial Training/ In-Service Education and Training) and, not least, the secondment of college staff into schools to gain relevant experience. As a result of the B.Ed. degree in its full- and part-time modes and the availability of higher degrees in education, a cadre of talented, well-qualified graduates with long experience of teaching and administering primary schools has developed within the schools. A considerable number have joined college staffs, bringing with them a wealth of ability and experience invaluable in the development of the revised courses required by the introduction of the National Curriculum. These developments have all contributed to give a greater sense of professionalism and involvement to college staffs, who now enjoy closer association with their colleagues in schools.

When, in 1962, those students stood 'to commemorate the end of an era', they could not have appreciated how prescient was their action. They were observing the passing of an attractive, socially memorable provision mainly for primary-school teachers, based on small, single-sex, largely residential colleges. In these, the great majority of students were following a two-year certificate course for which the entry qualifications were not overly demanding, but which was able to produce good school practitioners for the provision of the existing school curriculum. The college staffs at that time appeared content that, within the Area Training Organization of the University of Wales, their academic and professional roles were related, though in practice subservient, to the university education departments operating through the Faculty of Education.

In the three decades since that commemorative dinner, the colleges have undergone difficult and demanding trials. All have changed radically, some have disappeared, others have reached the brink of extinction only to be rescued by the strange twists of political fortune whilst most, even in their present forms, have uncertain futures. In the face of incessant criticism and ever-increasing demands the colleges, like Tennyson, have seen a life of 'ever climbing up an ever climbing wave', and even today a further round of examination of teacher training seems likely, as politicians thrash around for scapegoats to explain policy failures.

Despite, or perhaps because of, all this pressure over many years, the colleges and faculties of education in the non-university sector are now more entitled than ever before to consider themselves as fully capable of fulfilling their role as an essential element in higher education. The quality, qualifications and relevance of experience of their staffs makes them fully capable of meeting the demands of the present school curriculum. Their increased professionalism has been developed through long, sometimes painful, experience in course validation and evaluation by their peers, through exposure to staff in schools through extensive in-service activities and through greatly increased involvement in schools through secondment. Teaching and research for initial or higher degrees in which staff have now been involved for over twenty years, often in direct partnership with colleagues from university departments, have developed a range of expertise fully capable of meeting the academic and professional demands of their students.

The maturity of the academic staff and the competence and experience of college managements and administrators have now resulted in the establishment of the colleges and institutes as corporate bodies responsible for their own development with funding directly from the Welsh Office. Many new problems are likely to face the colleges and institutes but the competence and confidence they now exhibit will enable them to cope as they have coped with severe crises over the last thirty years. This attitude and ability entitles the public-sector and voluntary institutions to a higher profile and status — a feature which hopefully will be recognized when unified higher education for Wales is finally established.

Problems of Teacher Education in the 1990s

DENIS LAWTON

Introduction

My links with Roger Webster are through teacher education. For a while both of us represented that constituency on various committees of the Schools Council, and we still meet regularly at the Universities Council for the Education of Teachers. Yet we have all too rarely discussed major issues of teacher education, and I have not — yet — taken the opportunity to question him about his experience on the James Committee which reported twenty years ago. I look forward with interest to his response to some of the views in this chapter.

Peter Gosden[1] has pointed out, in a review of the James Report and its effect on more recent events, that one of the main characteristics of the last twenty years of teacher education has been strong criticism of the system for failing to produce the kind of teachers thought to be needed. Whenever criticisms are made of schools, it is not long before some, if not all, of the blame is directed at the training institutions.

The James Committee, appointed by Margaret Thatcher when she was Secretary of State for Education, with a chairman (Lord James) known to be critical of teacher training, inevitably gave weight to some of the complaints — for example, that there was too much irrelevant theory and too little emphasis on classroom competence. But on the whole, the recommendations were positive: three cycles of teacher training were envisaged: first, academic; second, pre-service plus induction; and finally the right to in-service education (one term in seven years). The debate about teacher education now is very different!

The James Report never became policy, however, and later in 1972 the Department of Education and Science (DES) produced its own agenda in the White Paper jokingly entitled *Education: A Framework for Expansion*.[2] Initial teacher training soon began to decline very rapidly (from 114,000 in 1971 to about half that number in the early 1980s). In-service training (INSET) did expand, for a while. But the teacher education enterprise overall is much smaller now than twenty years ago. But criticisms still abound. In fact, they have intensified and become more ideological. Why?

One of the features that has remained constant over the years is the inability of teacher educators to convince the public in general, and politicians in particular, of the need for educational theory and for institution-based training as opposed to an apprenticeship model of school-based induction. This is, of course, not unconnected with two aspects of English (but *not* Welsh) culture — distrust of professionals or professionalism and the low prestige of teaching as an occupation. Distrust of professionalism is part of the upper-class Englishman's dangerous admiration for amateurism (there are dozens of jokes such as 'The *Titanic* was built by professionals'). Similarly the dominant right-wing view of teaching is that secondary teachers need only to know their subject well, and that primary teachers should inculcate basic skills patiently but firmly — hardly a justification for a four-year B.Ed. degree.

One of the things we really need to do is to convince the public that teaching is — at all stages — a difficult, very demanding but worthwhile profession. To do that we need to spell out the kind of knowledge and skills required by teachers, and then, only then, to show how that knowledge and those skills are related to 'theoretical' matters contained in the Postgraduate Certificate of Education and other courses of teacher education.

There is another urgent need — to convince the public that some (but not all) 'modern methods' are superior to and more effective than traditional routines in terms of the quality and quantity of learning. For example, it is quite easy to make a child learn the multiplication tables and test pupils afterwards. It is much more difficult to be sure that children know how to apply such knowledge — for example, in working out the cost of real items in a shop. Theory and research, far from justifying 'cranky' innovations, help to sort out what are improvements from what are mere fads or fashions.

That weakness in the image of teacher education needs to be addressed, but there are other problems which are pressing on teacher education and, in my view, will persist for several years. The intention of this chapter is to analyse some of the important trends affecting initial teacher education — political, educational and demographic — and to speculate about the outcome of the tensions and contradictions within the system. Then I will rush in 'where angels fear to tread' and propose a solution to the problem of teacher education in the 1990s.

Political trends

I have elsewhere[3] described the growth in central control generally within education and, since 1982, particularly in teacher education. The most obvious manifestation was the invention of the Council for the Accreditation of Teacher Education (CATE) in 1984, and its renewal with increased authority in 1989.

Although the origins of CATE were highly controversial, it is clear that the Council has established national standards for initial teacher education, and has influenced standards for entry into the profession. Most educationists would accept the desirability of having some national guide-lines for courses which carry qualified teacher status (QTS), as well as the desirability of raising standards for entry into the teaching profession. The unacceptable face of politics is, however, that, at precisely the time standards were being raised, there were pressures from the political right to abandon all such controls and restrictions, even to abandon teacher training altogether.[4] The strange compromise of the late 1980s was to retain teacher training with higher standards and, at the same time, to introduce new routes into the profession such as by means of becoming licensed teachers and articled teachers where the emphasis is placed on training within the school rather than in institutions of higher education. What were the political reasons for promoting the new school-based routes?

In *The Tightening Grip*[5] I suggested that it was a mistake to talk of Department of Education and Science views or DES policies, since the DES was made up of at least three different groups, each with its own ideology:

1. The politicos (Conservative politicians and their political

advisers) whose beliefs and values include the supremacy of 'the market' and freedom of choice in education.
2. The bureaucrats (civil servants) who place a very high value on good administration and efficiency.
3. The professionals (Her Majesty's Inspectorate) who would give priority to professionalism and quality.

Since then I have extended the model[6] by suggesting that the politicos at the time of the Education Reform Act were themselves divided into at least two main groups — the privatizers and the minimalists (the privatizers favour the free market: minimalists want an inexpensive state system which they will take care not to use themselves).

Applying this model specifically to teacher education we might arrive at the following:

1. Most politicos would like to improve the supply of teachers at the lowest possible cost (whilst preserving the distinction between independent and state education), but a minority would favour abolishing the professional status of teachers and teacher education.
2. The bureaucrats would prefer clear-cut criteria for entrants to the profession and for qualified-teacher status — that is, promoting efficiency by qualifications.
3. The professionals would advocate better initial teacher training (ITT) courses, closer links between schools and ITT, as well as improved follow-up by way of in-service training — that is, enhancing professional standards.

I suggest that the major conflict will be between the need for greater professionalism and the unwillingness to pay for a larger and better-paid teaching force.

Educational trends

As far as decisions about official policies are concerned, it is probably reasonable to suggest that questions of educational theory are the least important! Yet there have been very interesting and professionally relevant developments in the last ten years which should not be ignored.

Possibly the most significant development has been the change in thinking about educational theory and its relation to practice. Paul Hirst[7] has, for example, described how during the 1960s attempts were made to derive education theory from the disciplines of psychology, philosophy, sociology and history. He has shown how these attempts failed, and why it is now necessary to concentrate on generating educational theory out of good educational practice. At about the same time, Donald Schon[8] invented the term 'reflective practitioner' to sum up the relation between theory and practice in other practice-based professions as well as in education. In the USA and elsewhere there is now a massive amount of research on the application of the 'reflective practitioner' concept to teacher education. One interpretation of these 'theoretical' changes is that initial teacher training (ITT) should now be regarded as the first stage of initiation into the profession of teaching rather than a licence to practise for the next forty years. If ITT were accepted only as Stage I then it could legitimately concentrate more on practical classroom skills and techniques, and would make no claims about providing a basis of philosophy, psychology or sociology for the rest of a professional career. This would not mean that the traditional educational disciplines cease to possess any relevance — simply that they would perform a different function at a later professional stage. It would reinforce some of the arguments of the James Report[9] which suggested that ITT should be followed by an induction period, and that later in their career all teachers should have the right to further professional study on a full-time basis. As well as the Schon-inspired work in the USA and elsewhere, there are good examples within the United Kingdom, for example, Wragg[10] and Stones.[11] Criticisms about the gap between theory and practice were not completely wrong, but they are now out of date. Professor Norman Graves[12] has neatly summarized the present state of the art.

Full-time study may well be difficult to achieve during the 1990s, but that is no reason for not expanding part-time provision. I would see a clear three-stage process of professionalization: initial training/licensing (ITT); followed by a period of probation/induction which would include further study before obtaining qualified teacher status (QTS); finally, after a period of experience (three to five years?) and further courses, full professional teacher status would be gained with an appropriate advanced qualification in education, probably — but not necessarily — at Master's degree level (as is the practice in some states in the USA). Each of the three stages would be separated by meaningful and relevant professional hurdles;

passing on to the next tier of professionalism would be accompanied by a much higher salary.

A phased approach to full professional qualification of this kind would help to reconcile some of the conflicts and contradictions described above. Moreoever, implementation of the National Curriculum will, during the 1990s, be placing much greater responsibilities on teachers, not only in the organization and implementation of a highly structured and detailed curriculum, but also in its assessment.

I suggest that the statutory requirements of teacher assessment and standard assessment tasks (SATs) will be such as to be properly the responsibility of senior *professional* teachers — not licenced teachers, probationers or those who have just reached qualified teacher status (QTS). The logic of this situation would be that all the Masters' degrees in education giving full professional teacher status would have to include appropriate courses covering the National Curriculum and its assessment. Thus the core curriculum idea would apply not only to ITT but to an important aspect of INSET. The Universities Council for the Education of Teachers (UCET) should now be embarking upon detailed studies of this kind — before the politicians start doing it for them.

Demographic trends

I suggested above that educational developments were likely to be the least influential on government policies. Perhaps the most influential factors will be the demographic trends influencing teacher supply and demand.

The first important fact to discuss is the clear rise in the school population during the 1990s; the numbers for primary schools are, of course, known up to 1995, and can be projected for the rest of the decade. For secondary schools the basic data is available, but choices cannot accurately be predicted — that is, the percentage of children staying on at school after the age of sixteen. But the trend is likely to be upwards. The Institute of Manpower Studies (IMS) Report[13] projected an increase of over half a million primary pupils in the years 1990 to 2000, plus 365,000 in secondary schools. Other things being equal, and assuming roughly the same pupil-teacher ratio, this would seem to indicate an increase in the demand for teachers of at least 40,000 by the end of the decade (less conservative estimates would double that number).

The rise in pupil numbers would not in itself be unduly disturbing if it were not for other demographic factors operating at the same time. During the 1990s there will be a fall in the number of school-leavers, and a shortage of (or at least a greater demand for) graduates. In other words, there will be much greater competition for 'teacher material' than in previous years. This will provide a classic situation of increasing demand and diminishing supply which would — in a free market — lead to much higher salaries. But, of course, the market is not free; it is to some extent controlled by government — there are, for example, many ways of influencing the very important factor of pupil/teacher ratio.

There are other factors in the supply-demand relationship which complicate the calculations (and almost certainly aggravate the recruitment problem). One of the complicating features of teacher supply is that it is heavily dependent on females: in 1986-7 of the overall under-25 intake, only 21 per cent were male (32 per cent of secondary; only 9 per cent of primary).[14] But during the 1990s other employers in search of graduates will almost certainly be trying to attract women into a variety of other occupations where the salary structure and conditions of service may well be more attractive than teaching.

A further difficulty: in 1986-7 of the 14,500 female teachers recruited to primary schools, only about one-third were new entrants to the profession; approximately two-thirds were 're-entries' — that is women who had temporarily interrupted their career for child-rearing or other reasons. When questioned about teacher supply, DES politicians and civil servants tend to make much of the fact that there are large numbers of trained teachers in the PIT (the 'pool of inactive teachers'). But they are, of course, a rather unpredictable group, often limited to one locality and increasingly open to other offers of employment. Professor Smithers[15] has also provided startling evidence about the increasing rate of wastage in the profession. This adds up to a picture of teacher supply during the 1990s which could become disastrous — unless appropriate action is taken. (Smithers's research indicates that teachers are leaving the profession at about five times the rate of official DES figures. This is a very important factor because in the past a comforting feature of the teaching force was its very low wastage rate.)

It may not just be difficult to recruit enough teachers during the 1990s — it may be impossible, if only traditional routes are relied upon. Pressures to recruit more and more unqualified teachers or under-qualified licensed teachers will be enormous. The alternative may be to send children home from school untaught, or to resort to 'part-time schooling' — an outcome already predicted by the National Association of Schoolmasters/Union of Women Teachers (NASUWT). Given such stark choices, it would be difficult for the teacher unions to resist pressures to employ the unqualified or under-qualified. A better strategy for them would be to welcome such recruits as teacher *assistants*, to concentrate on proper professional standards for those reaching full professional teacher status, and to delineate carefully the professional aspects of the teacher's role from the others. Studies of how teachers spend their working time show clearly that they are overburdened with necessary but quite 'non-professional' chores. There are now many schools where teacher assistants are used to great advantage.

Conclusion

All three trends — political, educational and demographic — seem to be taking teacher education in the same direction. Teaching is already a difficult and demanding job, and in the 1990s it will become more so, especially as a result of the National Curriculum and its assessment. The least damaging solution will be to have a more stratified teaching force where only the best qualified are regarded as fully professional teachers. Finding appropriate titles will be difficult: 'teaching assistant', 'qualified teacher', 'senior teacher' are some of several possibilities. (CATE should also take on the task of specifying suitable training for 'teaching assistants'.) The role of the teacher will be changing considerably in any case. During the 1990s there will certainly be a change in teaching, but it need not be to the detriment of the pupils. Teachers will spend more time assessing pupils, but they will also spend more time on curriculum planning — curriculum planning for individual pupils and small groups as well as the whole class.

In the past when teachers talked about individual differences in pupils, they tended to be thinking in one-dimensional terms about intelligence, and some teachers grouped children accordingly. But there is increasing evidence that intelligence is only one of many factors influencing how children learn. One of the tasks for professional teachers in the 1990s will be to diagnose other factors contributing to learning (or learning difficulty). Children certainly differ in terms of intelligence, but the IQ test is far too blunt an instrument as a diagnostic guide for improving performance. Some systems, for example, in Ontario,[16] are far in advance of the UK in this respect.

It is clear that teacher education will flourish in the 1990s, but it will be very different from the kind of programmes typical of the 1980s. Initial teacher education will concentrate on shorter, more intensive courses, involving preparation for the classroom, perhaps deriving something from studies of the skills and competences required in the classroom — without going to the extremes of some of the American competency-based courses. More of this training — but not all — will be school-based. It is already being acknowledged that professional training restricted to the experience of only one school is likely to be much too limited.

During the second stage, induction/probation, the emphasis will change, encouraging teachers to reflect about practice as well as to become better practitioners. The third stage will concentrate on developing professional expertise, encouraging teachers to understand the curriculum as a whole, for example, and to reflect on teaching with reference, when appropriate, to the potential contributions of such disciplines as philosophy, psychology and sociology. But that will not be the end of the story. Professional teachers will need opportunities for continuous periods of education, not only to update their skills and rethink their methods, but to develop as human beings and professional teachers in a variety of ways. Part-time research into the process of teaching and learning should be a high priority for them. Some will want to work for research degrees, and should be encouraged to do so.

As for the teacher educators, there will also be greater pressure on them to reflect on their practice, and to demonstrate the relevance of whatever they profess to the real world of teachers. Unless the teacher educators, in co-operation with the teachers, embark upon the kind of reform outlined above, I would suggest that the future is very bleak indeed.

REFERENCES

1. P. Gosden, 'The James Report and recent history', in J.B. Thomas (ed.), *British Universities and Teacher Education* (London, 1990).
2. Department of Education and Science (DES), *Education: A Framework for Expansion*, Cmnd 5174 (London, HMSO, 1972).
3. D. Lawton, *The Tightening Grip* (London University Institute of Education Bedford Way Papers, 1984).
4. Hillgate Group, *Learning to Teach* (London, 1989); C. Cox, 'Unqualified approval', *Times Educational Supplement* (6 January 1989); A. O'Hear, *'Who Teaches the Teachers?'* (London, 1988).
5. D. Lawton, op. cit.
6. D. Lawton, *Education, Culture and the National Curriculum* (London, 1989).
7. P. Hirst, 'Educational theory', in P. Hirst (ed.), *Educational Theory and its Foundation Disciplines* (London, 1984).
8. D. Schon, *The Reflective Practitioner* (London, 1983).
9. Department of Education and Science (DES), *Teacher Education and Training* (Report of the James Committee) (London, HMSO, 1972).
10. E.C. Wragg, *Teaching Teaching* (London, 1984).
11. E. Stones, *Supervision in Teaching Education* (London, 1984).
12. N. Graves, 'Thinking and research on teacher education', in N. Graves (ed.), *Initial Teacher Education: Policies and Progress* (London Educational Studies, London, 1990).
13. J. Buchan and C. Weyman, *The Supply of Teachers: A National Model for the 1990s* (London, Institute of Manpower Studies (IMS), 1989).
14. Ibid.
15. A. Smithers et al., *A Study of Teacher Loss* (London, 1989).
16. P. Huff, et al., *Teaching and Learning Styles* (Canada, Ontario Secondary School Teachers' Foundation, 1986).

The Control of Teacher Education

ALEC M. ROSS

The world of teacher education in England and Wales today is very different from that which existed when Roger Webster (and the present author) first moved from the school classroom to the university lecture theatre. There we began the task of seeking to develop in a new generation of teachers the ideas, skills, attitudes and values which would in due course provide them with the means to develop that personal philosophy of education which all successful teachers need. Without such a worked-out view of the educational process, itself a result of the interaction between theory and practice, an individual cannot lay claim to the honoured title of teacher. The choice of experiences to which the individual is exposed itself influences the outcome in some measure, and this essay concerns the extent to which control of the choice of those formative influences has moved to central government. This account is most certainly not an elegy for an imagined golden age that has passed; nor is it a paean for what has replaced the earlier arrangement. It is, however, intended in part as an appeal to the teaching profession so to organize its affairs that it shows itself worthy to be given a significant role, especially in determining entry to the profession, for that is one of the defining characteristics of a true profession — it controls entry to its ranks.

The changes which have taken place over the last two decades represent a virtual revolution in the relationship between central government and the various 'partners' who formerly played a leading part in the control and management of the education system. These partners include the local education authorities, the churches and other voluntary bodies, the various institutions of higher education and the teaching profession itself, in particular as it is represented by its professional associations; the list also includes the public at large and notably that part of it which owns, manages and makes use of independent schools, as well as the thousands of non-professionals who participate in the management of the maintained system. Most important of all are the parents of those for whom the school system exists. It is evident that education touches upon the interests of our whole society and that is why the control of teacher education is a matter of great significance.

We are dealing here with a system which arranges for an adult, specially trained to influence the young, being placed in an enclosed space for a large part of the school day with numbers of those whose immaturity leaves them exposed to the ideas and attitudes of the significant adults around them. Education has come to be regarded by the politicians as too important to be left to what has, disparagingly, been called 'the educational establishment'. Teacher education has, by the same argument, been judged to have become too important to be left to those who by custom and tradition have come to dominate it. However valid this view is held to be, it is possible to question whether these matters should be left almost entirely to politicians and their advisers. The fact that teacher trainers have been manoeuvred out of their former positions of influence is of less importance than the fact that the profession itself — albeit through its own fault — has also been excluded from the control mechanisms.

The present style of detailed control of teacher training could be regarded as merely a return to earlier practice. Sir James Kay-Shuttleworth, the founder of state-provided education in England and Wales, sought to control the whole operation from the Privy Council office. Though the effort broke his health, he thought nothing of prescribing in great detail what had to be done even to the extent of producing teachers' manuals to be used in the training colleges he established.[1] The standard histories of education explain how power came to be shared with other bodies, most notably those which emerged locally when local government came to be organized.[2] A partnership developed between the centre and a range of bodies at the periphery; the arrangement rested upon an agreement between the main political parties that a change of political balance would not upset the arrangements for educational provision. In the case of teacher training, the process of passing a measure of responsibility to other bodies can be followed in studies such as those by Jones,[3]

Ross,[4] Tuck,[5] Thomas,[6] and Armytage.[7] Perhaps the most important of these acts of self-denial which the centre undertook was that which followed the implementation of the McNair Report[8] of 1944 which led to the training colleges being brought into a relationship with the universities in their region through the newly created institutes or schools of education, which also included the universities' own departments of education. The aptly named book *The University Connection* by Niblett *et al.*[9] gives a full account of how teacher education was thus brought into the ambit of higher education. For present purposes it has to be noted that this arrangement meant that control of the content and, indeed, style of teacher education was now powerfully influenced by the university-based Area Training Organizations.[10]

The Prime Minister's Committee on Higher Education, which produced the Robbins Report in 1963,[11] completed the task of bringing teacher education fully into higher education. At last, teachers were, as in other professions, educated and trained in an atmosphere of research and scholarly activity. This was coupled with the decision to move at a steady pace towards making teaching a graduate-entry profession. Control of the size of the profession, that is the numbers admitted to training courses, remained with the Department of Education and Science (as the Ministry had become in 1964), this being necessary if the Secretary of State was to be in a position to fulfil the tasks specified in the Education Act of 1944.

The new department of state had a much enlarged area of responsibility and it would appear that there was an intention to make a break with a past which had left the central department in a position of somewhat diminished influence. The DES felt frustrated by the realization that, unlike other (proper?) ministries, though it had responsibility for a large and hugely expensive system, it had somewhat limited control over its operation. It could stop a building being put up or strike a teacher off the roll but the larger decisions seemed to lie to a surprising extent with others, especially the local education authorities and the professional associations of teachers. The larger story of how the DES managed gradually to claw back some of the influence which its predecessor bodies had willingly devolved need not be detailed here, but it should be kept in mind when considering how the influence of the centre was gradually increased in the area of teacher education.

Practice until the later 1960s had been that major issues of policy, such as the raising of the school-leaving age or the reform of the secondary-school examination system, were first discussed, often at great length and over a considerable period, in committees made up of 'the good and the great'. The names of those who chaired these committees passed into the language of education and their reports became standard texts for those preparing for entry to the profession. Officials ruefully regarded such committees as having power without responsibility, that is power to make all but binding recommendations without the responsibility of finding the resources required for their implementation. The principal vehicles for the 'education establishment' were the two (one for England and one for Wales) Central Advisory Councils.[12] A stream of important reports flowed from these bodies. The Welsh Council, for example, produced in 1960 an important study of education in rural Wales[13] and in 1967 published the Gittins Report on *Primary Education in Wales*.[14] After the Gittins Report and its English equivalent, the Plowden Report,[15] there would appear to have been a decision in favour of masterly inactivity to ensure that the Advisory Councils were not reactivated. The plot (if such it was) soon became known and led to the Permanent Secretary and his senior colleagues being interrogated extremely sharply by the Select Committee of the House of Commons in the 1969–70 session; the skill with which these officials avoided admitting to the fact that they had not taken the steps necessary to implement what was, after all, a legal requirement under the 1944 Education Act has to be admired. The minutes of evidence for that day[16] read like a script for the television programme 'Yes, Minister', which at a later date sought to make fun of the devices used by civil servants wishing to get their own way. The fact remains that the Central Advisory Councils were never again convened; the position was not regularized until 1986 when Sir Keith Joseph, ever a person to make sure that the law should not be abused, legislated for their demise in the 1986 Education Act. Henceforth policy was, as far as possible, to be worked out 'in-house'; if for political or other reasons it was necessary to have a committee, it would be a small one with, as some have thought, personnel chosen with a view to the desired outcome. The policy of dispensing with advisory committees, especially large committees with all interests represented, has become explicit in the 1980s. It has also to be pointed out that it became more evident, as the debate on comprehensive secondary schooling developed in the 1960s, that the consensus on education between the two main political parties was breaking down; by the mid 1970s it had entirely disappeared. The 'good and the great' can be allowed to pontificate on education as long as there is general agreement as to where the system should be heading; once that agreement begins to break down, policy issues have to be determined by the ministers alone, advised by their civil servants. Large representative committees cannot be relied upon to produce the required set of recommendations.

If a civil servant were to have sought for the means to obtain a better grip on teacher education, clause 62 of the 1944 Education Act would have provided plenty of scope, for it gave the Minister the task of making 'such arrangements as he considers expedient for securing that there shall be available sufficient facilities for the training of teachers. . .' By custom and tradition this power had been exercised by the Minister principally in relation to controlling the numbers being trained and undertaking special measures to cope with shortages as they emerged. The Inspectors of Schools had made valuable suggestions from time to time, especially in establishing the case for increasing the length of the training college course from two years to three in 1963. Nevertheless, here in the Act was a general power which could be used to bring the training system under control. In 1967 the Teacher Training Regulations were reissued and the opportunity was taken to firm up the Secretary of State's powers over teacher training, including the 'nature of the courses'.

There was, however, one important difference in the case of teacher education. Though the DES would have preferred to do without them, it became apparent, especially at times of difficulty, that representative committees, especially if they were serviced and firmly controlled by the Department, could be used, as Kogan and Packwood[17] put it, 'to bring out for discussion and assimilation many policies which the Department would otherwise have found it difficult to negotiate through the complex of local authority, teacher and teacher education interests'. Although there were gaps between committees, through the seventies and the first part of the eighties large, representative, specialist committees were used to assist in the task of making the adjustments needed. A major reduction in the number of teacher-training institutions in the mid 1970s was, for example, more efficiently accomplished because it had the imprimatur of representatives of the people most affected.

Throughout those post-war years when extremely difficult supply questions arose because of the fluctuations in the birth rate, there had always been committees to discuss these issues and advise. The National Advisory Council on the Supply and Training of Teachers, established in 1949 on the model of the large 'good and great' councils, produced, under a series of distinguished chairmen, eleven excellent reports on teacher supply questions. In 1966, however, it was quietly stood down. The then Secretary of State, Anthony Crosland, was later to explain that it 'was concerned with the future supply and demand for teachers. I thought that was a job that should be done inside the Department and not by an amorphous outside body. If the Department couldn't do that job, which was central to all its activities, it ought to pack up.'[18] However, the task of adjusting the training system to a sharp decrease in the demand for teachers would certainly involve the closure of institutions (all of which would have Members of Parliament ready to make life difficult), and Crosland's successors in the early 1970s decided that it would be expedient to create a committee to deal with the problem.

The Advisory Committee on the Training and Supply of Teachers (ACSTT) was in being from 1973 to 1978; this was a representative body and concentrated upon questions of numbers. It is interesting to note that the word 'Committee' rather than the previous term 'Council' was used. After its five-year term was completed there was another pause before it was found desirable to create a successor body, the Advisory Committee on the Supply and Education of Teachers (1980–5). This time the problem to be tackled had less to do with numbers and more to do with the sensitive issue of the content of the training courses. The slight change in the title of the committee made it a little easier for the Department to move into the areas of academic and professional significance which had begun to interest ministers.

All these committees were serviced by the DES and worked on documents largely supplied by the Department and Her Majesty's Inspectors. The DES had thus created, under its administrative control, what was virtually a professional body for teacher education. The professional associations of teachers and the other educational organizations represented on these committees were glad to take part since it offered an opportunity to seek to influence policy and also acted as an important channel of statistical information on the teaching force. They all recognized that, at that time, so deep were the differences between them that they would be unable to reach agreement on the formation of a proper professional body, that is a General Teaching Council, and so they settled for this interim substitute. The Advisory Committee on the Supply and Education of Teachers (ACSET), in its advice to the Secretary of State in January 1983,[19] resignedly reported thus:

> There is a wide measure of agreement both within and beyond ACSET that the establishment of a General Teaching Council, which among other things might advise on the control of entry and approve courses of training, remains a desirable objective... It has so far proved difficult to achieve agreement about the form and constitution of such a Council and despite independent initiatives such as those of the College of Preceptors, the future existence of a General Teaching Council cannot be relied upon as a basis for immediate policy decisions.

The conclusion that followed from this somewhat sad confession of failure by representatives of all the key bodies involved in teacher education, was that the Secretary of State should be invited to take charge.

> We believe that the Secretary of State should establish criteria which he will take into account in deciding whether or not to approve, or to continue to approve, individual courses.

The committee had now served its purpose and even before its term of office was complete — it was never replaced — a new-model, small, ministerially appointed body took over, but only as an agent of the Secretary of State, not as an independent body. That body, the Council (the older usage returned) for the Accreditation of Teacher Education is dealt with below. For the moment it has to be noted that the teaching profession at this point acquiesced in the loss of whatever small measure of control over entry to its ranks it still at that time retained.

Debates such as those described above do not take place in isolation from the world of everyday affairs and it is necessary at this point to fill in the background against which the administrative procedures outlined were carried out. This is particularly so in the case of teacher training, for that activity has always found itself to be a matter of public debate. Rightly or wrongly, teacher training has regularly been criticized; as these words are being written there is fierce discussion as various political groups produce their solution to what they describe as the teacher-training problem. As the new policy of 'Thorough', initiated in the DES in the middle 1960s, was developed, it could be well justified in the field of teacher training by reference to the increasing amount of public and even professional criticism of current arrangements. Ministers and their advisers have a duty to respond to such complaints. As the 1960s proceeded, student unrest and disruption, especially in 1968, seemed to give further grounds for public complaint about what was happening in higher education, including teacher education which had now become part of that great — and expensive — enterprise. The Robbins Committee had proposed that a special degree in education should be created for those teachers who entered the profession via the college route rather than the university degree route. That had been delivered in a remarkably short period of time.[20] The academic bodies concerned, the universities which agreed to validate the degrees and the Council for National Academic Awards, were determined to ensure that this new degree would, in its field, be comparable with degrees in other fields. The programmes of study were therefore constructed with appropriate rigour, offering plenty of opportunity for the student teachers to display their higher-level cognitive skills and their grasp of complex concepts. The most convenient way to bring this about was to require substantial amounts of study in what were called the 'foundation' disciplines of psychology, history, philosophy and sociology in their applications to the educational process. This brought out what has always been a problem to be faced in teacher education and training, that is achieving the right balance between the practical and the theoretical in a course which seeks to provide an academic education within the context of a professional preparation.

The Association of Chief Education Officers, in its evidence to the Select Committee of the House of Commons on Education and Science (Session 1969–70) when it was discussing teacher training,[21] was typical of many bodies which had been calling for a major inquiry into teacher education. Some thought that this was the kind of task which could be tackled by the Central Advisory Councils but as we have seen these bodies were not favoured by the DES. In fact the DES resisted pressures to set up an inquiry, though it did make some contingency plans for a more limited investigation into training for primary education if the pressure on ministers became too great. Advising ministers is one thing but keeping shadow ministers in the picture is another, and in the run-up to the 1970 general election the shadow Secretary of State (a Mrs Margaret Thatcher) promised that if elected she would have an inquiry into teacher training. Her party was elected and being a woman of her word she told her civil servants to set up an inquiry. Given the Department's dislike for large-scale, expensive and potentially far-reaching inquiries, the solution produced was ingenious. It was to be a small group on a strictly limited time-scale (one year) and would not explore the many thickets which lay around the topic. It is, for example, remarkable that the 'inquiry' did not look into the question of the very considerable over-supply problem which the well-informed knew had to be tackled at once. The inquiry was fortunate to have a chairman of known views and with impeccable qualifications. Lord James of Rusholme, the Vice-Chancellor of one of the new universities, had formerly been High Master of Manchester Grammar School. The Report[22] was produced on time and, though it had excellent recommendations to make on the question of the in-service education of teachers, its proposals on initial training were, perhaps, too revolutionary. Within months of the publication of the James Report, the Department produced in December 1972 a White Paper, *Education: A Framework for Expansion* (Cmnd 5174), which not only displaced the James Report but effectively set the agenda in teacher training and a range of other matters for the rest of the decade. It accepted some of the James suggestions but dismissed the rest. Policy-making was again firmly within the walls.

In the context of the occasion of this volume it is important to record that, though the great majority of teacher trainers took little comfort in the James recommendations on initial training, they found welcome recognition of their work in a 'Note of Extension' which two of the members had appended to the report. One of the signatories to that note was Professor Roger Webster. It did much to encourage those who felt that their recent efforts on behalf of the profession had perhaps been unduly disparaged. The 1970s set teacher trainers a series of demanding challenges: the new Bachelor of Education (B.Ed.) degree, as proposed in the White Paper of 1972, had to be developed and the colleges of education had to be transformed into 'diversified' colleges of higher education as institutions widened their range of courses in order to adjust to the reduction of teacher-training courses made necessary by the demographic swing.

The pattern of public concern about teacher training re-emerged as part of the 'Great Debate' on education initiated in 1976 by the then Prime Minister, James Callaghan, on the basis of confidential briefings from within the DES. One small measure, brought through on the recommendation of ACSTT, was Circular 9/78 (Welsh Office 99/78) of August 1978 which made it mandatory for all students admitted to teacher-training courses, regardless of what they intended to teach, to possess GCE Ordinary-level qualifications (Grade C or better) in mathematics and in English language. This very sensible requirement could be thought to mark the start of the process whereby the centre began to prescribe in ever-greater detail what should be done in teacher-training courses. This process was not, of course, unique to teacher training. The parallel movement in the field of the curriculum has been described by Lawton[23] and was in due course to lead to a national curriculum being specified in the 1988 Education Act.

The 1979 General Election was a bitterly fought contest and brought Margaret Thatcher back into government, though this time in a somewhat more senior position. There was clearly, in the light of the 'Great Debate', a mandate to 'get a grip on' education including teacher education, not least because of the obvious strides forward being taken by fellow members of the European Community. There had to be an end to what was called 'the cosy consensus' which allowed 'the educational establishment' to gain undue influence and even to thwart the intentions of radical governments. However, the full force of the new thrust was not felt until September 1981 when Mrs Thatcher's mentor, Sir Keith Joseph, came to the DES. The officials had prepared the way for the positive top-down, command-structure approach to the management of a system which little more than a decade before had been a classic bottom-up, consultative system. The machinery was in place and was used by the new Secretary of State to reshape the whole operation. Sir Keith (who became a peer on his retirement) held office for a remarkably long period till May 1986 and thus stayed long enough to see through the reformation, as he saw it, of the Department and the transformation of relations with the former 'partners'.

In the field of our concern, his first major policy statement came in a White Paper of 1983, *Teaching Quality*,[24] which provided a *tour d'horizon* of the world of teacher education as seen by the Secretary of State. The ACSET advice that he should himself issue criteria for teacher education was gladly taken and forthwith implemented.

Schedule 5 of the Education (Teachers) Regulations Act of 1982 established the legal basis for the new arrangement by giving to the Secretary of State power to approve courses of initial teacher training for teachers as being suitable for those who satisfactorily complete them to be recognized as qualified teachers. 'Qualified Teacher Status' was essential if a person were to teach in a maintained school. Following the White Paper, the Secretary of State moved rapidly; in April 1984, Circular 3/84 (Welsh Office 21/84) laid down precise criteria by which courses would be judged and set up the Council for the Accreditation of Teacher Education (CATE) to advise the Secretary of State as to whether a particular course met the criteria or not. The criteria were not determined by CATE but by the Secretary of State, though when CATE was renewed in 1989 it was given extended powers allowing it to make suggestions which the Secretary of State could consider in any future revision of the criteria. CATE was, and is, chaired by a distinguished Vice-Chancellor who also happens to be a leading expert on teacher education. Sir William Taylor's Council consists of the Secretary of State's nominees, many of whom came from outside the world of professional education. An account of the Council and its work, written by Sir William himself,[25] makes a clear distinction between 'validation', that is the decision by a university or another chartered body such as the Council for National Academic Awards to make an award, and 'accreditation', the recognition of that award as conferring certain professional rights. Though the distinction is a sound one, it has to be said that the tighter the criteria for accreditation become the less is the room for manoeuvre left to those who have to make validation judgements. The present writer has put some arguments against the position in which a profession's accrediting body is in effect the creature of the politician who *pro tempore* holds the post of Secretary of State and in which the criteria can be changed at will and without reference to the profession which is the subject of that body's decisions.[26] A profession must always think in terms of the longer term whereas politicians cannot think in terms of anything but the short term. The CATE system has not yet had to face the implications of a change of government involving a change of political party. Given the plenitude of power over entry to and training for the profession now in the hands of the Secretary of State, it would not be at all surprising if, after a change of government, the new Secretary of State decided to change the criteria to bring them into line with the new educational philosophy, to dismiss the present membership of CATE and bring in another team, and to require Her Majesty's Inspectors (who have to inspect each course before it can be accredited) to alter the list of things they have to check. The training institutions and their validating bodies would have to re-design all initial training courses. It is not a sufficient defence to say, 'It would never happen like that.' It could and it probably will. There is certainly an important part for the Secretary of State of the day to play in the task of controlling entry to this vital profession, but it is, in the writer's view, wrong for that person (who will almost never be even a member of the profession) to have virtually unlimited power to determine how teachers shall be trained. This is not an argument for that power to be left with teacher trainers, validating bodies or the profession alone but it is a case for spreading the responsibility in such a way that the profession is not exposed to the short-term vagaries of politics. We turn below to what the profession itself might do to redress a balance which has gone too far in favour of the government.

Something of the flavour of the drive towards detailed control can be obtained from a memorandum issued by CATE (undated but thought to be January 1991) to the new local committees which were added to the structure when it was renewed in 1989, and entitled 'The monitoring of initial teacher training'. One section reads:

> It is also Council's intention to review, starting in the summer of 1991, how institutions are adapting their courses to take account of the criteria-related National Curriculum and assessment requirements. This will include a reference to the hours-requirement for English, Mathematics and Science. The associated requirement for a minimum number of contact hours is likely to lead Council into a wider review of contact hours and their interpretation, in subject studies and subject application.

Such almost obsessive concern with entry characteristics and process variables does not match with a view which places more weight on outcomes. But far worse than this is the assumption that it is legitimate for binding decisions involving academic, pedagogical and professional judgements to be taken at the centre without reference to the people whose profession is thereby being controlled.

The final part of this essay deals with an element which has been missing from the discussion so far: the teaching body as a profession. It is most unfortunate that throughout the debates reported above there has at no time been representation of the profession as a profession. Scotland has had a General Teaching Council, modelled on other professional bodies, since 1965 and has greatly benefited thereby. Such a body does not exist for England and Wales. The Secretary of State for Scotland most certainly has his views heeded and develops his policies in a context which includes a General Teaching Council as an important and permanent part of the structure. Lately the Secretary of State for Education and Science, acting for England and Wales, has brought in a system whereby an untrained person, including a non-graduate, can be employed as a teacher in schools and trained 'on the job' without any necessary contact with a teacher-training establishment. Such a person does not receive an award from a chartered body such as a university or the Council for National Academic Awards, but, if successful, is granted qualified teacher status by the Secretary of State's fiat under his powers to declare who shall be recognized as a qualified teacher. Such a scheme was not even attempted in Scotland because there the General Teaching Council of Scotland would have had powerful objections to an untrained person undertaking the responsibility of being a teacher.

That is not the situation in England and Wales. What is particularly unfortunate is that a General Teaching Council for England and Wales was offered to the profession by government in 1970,[27] but was not taken up because of inter-union differences. The present author has provided a short account of the failure of the profession south of the border to emulate their Scottish colleagues.[28] The failure in 1970 turned out to be crucial, for the tide in favour of professional bodies began to ebb in the 1970s and disappeared in the 1980s amidst talk of 'conspiracies against the laity' and 'professional cartels'. From this the conclusion must be drawn that a new professional body would have to be more broadly based than the nineteenth-century models which other professions have; even the General Teaching Council (Scotland) would today be thought to give insufficient weight to other professions, the employers and the general public interest. Those who have continued to make the case for a General Teaching Council for England and Wales have certainly recognized this point; their model constitution acknowledges the strength of the case for a broadly based body. There has been little encouragement from the DES; at a time when the concern has been to keep as much control as possible within the Department this is not surprising. The main reservation comes from the thought that a General Teaching Council might begin to behave like a large trade union. In fact a professional body leaves all matters to do with pay and conditions of service to be dealt with by unions and itself concentrates on the professional side.

There are matters which a General Teaching Council could itself *determine*; there is, for example, no reason why the DES should continue to maintain the register of qualified teachers. Nor is the DES the appropriate body to determine disciplinary cases. There are other matters on which the Council could give the DES *advice*, such as questions of supply, whilst recognizing that final responsibility lay with the DES. There is also a range of topics on which the Council could offer *consultation*. The important questions about the nature of teacher training which have been raised in this essay are examples of the kind of issue to which a General Teaching Council could make a well-informed and authoritative contribution.

A move towards a General Teaching Council would be in keeping with modern management styles. The present arrangement, which relies on prescriptions being presented without prior involvement on the part of those whose commitment is essential to their achievement, can be counter-productive. In short it is time for England and Wales to have a General Teaching Council, and for one of the duties of that body to be the creation of an appropriately balanced teacher education committee which could work with the DES to regulate supply questions and to keep under review the content of teacher education courses. In the mean time, if it is too difficult a task to be accomplished for the two nations, let a start be made by creating a General Teaching Council (Wales) so that all who wish to teach in the Principality would have to be registered with a Welsh Council. A nation which, like the distinguished educator honoured in this volume, has always stood for the highest ideals in education, would readily respond to an invitation to match the achievements of the profession in Scotland.

REFERENCES

1. For Kay-Shuttleworth, see F. Smith, *The Life and Work of Sir James Kay-Shuttleworth* (London, 1923; republished Bath, 1974).
2. See, for example, P. H. J. H. Gosden, *The Development of Educational Administration in England and Wales* (Oxford, 1966).

3. L. G. E. Jones, *The Training of Teachers in England and Wales: a Critical Survey* (London, 1924).
4. A. M. Ross, 'The development of teacher education in Colleges of Education', in D. E. Lomax (ed.), *The Education of Teachers in Britain* (London, 1973), 135–47.
5. J. B. Tuck, 'From Day Training College to University Department of Education', in D. E. Lomax (ed.), op. cit, 71–94, n.4.
6. J. B. Thomas (ed.), *British Universities and Teacher Education: a Century of Change* (London, 1990).
7. W. H. G. Armytage, 'From McNair to James', in R. J. Alexander, M. Craft and J. Lynch (eds.), *Change in Teacher Education* (London, 1984), 3–15.
8. *Teachers and Youth Leaders* (McNair Report) (London, HMSO, 1944).
9. W. R. Niblett, D. W. Humphreys and J. R. Fairhurst, *The University Connection* (Slough, 1975).
10. For an account of these important bodies of regional control see J. D. Turner, 'The Area Training Organization', in J. B. Thomas (ed.), op. cit., 39–57, n.6.
11. *Higher Education*, Report of a Committee appointed by the Prime Minister (Chairman: Lionel Robbins), Cmnd 2154 (London, HMSO, 1963).
12. See M. Kogan and T. Packwood, *Advisory Councils and Committees in Education* (London, 1974).
13. *Education in Rural Wales*, Report of the Central Advisory Council for Education (Wales), (Chairman: Alun Oldfield-Davies) (London, HMSO, 1960).
14. *Primary Education in Wales*, Report of the Central Advisory Council for Education (Wales), (Chairman: Charles Gittins) (London, HMSO, 1967).
15. *Children and their Primary Schools*, Report of the Central Advisory Council for Education (England), (Chairman: Bridget Plowden) (London, HMSO, 1967).
16. Select Committee on Education and Science, Session 1969–70, *Teacher Training*, minutes of evidence, Department of Education and Science, 21 and 23 April 1970 (London, HMSO) 30–xiii and 30–xiv (see Q. 1244ff). When explaining why the National Advisory Council on the Supply and Training of Teachers had also been allowed to lapse, Sir Herbert Andrew, the Permanent Secretary, said, 'We had to write all the stuff for it. We could write it for ourselves just as well.' (Q. 1276).
17. M. Kogan and T. Packwood, op. cit., 22, n.12.
18. Ibid.
19. The most accessible source for this important memorandum is Appendix B of *Teaching Quality*, White Paper, Cmnd 8836 (London, HMSO, 1983).
20. A. M. Ross, 'The universities and the B.Ed. degree', in J. B. Thomas, op. cit., 58–72, n.6.
21. Select Committee on Education and Science, Session 1969–70, *Teacher*

Training, Documents, Appendix 4, 14–18, 30–xv (London, HMSO, 1970).
22. *Teacher Education and Training*, Report by a Committee of Inquiry (Chairman: Eric James) (London, HMSO, 1972).
23. D. Lawton, *The Tightening Grip: Growth of Central Control of the School Curriculum*, Bedford Way Papers No. 21 (London, University of London Institute of Education, 1984).
24. *Teaching Quality*, Cmnd 8836 (London, HMSO, 1983).
25. W. Taylor, 'The control of teacher education: the Council for the Accreditation of Teacher Education', in N. J. Graves (ed.), *Initial Teacher Training: Policy and Progress* (London, 1990), 109–23.
26. A. M. Ross, 'The control of teacher education: a General Teaching Council for England and Wales', in N. J. Graves, op. cit., 124–43, n.25.
27. Department of Education and Science, *A Teaching Council for England and Wales* (Chairman: Toby Weaver) (London, HMSO, 1970).
28. A. M. Ross, op. cit., n.26.

Whither the LEA?

W. J. PHILLIPS

For those educational administrators who forsook the classroom in the sixties and early seventies to enter the portals of county hall there was the certainty that the local education authority (LEA) was very much a force to be reckoned with. They were after all heirs to that stalwart band of professional officers charged with the task of implementing the 1944 Education Act. This legislation ensured that county councils in their capacity as LEAs would be the vehicles for implementing the educational reforms designed to improve opportunities for young people in post-war Britain. Education was to be a national service but locally administered, with the duties of the Minister of Education and of the Local Education Authorities defined. The Minister had the duty to 'promote the education of the people of England and Wales' and to 'secure the effective execution by local authorities, under his control and direction, of the national policy for providing a varied and comprehensive education service in every area'.

In order to 'execute' national policy a wide range of duties and powers were conferred upon the LEAs, particularly the duty 'to secure the provision of sufficient primary and secondary schools for their area'. The fulfilment of this obligation required the provision of sufficient facilities and equipment. It also demanded a sufficient variety of instruction and training as would be desirable to educate pupils according to their ages, abilities and aptitudes. Thus the LEA was charged with a wide range of responsibilities from the appointment of teachers to the provision of transport, from the supply of school meals and milk to the provision of school clothing where necessary. The total well-being of the child at school was to be the concern of the LEA.

The Butler Act was the progeny of a political consensus and was widely hailed as a reforming piece of legislation geared to meet the needs of a society emerging from the consequences of a World War. It contained aspirations for a more egalitarian society aiming at equality of opportunity for all its citizens. There was an inherent acceptance that education would play an essential role in achieving these goals. This was particularly evident in the principle of providing secondary education for all. The provision of such opportunities within two distinct types of secondary school seemed immaterial as the ideal of 'parity of esteem' between grammar and secondary modern schools was to prevail. Each was to develop its own particular ethos and there was to be no suggestion that one was an inferior institution as compared with the other. They were to provide an education relevant to the needs of their pupils classed as academic and non-academic. The former would require traditional grammar-type courses and the latter a more practical form of education. The grammar school was already a much venerated institution but the modern school would need to develop its own traditions and to establish a distinct role within the educational system. Many secondary modern schools managed to do that, but others found it difficult to contend with the popular perception that they were schools for those who had 'failed' the eleven-plus examination.

The relationship between central and local government in England and Wales is not always easy to grasp. To seek to explain the actual functioning of the Education Act of 1944 to groups of overseas students familiar with a more centralist system is sometimes difficult. It seemed anomalous that the law prescribed standards for school sites and even decreed the number of toilets and wash-basins in new schools but did not prescribe minimum standards for the number of teachers or the expenditure on books. It seems strange to many of them that central government, while imposing legal requirements for the teaching of religious instruction, was content to leave the remainder of the curriculum totally in the hands of the LEA. This in practice was to mean in the hands of the schools themselves. It appeared that governments in the fifties and sixties were content to allow the principle of a national service to be subordinated to the expediencies of local control. Education was not a live political issue on the national stage and educational administrators felt no seismic shifts when a government of one political party was replaced by one of another.

The 1944 Education Act does, however, contain definite powers enabling Secretaries of State to intervene when it was felt to be necessary. Section 68 empowers him to intervene to prevent the unreasonable exercise of functions by an authority or by a governing body. Section 99 allows him to take action if an authority or a governing body fails to discharge any duty imposed upon it. Section 67 provides that the Secretary of State should determine any disputes or questions arising between one LEA and another, or between an LEA and a governing body. Even so, these provisions have been used sparingly and, during the years following the 1944 Act, successive Secretaries of State preferred to work on the principle that a light hand on the tiller was preferable to direct intervention.

In those councils charged with responsibility for education the status of the service was well assured. It did after all account for sixty per cent of the Council's total expenditure. The post of chief education officer was a statutory one requiring the Secretary of State's assent before the council's appointee could take up the post. It was also a statutory obligation to set up an education committee to administer the service and substantial powers were delegated to it. In most instances, particularly in Wales, all members of the council were members of the education committee and they exercised a great deal of influence. There was ample scope for enlightened committees to innovate and to promote high standards within their areas. Governing bodies of schools were also endowed with distinct powers under the Education Act of 1944, but the majority of the members were councillors drawn from the education committees and they were more or less content to function as watchdogs conveying the concerns of headteachers to the LEA. They were responsible for appointing staff but they rarely ventured into the 'secret garden' of the curriculum. All too often they were diverted into interminable discussions concerning minor improvements to buildings or the need for new facilities at a school.

The political consensus which had largely existed since 1944 was tested in 1965 with the publication of Circular 10/65. This required LEAs to produce schemes for the introduction of non-selective education on comprehensive lines and involved changing the character of direct-grant grammar schools. The Labour Government of the time felt that the equality of opportunity enshrined in the Butler Act was not being realized for a large number of pupils with the continuance of a selective system of education. It was asserted that the eleven-plus examination was divisive and that the 'parity of esteem' as between grammar and modern schools had not become a reality. Even so, the political battle-lines were not firmly set. Some Conservative LEAs were already wedded to the comprehensive principle but others remained firm adherents of the grammar-school principle. Some Labour LEAs were also less enthusiastic than others in their desire to implement schemes for secondary reorganization. Nevertheless, Circular 10/65 is significant in marking a direct involvement by central government in seeking a fundamental change in the form of education provision within LEAs. With the election of a new Conservative Government and the appointment of Margaret Thatcher as Secretary of State, an attempt was made to temper the more rigid approach contained in Circular 10/65. The element of compulsion imposed upon authorities was removed by Circular 10/70. Authorities were allowed to organize secondary education as they wished but there was no attempt to stem the tide of non-selective education which had by 1970 achieved a momentum of its own.

The late sixties and early seventies were dominated by the arguments for or against comprehensive education. The implementation of schemes of reorganization absorbed much of the energies of LEAs and also took up a great deal of their resources. What was actually happening within the classroom went largely unnoticed by those exerting an influence in the corridors of power. The general emphasis upon child-centred learning had not as yet raised the spectre of declining standards which was to be exploited a few years later as evidence that the system was failing the country. A general feeling of unease was beginning to emerge, however, during the mid seventies when the general question of standards was to be put into sharp focus.

Even within county councils themselves the independence traditionally afforded to the education service seemed to be under threat. The Local Government Act of 1972 created a new pattern of councils but it also provided an opportunity for looking afresh at the management of local government. The Bains Report emphasized the need for a corporate approach to the work of councils. New corporate management structures were to be a feature of the arrangements for the new authorities. The independence and influence traditionally enjoyed by education committees were seen as an obstacle to this new corporate vision, and efforts were made to release authorities from such statutory obligations as the appointment of chief education officers and the setting up of education committees. The powerful education lobby managed to thwart such designs and it is still an obligation for county councils to receive a report from their education committees 'before exercising any of their functions with respect to education'. In spite of this, the degree of delegation granted to education committees has diminished since the formation of the new authorities in 1974 and chief education officers now function within corporate constraints.

Resources have never really matched the needs of public services nor the aspirations of those charged with their provision. The sudden shock of the financial discipline imposed by the International Monetary Fund in 1976 led to the requirement to make instant cuts in education expenditure. This was merely a precursor to the harsh realities that were to confront local government during the eighties. In the case of local education authorities financial constraint was exacerbated by the sharp drop in pupil numbers as a result of the declining birth rate. There was also a general perception that standards were dropping and that the nation was not getting full value for money from its education service.

Governments confronted with economic difficulties tend to look for reasons and it is too easy to link the nation's declining fortunes with a perceived decline in standards within schools. On 18 October 1976, in a speech at Ruskin College, the Prime Minister James Callaghan outlined the need for a 'Great Debate' on educational standards and on the relevance of our system of education to the economic needs of the country. The content and the delivery of education now emerged as live issues to be considered in terms not only of the needs of individual pupils but also of those of society at large. Four main concerns emerged:

(a) The unacceptable differences between schools in the content and quality of learning, leading to inequalities of opportunities for pupils.
(b) The overcrowding of the curriculum and the placing of too much emphasis on social rather than educational aims.
(c) The feeling that too few young people were mastering necessary skills, knowledge and understanding of the economy.
(d) The belief that there were too many differences in the teaching

approaches or methods of schools, adding to the difficulties of children changing schools.

The Prime Minister stressed that 'parents, teachers, learned and professional bodies, representatives of higher education and both sides of industry and the Government' have an important part to play in setting the aims and achieving the required standards needed. Thus, the position of the LEA as a monopoly for the provision of state education was being questioned.

During the consultations which took place early in 1977 a wide spectrum of views emerged. The National Union of Teachers contended that the purpose of schools was not confined to providing employers with 'young people equipped with defined desirable skills' but to develop the 'intellectual potential' of individual pupils. Even so, they accepted the need for stronger links between schools and industry. The Association of University Teachers concluded that 'the school system is not alone responsible for the present economic state of the country.' The Secretary of State Shirley Williams had already dismissed the fears that the Government intended to impose state control over the curriculum adding: 'Among the splendours of the English system are its flexibility, imagination and the freedom of the teacher in the classroom.' This reassurance was applauded by the Confederation of British Industries although they favoured stronger central control and influence through Her Majesty's Inspectorate and LEA advisers and inspectors within schools.

Shirley Williams also dismissed the suggestion that pupils would be bombarded with batteries of tests as 'wild conclusions'. Nevertheless, there were calls from the CBI, the Trades Union Congress and the National Consumer Council (NCC) for a closer monitoring of schools. The NCC complained that the 'providers of the service were also its judges' and called for the publication of reports on individual schools by local inspectors and the Inspectorate. It also called for increased representation for parents and teachers on governing bodies. The Taylor Report addressed many of these issues and was to suggest a reappraisal of the composition of governing bodies of schools and a reassessment of their relationship with the LEAs. In 1979 the Society of Education Officers concluded that although the Great Debate on education had not as yet 'inspired programmes or created instruments for change', it might eventually have 'important effects on management at institutional level'. Nevertheless, it noted that the Secretary of State had disclaimed any intention of upsetting the existing partnership arrangements but it posed the question: 'Suppose the DES deems that in some matters, practice does not meet national needs? What then? The present balance of interests and function could not long survive a shift from counsel and persuasion to fiat.' Over the next decade such a hypothesis was to become a reality.

The incoming Conservative Government of 1979 was firmly wedded to the belief that standards in the public services could only be enhanced by an injection of free-market principles. This required the breakdown of public monopolies, the encouragement of competition as a prerequisite for raising standards, and greater accountability to the consumers of those services. As the LEAs exercised a monopoly in the provision of state education they were clearly vulnerable and their cause was not well served by the excesses of a few. The recession of the early eighties and the need to reduce public expenditure added to the pressures on LEAs, leading to accusations that they were profligate and wasteful and did not provide value for money. Many of the allegations adumbrated during the Great Debate concerning declining educational standards now surfaced with greater vehemence as did the belief that schools were not sufficiently responsive to the needs of business and industry. Bolstered by a large majority and propelled by a distinct philosophy, the new government embarked upon legislative proposals designed to reshape the educational system that had survived virtually intact since 1944.

The first target was the actual management of schools and colleges. Measures were to be taken to reduce the direct influence of LEAs on the governing bodies of these institutions. During the Great Debate, and subsequently in the Taylor Report, the predominance of LEA representation and the absence of parent and teacher influence were called into question. The 1980 Education Act sought to redress this by making it a legal requirement that both of these interests should be well represented on such bodies. It also sought to increase the accountability of schools by extending the principle of parental choice and allowing parents to express a preference for a school. In order to assist them in making a choice, schools were to be obliged to publish prospectuses containing relevant information including admission arrangements and examination results. Independent appeal committees were to be set up to adjudicate between the LEA and those parents whose preferences for schools had not been assented to.

The eighties became a decade of legislation as changes to the system of education became a priority in the eyes of the government. The publication of the White Paper, *Better Schools*, in March 1985 set the aims. These were:

(1) to raise standards at all levels of ability;
(2) to secure the best possible return from the resources which are invested in education.

In order to realize these aims the government expressed its intention of looking at the curriculum, the examination system and assessment, the professional effectiveness of teachers and school government itself. A new initiative, the Technical and Vocational Education Initiative (TVEI), had already been introduced on a pilot basis in order to equip pupils for working life and with the basic aim of ensuring that work-related skills were given due emphasis within schools. The White Paper expressed the government's intention of considering the wider application of the lessons of TVEI and to raise pupil performance generally at all levels of ability. At this stage, however, there was apparently no intention to introduce national syllabuses and Sir Keith Joseph mirrored the views of his predecessor in lauding the fact that 'diversity at local education authority and school level is healthy and accords well with the English and Welsh tradition of school education, and makes for liveliness and innovation'.

The 1986 Education Act was further to weaken the direct influence exercised by LEAs at school level by fundamentally changing the balance of representation on governing bodies. No longer would they appoint the majority of governors as the new legislative arrangements required a balance between the parent representatives, the teachers, the co-opted members and the LEA nominees so that no group has overall control. The accountability of governors to the parents generally was increased by a requirement that they should account for their stewardship in an annual report and by holding an annual meeting of the parents. Although the LEA is still required to keep a written statement of policy for the secular curriculum the governors are now charged with setting the aims of the curriculum for their particular schools. Under the 1986 Act, they were also empowered to 'modify' the LEA's curriculum and, if the modified curriculum conflicted with the authority's statement, the headteacher had to decide which to follow. This was clearly unsatisfactory and, under the terms of the 1988 Education Reform Act, the headteacher is obliged to implement the curriculum as 'modified' by the governors. In order to curb what were perceived as the excesses of a small number of authorities, governors were also given the power to decide whether or not sex education should form part of a school's curriculum. It was also decided to prohibit the promotion of the views of political groups within schools.

The Acts of 1980 and 1986 had been merely preludes to the Education Reform Act of 1988. The traditional reluctance of central government to impose a national curriculum was swept aside, and added to the imposition of the curriculum was the requirement to test pupils at the ages of 7, 11, 14 and 16. The requirement for LEAs to give greater financial control to governors of secondary schools and the larger primary schools under schemes for the local management of schools also marks a significant development in loosening the control of the LEA over individual schools. The requirement to produce a scheme for the allocation of funds on the basis of pupil numbers increases the element of competition between schools and will inevitably oblige them to be more entrepreneurial in their approach. Possibly the most significant development governing the relationship between central government and the LEA within the Act is the creation of a new category of school known as the grant-maintained school (GMS). Following a successful ballot of parents such schools can apply to receive their funding directly from the Secretary of State and can thus run their own affairs. In spite of vigorous efforts to promote the benefits for schools of such a change of status, to date only about seventy have taken this step throughout England and Wales. Even so, the intention of the government is clear and ministers have expressed the hope that during the 1990s the majority of schools will have become grant-maintained and will have severed their ties with the LEAs.

Fundamental changes such as those implemented within the education service over the past decade have produced tensions as relationships are realigned and entrenched positions weakened. As the government sought to make the service more accountable it was deemed necessary to increase the accountability of the teachers themselves. The imposition of a defined contract requiring them to work for 1,265 hours and the termination of their right to negotiate their salaries with their employers, the LEAs, provide examples of this. The burdens of implementing the National Curriculum and, in particular, the requirements of testing have undoubtedly had an effect on morale within classrooms and have prompted larger numbers to opt for early retirement. The lack of confidence expressed by some politicians in teachers has not improved matters, and recently a former minister, George Walden, claimed that testing was not after all for the benefit of pupils but was designed to test the teachers:

> The real reason for testing small children in state education is that people have lost confidence in primary teachers... In effect we are testing not the pupils but the teachers. (*Daily Telegraph*, 17/4/91)

Where does all this leave the LEAs as they see their responsibilities whittled away in a piecemeal or — as many assert — an *ad hoc* fashion? They have lost control of higher education institutions and in 1993 further education colleges will no longer be administered by them. Their task of administering schools is constantly being frustrated and their potential for strategic control over the educational provision within their areas is being eroded. Following the contraction in pupil numbers LEAs have been exhorted by central government, in the interests of economy, to take out of use 'spare places' in schools. This must involve the closure of schools. But the avenue opened to schools to seek 'grant-maintained' status has also opened an escape route to those who seek to avoid closure. The apparent willingness of central government to grant such status, even if this frustrates an LEA's plan to rationalize educational provision, makes it increasingly difficult for authorities to fulfil an essential part of their responsibilities. The only school to opt out in Wales to date has been Cwmcarn in Gwent, a school of 300 pupils threatened with closure as a result of the LEA's efforts to reduce empty places in its secondary schools. In his letter granting grant-maintained status, the Secretary of State affirms to the LEA 'that it remains his policy to encourage local education authorities to take appropriate measures to remove surplus school places and to make savings'. Even so, he adds that this cannot be regarded as an overriding consideration 'irrespective of all other policies or circumstances'. Although the prospective numbers in this case were well below those suggested for an effective school in *Better Schools*, the Secretary of State recognized that 'certain factors may sometimes necessitate unusually small schools'. This has always been recognized in sparsely populated rural areas but in this case he concluded that the 'interests of parental choice' provided 'a case for continuing to retain a small school as a grant maintained school'. Such decisions pose a dilemma for authorities contemplating the closure or reorganization of schools for they will now have to contend with the threat that such schools will seek grant-maintained status and opt out from their control.

Faced with so many constraints, is there a future role for LEAs? In considering this question the present Secretary of State, Kenneth Clark, pointed to such issues as the need to control truancy and to listen to parental appeals against exclusions from schools as being roles still required of LEAs for the future. The execution of such roles will surely not be sufficient justification for the retention of LEAs. The government itself sees the future role of authorities as 'enabling authorities' with, to quote from Michael Heseltine's speech to Parliament on 23 April 1991, 'greater opportunities to choose the best source of services'. In other words they will still retain the duty to provide services but without the necessity of providing those services themselves. They may still be responsible for ensuring the quality of the services provided and continue to be under an obligation to ensure that they are adequate, but the actual providers may well be from the private sector.

The Audit Commission in one of its occasional papers *Losing an Empire, Finding a Role: The LEA of the Future* (1989) acknowledges the dilemma confronting LEAs in seeking to define their relevance in the future. It emphasizes the need for education authorities to recognize the fact that they will have to exist in a pluralist environment where actual power is diffused. It sees the LEA continuing as a leader, a partner supporting schools, a planner of future facilities, a provider of information, a regulator of quality and a banker channelling funds into schools. If, however, the majority of schools 'opt out' it may well be more efficient to accord grant-maintained status to all schools, thus making it difficult for LEAs to fulfil these roles adequately.

Cambridgeshire, a pioneer authority in the introduction of financial delegation to its schools, has produced an issues paper delineating its future role as an LEA. Already committed to a 'buyer-driven role' for its support services, it anticipates a situation where the schools themselves will determine the extent of the services they require and the money spent on them. Nevertheless, they still see for themselves a strategic role in the provision of education while relinquishing operational power and allowing full freedom to manage at establishment level. The document is in line with the views expressed by the Audit Commission and it accepts that its provision of support services will be governed solely by the market. The provision of such services will be separate from the main responsibilities of planning, quality control and the other statutory duties. It bases the LEA's future role on the assumption that a variety of county, voluntary, special and grant-maintained schools will continue to exist in Cambridgeshire.

Recent pronouncements on behalf of the government suggest that the regulations concerning the balloting of parents are to be revised, thus making it easier for schools to attain grant-maintained status. The restriction which prevents such schools from changing their character within five years of opting out is also to be reviewed. This will open the way for some comprehensive schools to operate a system of selection and could be an added inducement for some schools to leave LEA control. Such schools could well become quasi-grammar schools leading to a greater dichotomy between those schools directly funded by central government and those remaining within the LEA.

Local authorities are still charged with the duty of securing the provision of sufficient schools for their area, for the requirements of the Education Act of 1944 are still in place. It does not suggest that such schools need be under LEA control. Certain anomalies do arise, however, even in the relationship between the LEA and its own institutions. Teachers are still employed by LEAs but as employers the latter are no longer involved in the national salary negotiations with the teachers' organizations, nor are they responsible for appointments, dismissals and redundancies at school level. Such a situation is totally at variance with the normal relationship between an employer and employee. The system of 'charge capping' also limits the power of county councils to spend money on their services, thus limiting further the ability of LEAs to provide the resources they deem necessary for the education service.

All the main political parties have now ensured that education and connected concerns have reached the top of the national agenda. There is a reaction against the teaching methods popularized in the sixties which emphasized the need to nurture individual development. This so-called 'child-centred education' is blamed for an assumed drop in standards and increasingly there are calls for a return to the traditional methods. The traditionalists blame the LEAs in large part for the trendy innovations which they believe have marred standards within schools and they argue vehemently for control of the service to be delegated to the schools themselves. They argue that standards will be best maintained by making all schools grant-maintained and dependent upon parental choice for their funding. There appears to be little or no role for the LEA as such in this kind of scenario. Indeed Sir Rhodes Boyson appears to see the choice in the future as between a centralist educational policy based upon a national curriculum, inspection and direction of teachers and a free-market system based upon competing schools free to determine their own policies. Whether or not LEAs continue to have a direct involvement in education will be determined eventually by central government, but the continued erosion of their powers and the gradual dismemberment of their services does not augur well for their future. Clearly, they have to adapt to their changing role but their discontinuance would remove a layer of local control over education by bodies which are still directly accountable to the electorate, for schools belong to communities as well as to parents.

Sylwadau ar Addysg Gymraeg Heddiw

D. GARETH EDWARDS

Cyflwyniad

Bu cyfraniad Adran Addysg Coleg Prifysgol Cymru, Aberystwyth i addysg Gymraeg yn sylweddol ar hyd y blynyddoedd. Yn ystod y cyfnod y bu'r diweddar Athro Jac L. Williams yn bennaeth datblygwyd y dull dwyieithog o ddysgu ail iaith dan arweiniad Carl Dodson, arloeswyd ym maes dysgu'r Gymraeg i oedolion dan gyfarwyddyd R. M. Jones a Dan Lyn James, a chyflawnodd yr Athro Jac L. Williams ei hun waith safonol mewn gwahanol agweddau ar addysg ddwyieithog; golygodd nifer o gyfrolau yn ymdrin â sawl maes addysgol yn y Gymraeg, lluniodd restri niferus o dermau technegol ar gyfer cyflwyno gwahanol bynciau trwy'r Gymraeg, a bu'n erthyglwr brwd ac yn llythyrwr toreithiog yn arbennig wrth ymgyrchu dros addysg feithrin a rhaglenni Cymraeg ar bob un o'r sianelau teledu.

Fodd bynnag, gyda dyfodiad yr Athro J. R. Webster ddeng mlynedd yn ôl sylweddolwyd bod y gyfundrefn addysg, o'r bôn i'r brig, ar drothwy cyfnod o ad-drefnu sylfaenol. Gwelodd y pennaeth newydd y byddai'n rhaid rhesymoli adnoddau ac egni trwy ganolbwyntio ar ychydig feysydd dethol, yn arbennig gofynion addysgol ac ieithyddol y gymuned yr oedd yr adran yn rhan naturiol ohoni, sef y Gymru wledig a'r Gymru Gymraeg. Ar sail ei brofiad fel aelod o nifer o bwyllgorau cenedlaethol lle y synhwyrodd i ba gyfeiriad yr oedd y gwynt yn chwythu, penderfynodd roi ffocws eglurach ac ehangach ar weithgareddau Cymraeg yr adran. Ei nod oedd adeiladu ar seiliau cadarn ei ragflaenydd a sicrhau bod Adran Addysg Aberystwyth yn datblygu yn ganolfan rhagoriaeth yn y byd academaidd Cymreig a Phrydeinig. Un o'i benderfyniadau polisi cyntaf felly oedd sefydlu'r Ganolfan Astudiaethau Addysg, dan arweiniad Glyn Saunders Jones.

Y Ganolfan Astudiaethau Addysg

Prif swyddogaeth y ganolfan yw datblygu meysydd penodol o'r cwricwlwm cynradd ac uwchradd yn ôl gofynion y Cwricwlwm Cenedlaethol, darparu adnoddau dysgu priodol ac ymgymryd â gwaith ymchwil a fydd yn hyrwyddo arferion dysgu da, yn arbennig o safbwynt addysg trwy gyfrwng y Gymraeg ac addysg wledig. O'r cychwyn cyntaf rhoddwyd y pwyslais pennaf ar gynnig gwasanaeth i athrawon, ac felly daeth y ganolfan yn gyrchfan gyson i grwpiau bychain o addysgwyr profiadol a blaengar i ymgymryd â gwahanol brosiectau cenedlaethol sydd bellach yn gaffaeliad i athrawon a disgyblion ar hyd a lled y wlad. Mae'r ganolfan hefyd yn llyfrgell i gasgliad cynhwysfawr o ddeunyddiau dysgu yn y Gymraeg, gan gynnwys rhai a gyhoeddwyd gan weisg ac eraill a ddarparwyd gan athrawon ac ysgolion unigol. Hefyd cyhoeddir catalog manwl o'r adnoddau bob rhyw ddwy flynedd.

Ar adeg pan mae gorwelion ein prifysgolion yn ymledu'n gyflym, a'r gwahanol feysydd academaidd yn gymdeithasau byd-eang o arbenigwyr, hawdd yw i academyddion golli golwg ar y gymuned y maent yn aelodau ohoni. Eithriad prin yw'r Ganolfan Astudiaethau Addysg, gan mai hon yw un o'r prif ddolennau cyswllt rhwng Coleg Prifysgol Cymru Aberystwyth a'r genedl a'i sefydlodd dros ganrif yn ôl. Trwy ganolbwyntio ar y Gymraeg mewn addysg plant mae ganddi gyfraniad nodedig o arwyddocaol a gwerthfawr y dyddiau ansicr hyn yn hanes yr iaith. Roedd sefydlu canolfan o'r fath yn ddatblygiad naturiol o fewn adran weddol fawr lle mae'r mwyafrif o'r staff, ers dros chwarter canrif bellach, wedi bod yn dysgu trwy gyfrwng y Gymraeg. Gwelwyd potensial canolfan o'r fath yn yr adran hefyd ar sail y profiad a gafwyd pan benderfynodd y Swyddfa Gymreig leoli prosiect uchelgeisiol yno, ychydig flynyddoedd ynghynt, i ddatblygu adnoddau dysgu ar gyfer blynyddoedd 1 i 3 yn y sector uwchradd ym meysydd hanes, daearyddiaeth ac ysgrythur.

Bellach y mae'r ganolfan yn un o dri sefydliad tebyg sy'n perthyn i rwydwaith cenedlaethol a glustnodwyd gan y Swyddfa Gymreig i dderbyn cyllid blynyddol i wasanaethu anghenion cwricwlaidd ysgolion Cymru. Lleolwyd un o'r ddwy ganolfan arall yn swyddfeydd

Cyd-bwyllgor Addysg Cymru (yng Nghaerdydd a Threfforest) a'r llall, sef y Ganolfan Astudiaethau Iaith, ym Mangor. Felly, mae unrhyw sôn am addysg Gymraeg heddiw, ar raddfa genedlaethol, o reidrwydd yn gorfod cymryd i ystyriaeth gyfraniad Canolfan Astudiaethau Addysg Aberystwyth.

Y Pwyllgor Datblygu Addysg Gymraeg

Cefnogir llawer o weithgarwch y tair canolfan gan gyllid a ddaw o goffrau'r Llywodraeth. Cydlynir eu gwaith, ar ran y Swyddfa Gymreig, gan y Pwyllgor Datblygu Addysg Gymraeg (PDAG) a sefydlwyd ym 1987 gan Gyd-bwyllgor Addysg Cymru. Bellach ni ellir trafod addysg yn y Gymraeg y dyddiau hyn heb ystyried swyddogaeth y pwyllgor hwn.

Daeth PDAG i fodolaeth ar ôl ymgyrch faith, gan Gymdeithas yr Iaith Gymraeg a rhai o brif sefydliadau addysgol a diwylliannol y genedl, am gorff a fyddai'n datblygu addysg trwy gyfrwng y Gymraeg ym mhob un o'r sectorau addysgol. Cytunodd y Swyddfa Gymreig i ariannu PDAG am ddwy flynedd i ddechrau. Roedd y misoedd cyntaf yn rhai digon stormus, gyda charfan eithaf niferus yn barnu nad corff annibynnol mohono, ond llawforwyn i'r Swyddfa Gymreig. Pwyswyd yn drwm ar yr aelodau a'r swyddogion i ymddiswyddo. Ond roeddynt yn gytûn na ddylid rhoi'r gorau i'w cyfrifoldeb ar ôl brwydro mor hir i sefydlu'r pwyllgor. Ofn pennaf aelodau PDAG oedd y byddai'r Swyddfa Gymreig yn creu corff enwebedig i ymgymryd â'r gwaith, ac y byddai corff o'r fath yn gwbl groes ei gyfansoddiad i natur Cyd-bwyllgor Addysg Cymru sy'n asiantaeth addysgol a sefydlwyd gan yr wyth sir Gymreig.

Yn nhrafodaethau cynnar y pwyllgor daeth tyndra i'r amlwg, rhwng yr awydd i gael fforwm a fyddai'n gofyn cael pwyllgor eithaf mawr a chynrychioladol, a'r angen am gorff gweithredol a fyddai'n bwyllgor llawer llai. Ar ddiwedd y ddwy flynedd o arbrawf cytunodd y Swyddfa Gymreig i ymestyn PDAG am bum mlynedd pellach. Yr un pryd penderfynodd Cyd-bwyllgor Addysg Cymru leihau ei faint a chwilio am ddulliau eraill o ymgynghori'n eang, er enghraifft trwy wahodd arbenigwyr mewn meysydd penodol i'w hannerch a chynnal cyfarfodydd agored o bryd i'w gilydd. Mae'r pwyllgor newydd yn dal i fod yn gyfuniad o gynrychiolwyr yr awdurdodau addysg lleol, addysgwyr a gweinyddwyr.

Wrth addo'r cyllid angenrheidiol i gynnal PDAG, amlinellodd Ysgrifennydd Gwladol Cymru y swyddogaeth ganlynol iddo:

bod yn fforwm a fyddai'n gallu cynghori llywodraeth ganol a lleol ar bolisi iaith;

gwella cydlynu ymhlith asiantaethau sy'n cyfrannu at addysg yn yr iaith Gymraeg;

dynodi anghenion datblygiad, a blaenoriaethau oddi mewn i'r anghenion hynny, ac i fod yn gyfrwng i'w hateb;

dosbarthu gwybodaeth;

dynodi anghenion ymchwil.

Y meysydd datblygu a gefnogir gan PDAG

Bob blwyddyn caiff PDAG gyfle i gynghori'r Swyddfa Gymreig ynglŷn â'r meysydd y dylid eu datblygu. Mae hon yn broses hir a chymhleth gan fod raid ymgynghori'n helaeth â phob un o'r sectorau addysgol (meithrin, cynradd, uwchradd, pellach ac uwch, a Chymraeg i oedolion) er mwyn canfod eu hanghenion. Erbyn hyn sefydlwyd patrwm effeithiol o bwyllgorau ymgynghorol sydd bellach wedi dechrau cynllunio yn ôl gofynion y tymor byr a hefyd y tymor hir. Mantais y math hwn o gynllunio yw y gall PDAG gyflwyno i'r Swyddfa Gymreig raglen ddatblygu, gyda'r blaenoriaethau wedi eu nodi a'r costau wedi eu hamcangyfrif, ar sail gweithgarwch blwyddyn neu hyd at dair.

Ar ôl dyfarnu grantiau blynyddol y Swyddfa Gymreig (tua Dydd Gŵyl Dewi fel arfer) un o brif gyfrifoldebau PDAG yw monitro'r cynlluniau a gyllidir, yn arbennig ym maes paratoi adnoddau newydd i gwrdd â gofynion y Ddeddf Addysg. I'r perwyl hwn sefydlwyd bâs-data cynhwysfawr yn swyddfeydd PDAG sy'n nodi manylion gwariant a chamau datblygiad pob un o'r prosiectau.

Y drefn arferol yw bod prosiect neu grŵp o brosiectau yn yr un maes yn cael eu datblygu gan swyddog cyflogedig dros gyfnod o flwyddyn yn y lle cyntaf, ond gan mai hyd y mwyafrif o brosiectau yw tair blynedd, adnewyddir y cyllid yn flynyddol. Caiff pob swyddog gymorth grŵp o addysgwyr sy'n flaengar yn y maes i lywio'i waith ac i gyfrannu o'u harbenigedd pan fo galw. Caiff pob deunydd a baratoir ei arbrofi mewn ychydig o ysgolion er mwyn arfarnu addasrwydd ei gynnwys a'i iaith cyn ei gyhoeddi ar ei ffurf derfynol.

Ers nifer o flynyddoedd bellach bu grantiau'r iaith Gymraeg dan Adran 21 y Ddeddf Iaith (1980) yn gynhaliaeth werthfawr i awdurdodau addysg lleol a nifer cynyddol o sefydliadau a mudiadau i ehangu eu gwasanaeth ym maes addysg Gymraeg.

Mae cyfanswm y grantiau wedi cynyddu fesul blwyddyn. Gwelir bod yr ymateb yn gadarnhaol i geisiadau PDAG ers ei sefydlu ym 1987, gyda'r cyfanswm wedi dyblu ers hynny:

1980-81	£501,775
1981-82	£790,630
1982-83	£857,567
1983-84	£1,025,306
1984-85	£1,004,701
1985-86	£1,317,657
1986-87	£1,439,300
1987-88	£1,735,000
1988-89	£2,019,000
1989-90	£2,700,000
1990-91	£3,303,000
1991-92	£4,100,000[1]

Y prif feysydd a gaiff eu noddi gan y grant iaith yw'r canlynol:

Datblygu adnoddau

Yn ystod y pum mlynedd ddiwethaf gwelwyd cryn gynnydd yn y deunyddiau dysgu cyfrwng Cymraeg a ddarparwyd ar gyfer ysgolion cynradd ac uwchradd. Nodir isod y meysydd a gaiff eu datblygu ym 1990-1 ym mhob un o'r tair canolfan. Y mae'n werth sylwi ar y flaenoriaeth a roddir yn y gwariant i baratoi adnoddau yn y pynciau hynny o'r Cwricwlwm Cenedlaethol sydd yn statudol yn y flwyddyn ysgol bresennol, sef Cymraeg, mathemateg a gwyddoniaeth; ar yr un pryd, rhaid cofio bod deunyddiau cyfoes wedi eu paratoi mewn llawer o'r pynciau hyn, ac mai llenwi bylchau a wneir mewn ambell faes.

Canolfan Astudiaethau Addysg Aberystwyth: Grant o £227,675: Mathemateg uwchradd (£40,000), cerddoriaeth (£2,500), addysg grefyddol (£8,500), astudiaethau busnes (£28,000), gwyddoniaeth gynradd (£55,750), hanes (lefel A) (£15,000), ieithoedd modern (geiriadur) (£17,000), canllawiau hanes a daearyddiaeth (£5,000), staff (£55,925).

Cyd-bwyllgor Addysg Cymru: Canolfan Uned Iaith Cymru (Trefforest). Grant o £225,000: Cymraeg ail iaith — 3 maes: babanod/cynradd/ uwchradd (£170,000), ieithoedd modern (£55,000)

Canolfan yr Adran Gymraeg (Caerdydd). Grant o £323,200: Mathemateg (£33,500), technoleg (£36,000), gwyddoniaeth uwchradd (£128,500), staff (£38,500), staff gwerslyfrau (£86,700)

Canolfan Astudiaethau Iaith Bangor. Grant o £184,862: Cymraeg (£14,000), mathemateg gynradd (£49,400), technoleg (£60,890), gwaith coed (£6,000), staff (£54,572).[2]

Athrawon bro

Cefnogir gwasanaeth athrawon bro gan y grant iaith ym mhob un o'r awdurdodau addysg lleol. Caiff ambell sir, yn arbennig y rhai mwyaf Seisnigedig, gefnogaeth sylweddol i gynnal y gwasanaeth hwn, tra nad yw eraill yn derbyn dim ond cymorth rhannol, gan gael eu gorfodi i ddarparu'r gwasanaeth o'u cyllid arferol. Erbyn hyn mae tua chant o athrawon bro drwy Gymru gyfan, a'r rhan fwyaf ohonynt yn treulio'u hamser yn dysgu ail iaith. Mae patrwm gwaith yr athrawon bro yn amrywio i raddau o sir i sir, ond y dull arferol yw eu bod yn ymweld ag ysgolion penodol, dros gyfnod o amser, ac yn gweithio law yn llaw â'r athrawon dosbarth. Rhoddant arweiniad ac enghreifftiau o fethodoleg dysgu ail iaith, a'u cynorthwyo i ddatblygu ac i gynnal cwrs addysg yn y Gymraeg. Ambell dro, oherwydd diffygion ieithyddol rhai athrawon, byddant yn gyfrifol am ddysgu ail iaith bron yn gyfan gwbl. Yn ystod y flwyddyn ddiwethaf, gyda dyfodiad y Gymraeg fel pwnc gorfodol yn y Cwricwlwm Cenedlaethol, mae eu rôl wedi ymestyn yn sylweddol mewn rhai rhannau o'r wlad. Er enghraifft, disgwylir i rai ohonynt roi arweiniad o safbwynt y cwricwlwm Cymraeg newydd trwy gynnal cyrsiau hyfforddiant-mewn-swydd, gofynnir i eraill ddysgu'r iaith i athrawon di-Gymraeg, tra bydd eraill wrthi'n ddyfal yn paratoi adnoddau dysgu deniadol, yn arbennig ar gyfer y plant lleiaf.

Ceir tystiolaeth yn adroddiadau Arolygwyr Ei Mawrhydi (AEM) i'w cyfraniad gwerthfawr.

> Y mae mewnbwn yr athrawon bro wedi bod yn sylweddol a chafodd eu gwaith ddylanwad arwyddocaol mewn llawer ysgol; y mae eu hymglymiad a'u brwdfrydedd, ansawdd a defnyddioldeb eu cynhyrchion, a'u heffeithiolrwydd fel athrawon dosbarth yn gyffredinol wedi gwella ymagweddiad tuag at y Gymraeg, a pherfformiad y disgyblion. Bu

iddynt ddangos bod gwell safonau a chyraeddiadau'n bosibl drwy rannu mentrau gydag athrawon dosbarth.[3]

Ar yr un pryd, mae'n bwysig bod athrawon bro yn ymateb yn greadigol i ofynion y Cymry Cymraeg sydd yn y lleiafrif mewn ardaloedd Seisnigedig gan ei fod yn hawdd eu diystyru. Ceir rhai enghreifftiau clodwiw o'r grant iaith yn cefnogi amrywiaeth o weithgareddau, y tu mewn i'r ysgol a rhai mewn sefyllfaoedd mwy anffurfiol y tu allan iddi, i gadw plant sy'n cael eu magu mewn sefyllfaoedd di-Gymraeg mewn cyswllt byw â hi.

Felly, yn sgil y galwadau amrywiol ar eu gwasanaeth yn ystod y cyfnod presennol o ddiwygio addysg, athrawon bro yw'r garfan fwyaf niferus o arbenigwyr sydd i'w cael yn ysgolion cynradd Cymru. Gyda'r pwyslais ar y Gymraeg, yn arbennig ail iaith, yn cynyddu rhagwelir y bydd angen cryfhau eu gwasanaeth yn sylweddol yn y dyfodol agos, ac mai cyfrifoldeb y Swyddfa Gymreig yn bennaf fydd eu cyllido naill ai trwy'r grant iaith penodol neu drwy ddarpariaeth ychwanegol i gronfa addysg flynyddol pob sir. Yn sicr, mae rôl yr athrawon bro yn allweddol i ffyniant yr iaith, yn arbennig o gofio mai plant cynradd a ddysgir ganddynt.

Canolfannau iaith

Datblygiad pwysig y degawd diwethaf, sy'n gymorth amhrisiadwy i leddfu effeithiau niweidiol y mewnlifiad di-Gymraeg i'n hardaloedd gwledig, fu sefydlu canolfannau iaith. Ynddynt ceir cyrsiau dwys yn yr iaith i hwyrddyfodiaid (rhwng 7 a 12 oed fel rheol) i'w galluogi i ymuno â dosbarthiadau arferol eu hysgolion. Yn ôl sawl tystiolaeth, mae agwedd rhieni at y Gymraeg yn gadarnhaol, a chroesawant y cyfle a gaiff eu plant i ddysgu iaith eu hardal newydd dan amodau pur ffafriol. Yn aml iawn bydd rhai rhieni hefyd yn ymuno â dosbarthiadau oedolion, gan ddysgu'r iaith yr un pryd â'r plant. Gwyddys am ambell enghraifft lle newidiwyd iaith yr aelwyd yn raddol o'r Saesneg i'r Gymraeg, ond mae honno'n broses sy'n gofyn am ymroddiad go arbennig.

Rhoddodd eu sefydlu chwistrelliad sylweddol o hyder a chalondid i athrawon a oedd yn cyflym weld eu disgyblion arferol yn cael eu boddi gan donnau diderfyn o Seisnigrwydd. Rhoesant hefyd obaith i arweinwyr barn gyhoeddus y cymunedau cefn gwlad hynny lle'r oedd yr iaith yn dihoeni'n frawychus o sydyn. Y gobaith yw mai ateb tymor byr fydd y canolfannau, ac y dylid eu cynnal cyhyd ag y pery'r mewnlifiad yn rhy rymus i'r gyfundrefn addysg arferol ei wrthsefyll. Oherwydd eu heffeithiolrwydd gwneir apêl daer, bob blwyddyn, gan PDAG a'r awdurdodau addysg am gyllid ychwanegol i ymestyn eu gwasanaeth, yn arbennig yn yr ardaloedd traddodiadol Gymraeg lle mae'r mewnlifiad yn rhy nerthol i ganiatáu'r broses naturiol o gymathu.

Wrth gwrs, mae canolfannau iaith lle y gall hwyrddyfodiaid mewnfudol o wledydd y Gymanwlad ddysgu Saesneg yn gyffredin mewn nifer o'n trefi mawrion, gan gynnwys Caerdydd. Ystyrir eu cyfraniad yn ffactor allweddol yn yr ymdoddi ieithyddol a diwylliannol sydd mor hanfodol i sicrhau bodlonrwydd cymdeithasol. Mae'r dadleuon o blaid canolfannau Cymraeg, felly, gymaint â hynny'n gryfach.

Cyrsiau preswyl

Dan nawdd y grant iaith, trefnir cyrsiau preswyl byr — yn arbennig ar gyfer dysgwyr y Gymraeg fel ail iaith — gan nifer o'r awdurdodau addysg lleol. Yn aml fe'u cynhelir yng ngwersylloedd yr Urdd yn Llangrannog neu Lan-llyn. Yno darperir amrywiaeth o brofiadau cyffrous sy'n rhoi cyfle i ddisgyblion ddefnyddio'u hiaith mewn ffordd newydd. Datblygiad diddorol arall y gellid ei ymestyn yn helaethach yw'r 'dyddiau dwys', sef cyrsiau un diwrnod ar y tro. Maent yn galluogi disgyblion o un ysgol neu nifer o ysgolion cyfagos i gydweithio, mewn dull mwy anffurfiol nag arfer, ar weithgareddau amrywiol trwy gyfrwng y Gymraeg.

Theatr mewn addysg

Mae'r grant iaith yn hybu cryn weithgarwch ym maes theatr mewn addysg. Yn flynyddol caiff yr wyth cwmni sy'n gysylltiedig â'r siroedd gyllid i'w galluogi i ymgymryd â rhaglenni drama amrywiol yn yr ysgolion, weithiau gyda babanod a chynradd, bryd arall gyda'r uwchradd, ambell dro gyda'r Gymraeg yn famiaith ac yna'n ail iaith. Mae hyblygrwydd eu cyflwyniadau yn adlewyrchu dyfeisgarwch theatrig ar ei fwyaf ffrwythlon.

Mae'r adroddiad ar y Gymraeg yn y Cwricwlwm Cenedlaethol yn croesawu gweithgarwch y cwmnïau drama mewn addysg.[4] Cyfeirir yn arbennig at eu swyddogaeth addysgol yn cynnig amrywiaeth o gyfleoedd i ddisgyblion gyfoethogi eu mynegiant. Rhoddant hefyd gryn bwyslais ar gyfraniad y disgyblion trwy eu gwahodd i gymryd rhan yn y gweithgareddau dramatig neu drwy ennyn eu chwilfrydedd i'w hannog i wneud gwaith creadigol pellach, yn llafar neu'n ysgrifenedig, yn y dosbarth. Croesewir hefyd yr arfer o gyflwyno perfformiad cyhoeddus o ddrama yn yr ysgol — profiad anghyffredin i lawer o ddisgyblion, mae'n bosibl. Rhydd ddimensiwn pellach i weithgareddau esthetaidd a dychmygus y cwricwlwm trwy drawsnewid neuadd ysgol neu ystafell ddosbarth yn fyd llawn cyffro a digwyddiadau dieithr.

Addysg feithrin

Nid yw'r Mudiad Ysgolion Meithrin yn derbyn ond cyfran o'i gyllid o'r grant iaith arferol gan fod y cyfraniad mwyaf sylweddol yn deillio o'r ffynhonnell sy'n cynnal gwasanaethau cymdeithasol. Mae'n debyg y daw addysg feithrin yn un o bynciau trafod yr Etholiad Cyffredinol nesaf gan fod sawl plaid wleidyddol yn cefnogi ymestyn y gwasanaeth i gynnwys plant iau a chynnig darpariaeth ehangach. Yn achos y Gymraeg byddai hyn yn ateb dyheadau cefnogwyr addysg feithrin ers blynyddoedd, gan mai gorau po ieuengaf y daw plant i ddechrau siarad yr iaith. Yn ddigwestiwn, byddai rhoi cyfle i bob plentyn fynychu uned feithrin leol am ddwy flynedd cyn dechrau ar ei yrfa yn yr ysgol gynradd yn bump oed yn datrys llawer o broblemau dysgu ail iaith.

Hanes llwyddiant yw hanes y Mudiad a dengys yr ystadegau a gyflwynwyd adeg dathlu ei ben-blwydd yn 18 oed faint y galw:

	1971	1989
Nifer y Cylchoedd Meithrin	68	535
Nifer y plant	950	7783
Nifer y Cylchoedd Mam a'i Phlentyn	–	318
Nifer y plant	–	3719[5]

Yn dilyn llwyddiant o'r fath cododd nifer o broblemau a all effeithio'n drwm ar ddyfodol y gwaith. Yng nghais cyfansawdd PDAG i'r Swyddfa Gymreig, dywed Cyfarwyddwr y Mudiad Ysgolion Meithrin wrth drafod y ffordd ymlaen:

> Nodwedd arbennig y blynyddoedd cynnar oedd y canran uchel o athrawesau trwyddedig oedd yn arwain ein Cylchoedd gyda 72% ohonynt yn rhai trwyddedig. Gyda'r newid yn economi a natur gymdeithasol y wlad newidiodd yr agwedd hon ar y gwaith a gostwng mae

nifer yr athrawesau trwyddedig hyn oddi ar hynny. Awgrymir y rhesymau canlynol am y newid:
* Daeth athrawesau trwyddedig yn fwy cyndyn i roi'r gorau i'w swyddi gydag awdurdodau lleol ar enedigaeth eu plant oherwydd prinder swyddi yn y sector statudol. Y tuedd yw ail ymafael mewn swydd dysgu wedi genedigaeth plentyn.
* Fe ddengys cyfrifiad 1951 fod nifer y plant allai siarad Cymraeg wedi gostwng yn sylweddol ers y Cyfrifiad blaenorol ac o blith merched a anwyd tua'r adeg honno, sef merched oddeutu 35–45 mlwydd oed heddiw, yr ydym yn chwilio am athrawesau i'n Cylchoedd. Nifer cyfyng sydd ar gael ac mae hyn yn rhwystro ehangu.
* Mae'r cynnydd yn nifer ein Cylchoedd wedi dwysáu'r broblem (gweler yr ystadegau uchod). Digwyddodd y cynnydd mwyaf yn y De-ddwyrain, sef yn yr ardal lle'r oedd Cymry Cymraeg brinnaf beth bynnag.[6]

Ffordd y Mudiad i ymateb i'r newidiadau hyn a goresgyn yr argyfwng staffio yw trwy gynllunio a chynnal sawl math o gwrs pwrpasol. Bydd rhai ar gyfer Cymry Cymraeg i'w hyfforddi yn nhechnegau addysg feithrin, a bydd eraill i rieni di-Gymraeg bedwar bore yr wythnos, a hyfforddiant yn elfennau addysg feithrin ar y pumed bore.

Addysg Bellach (16 + oed)

Dyma faes y mae gwir angen ei ddatblygu o safbwynt darpariaeth Gymraeg. Er mai darniog a digyswllt fu'r ymateb yn y sector addysg bellach yn gyffredinol, y mae darlun cadarnhaol i'w weld yn datblygu erbyn hyn. Gellid datgan bod ym mhob awdurdod addysg yng Nghymru ryw gymaint o ddarpariaeth ddwyieithog yn y maes — hynny yn amrywio o ran maint a natur, gan adlewyrchu lle'r Gymraeg ym mholisïau'r awdurdodau hynny. Y mae'r ddarpariaeth i'w chael mewn nifer o feysydd galwedigaethol, yn cynnwys busnes, gofal, arlwyaeth, twristiaeth a hamdden, amaeth a chrefft adeiladu. Ond anghyflawn iawn yw'r deunyddiau dysgu i staff a'u myfyrwyr. Yn amlach na pheidio rhaid i ddarlithwyr baratoi nodiadau i'w dosbarthiadau a gwneud y gorau o gyrsiau eraill, e.e. cynhyrchwyd defnyddiau gwerthfawr o dan nawdd yr Asiantaeth Hyfforddi ar gyfer cynlluniau ADAG (TVEI), ac y mae rhannau o gyrsiau TGAU yn berthnasol. Y mae i'r deunyddiau hyn eu defnydd mewn cyrsiau addysg bellach, eithr i raddau y mae hynny. Rhaid cofio bod i gyrsiau galwedigaethol anghenion arbennig ac felly mae'n hanfodol bod yr adnoddau a gynhyrchir yn ateb y gofynion o ran eu cynnwys a'r gwaith y disgwylir i'r myfyriwr ei gyflawni.

Dengys tystiolaeth ymchwil a gasglwyd ddwy flynedd yn ôl trwy arolwg Prosiect Datblygu Dwyieithrwydd mewn Addysg Bellach Is a noddwyd gan yr Asiantaeth Hyfforddi:

a. bod galw am berson â sgiliau dwyieithog ym meysydd busnes, gofal ac arlwyaeth, a bod cyflogwyr yn y sector cyhoeddus a phreifat yn eu hystyried yn bwysig a defnyddiol mewn amrywiaeth o swyddi. Gwelwyd hefyd bod ymwybyddiaeth y cyflogwyr o werth y Gymraeg yn y byd gwaith yn tyfu;
b. bod galw o du pobl ifainc sydd ar fin gadael yr ysgol am ddarpariaeth Gymraeg/ddwyieithog mewn colegau addysg bellach, yn bennaf yn y tri maes a nodir yn (a), er mwyn sicrhau parhad naturiol i'r profiadau ieithyddol ac addysgol a gafwyd cyn 16 oed ynghyd â pharatoad perthnasol ar gyfer cyflogaeth a bywyd yn y gymuned.

Ar sail y dystiolaeth ymchwil uchod i anghenion y farchnad lafur, datblygiadau diweddar yn y cwrs addysg cyn-alwedigaethol, gofynion y Cwricwlwm Cenedlaethol ac ar ôl ymgynghori â darparwyr rhaglenni hyfforddiant galwedigaethol, argymhellodd PDAG i'r Swyddfa Gymreig y dylid datblygu'r meysydd canlynol dros gyfnod o bum mlynedd:

1. Sgiliau cyfathrebu a datblygiad personol
2. Astudiaethau busnes
3. Arlwyaeth
4. Twristiaeth a hamdden
5. Astudiaethau gofal
6. Amaeth a garddwriaeth
7. Crefftau adeiladu
8. Celf a dylunio
9. Technoleg gwybodaeth[7]

Cymraeg i Oedolion

Dyma faes sydd wedi datblygu'n rhyfeddol o gyflym yn ystod y chwarter canrif ddiwethaf, ers cyhoeddi cyfrolau R. M. Jones, *Cymraeg i Oedolion*. Arbrofwyd y deunydd a'r dulliau dysgu arloesol mewn dosbarthiadau nos a 'chyrsiau carlam' blynyddol, a drefnwyd gan Gyfadran Addysg Coleg Aberystwyth. Bu llwyddiant yr ymgyrch yn symbyliad i fentrau cyffelyb ar hyd a lled Cymru. Gymaint fu'r cynnydd fel y bu'n rhaid penodi, rai blynyddoedd yn ôl, Swyddog Datblygu Cenedlaethol Dysgu'r Gymraeg i Oedolion i gydlynu'r gweithgarwch. Cyflogir y swyddog hwn, staff y swyddfa ganolog a nifer o ddiwtoriaid a threfnyddion datblygu yn y maes gan grant iaith y Swyddfa Gymreig.

Ar y raddfa leol, gweinyddir y gwasanaeth gan amrywiaeth o sefydliadau. Mae cyfraniad y Brifysgol i'r maes yn sylweddol gan iddi ddarparu canolfan sy'n arbenigo yn y gwaith yng Nghaerdydd, ac y mae prosbectws pob un o'r Adrannau Efrydiau Allanol, Coleg Politechnig Cymru a Chymdeithas Addysg y Gweithwyr yn cynnwys detholiad o gyrsiau ar wahanol lefelau. Mae pob un o'r siroedd hefyd yn cynnig dosbarthiadau yn ogystal â chanolfannau annibynnol megis Nant Gwrtheyrn a Chlwyd. Cyfoethogir profiadau'r dysgwyr hefyd gan y rhaglen amrywiol o weithgareddau cymdeithasol a diwylliannol a drefnir gan CYD (sef Cymdeithas y Dysgwyr).

Croesewir yn frwd y cynllun arbrofol, a noddir gan y Bwrdd Iaith, i godi ymwybyddiaeth ieithyddol cymuned Cwm Gwendraeth. Os yw addysg Gymraeg ein hysgolion i fod o unrhyw arwyddocâd i'r disgyblion, mae'n bwysig i'r iaith gael ei harddel y tu allan i furiau'r ysgol.

Diweddglo

Bedair blynedd yn ôl, yn haf 1987, pan ddechreuodd PDAG ar ei waith, prin y byddai neb wedi rhagweld y cyffroadau a gafodd effaith mor bell-gyrhaeddol ar y byd addysg ac ar addysg Gymraeg yn arbennig — ac y mae'r cyffro'n parhau. O fewn ychydig fisoedd i sefydlu PDAG cyhoeddwyd dogfen drafod y Llywodraeth ar Fesur Addysg newydd. Nid oedd y statws a roddid i'r Gymraeg wrth fodd cefnogwyr yr iaith, ac felly cafwyd ymgyrch ar y cyd rhwng y prif fudiadau addysg a chyrff cenedlaethol o'r un anian i gryfhau safle'r iaith ac i sicrhau diffiniad mwy derbyniol o'r hyn oedd 'ysgol Gymraeg'. Dan arweiniad yr Arglwydd Gwilym Prys Davies ac aelodau eraill cefnogol o Dŷ'r Arglwyddi, llwyddwyd i gynnwys cymalau yn y Ddeddf Ddiwygio Addysg (1988) sy'n sicrhau bod y Gymraeg yn bwnc craidd (neu sylfaen) a Chymraeg ail iaith yn bwnc sylfaen yng nghwricwlwm ysgolion Cymru.

Yn sgil y Ddeddf sefydlodd yr Ysgrifennydd Gwladol dros Gymru weithgor ar y Gymraeg yn y Cwricwlwm Cenedlaethol, dan gadeiryddiaeth yr Athro Gwyn Thomas. Cyhoeddwyd yr adroddiad ym mis Mehefin 1989, ac y mae'n cynnwys argymhellion ar dargedau cyrhaeddiad a rhaglenni astudio ar gyfer y Gymraeg a Chymraeg ail iaith.

Esgorodd y statws a roddwyd i'r Gymraeg ar nifer o gynlluniau allweddol a lansiwyd ym 1989-90 ac a ehangwyd ers hynny, yn sgil eu heffeithiolrwydd. Mewn perthynas â'r Grant Cynnal Addysg clustnodwyd £160,000 (y flwyddyn gyntaf) i ddarparu hyfforddiant-mewn-swydd ar gyfer y Gymraeg yn y Cwricwlwm Cenedlaethol. Gyda'r cyllid hwn penodwyd hyfforddwr cenedlaethol ac arweinydd hyfforddi ym mhob awdurdod addysg lleol. Y flwyddyn ganlynol penodwyd hyfforddwr cenedlaethol cynorthwyol. Rhoddwyd £223,000 (y flwyddyn gyntaf) ar gyfer Grantiau Hyfforddi'r Awdurdodau Addysg Lleol er mwyn hyfforddi athrawon sy'n trosglwyddo o'r cyfrwng Saesneg i'r cyfrwng Cymraeg; hyfforddi athrawon gyda rhywfaint o hyfforddiant cychwynnol yn y Gymraeg ail iaith, ond sydd angen hyfforddiant pellach i'w galluogi i ddiweddaru eu technegau dysgu i gwrdd â gofynion y cwricwlwm newydd.

Rhoddwyd Grant Bonws o £1,200 y pen i fyfyrwyr cymwys ar eu cwrs hyfforddiant dechreuol i ddysgu trwy gyfrwng y Gymraeg; hyn yn ychwanegol at y grant am ddysgu pynciau prin, megis mathemateg ac ieithoedd modern.

Ers i PDAG gychwyn ar ei waith ym 1987 sefydlwyd dau gorff cenedlaethol sydd, i raddau, yn effeithio ar y swyddogaeth y rhagwelodd PDAG yn perthyn iddi ar y dechrau. Yn wahanol i PDAG, sy'n cael ei gynnal yn ariannol gan y Swyddfa Gymreig ond bod ei aelodaeth yn cael ei benderfynu gan Gyd-bwyllgor Addysg Cymru, dau gorff a ffurfiwyd a'u haelodau wedi eu henwebu gan y Swyddfa Gymreig yw Cyngor Cwricwlwm Cymru a Bwrdd yr Iaith Gymraeg. Mae'n amlwg y gallai rhai o swyddogaethau'r ddau gorff newydd ymylu ar rai PDAG, a hyd yma, drwy gyd-ddealltwriaeth rasol, llwyddwyd i gydweithio'n effeithiol.

Fodd bynnag, mae lle i ddadlau y gallai — ac yn wir, y dylai — PDAG ymestyn ei weithgarwch a chael llais cryfach mewn penderfyniadau yn ymwneud â pholisi a chyllid. Beth yw'r ffordd orau ymlaen iddo felly? Mae gan PDAG sawl dewis o'i flaen: naill ai, gyda chefnogaeth lawn Cyd-bwyllgor Addysg Cymru, mynnu ei fod yn datblygu'n gorff statudol gyda brîff cadarnach a chyllid digonol fyddai'n sicrhau ei annibyniaeth; neu barhau yn rhan o gorff statudol arall. O benderfynu ymgysylltu â chorff cenedlaethol o natur addysgol neu ieithyddol — ac y mae manteision pendant i hyn yn wyneb yr holl gyrff sy'n bodoli — mae gan PDAG ddigon o ddewis;

naill ai parhau gyda'r un math o berthynas â'r Cyd-bwyllgor Addysg, neu ymuno â Chyngor Cwricwlwm Cymru gan greu Adran Gymraeg hyfyw o fewn y corff hwnnw, neu ddod yn sector allweddol dan adain Bwrdd yr Iaith Gymraeg.

Beth bynnag fydd ei ffawd, mae'r hyn y mae PDAG yn ei gynrychioli a'r llafur enfawr sy'n ei wynebu yn sicrhau ei ddyfodol yn gadarnach nag erioed.

CYFEIRIADAU

1. *Adroddiad Blynyddol PDAG* (Gorffennaf 1990), 17.
2. Ibid., 18-19.
3. *Edrych yn ôl: Cymraeg 5-18*, Sylwebaeth ar adroddiadau AEM a gyhoeddwyd yn ystod 1983-88 (Y Swyddfa Gymreig, 1989), 37.
4. *Cymraeg ar gyfer 5-16 oed* (Y Swyddfa Gymreig, 1989), para 7.23 a 24.
5. *Cais i Ddatblygu Addysg Gymraeg 1990-91* (PDAG, 1989), 88.
6. Ibid., 89-90.
7. Ibid., 70-2.

Hoffai'r awdur ddiolch i'r Dr Alun Ogwen a Mr Dafydd Kirkman wrth baratoi'r erthygl hon.

European Dimensions—Rhetoric and Realities

MICHAEL WILLIAMS

Introduction

The study of education is eclectic in nature, drawing on a wide array of disciplines, fields and subjects. Educational research is distinguished by the richness of its methodology, reflecting the variety of problems it wishes to resolve and the issues it seeks to clarify. Like other fields of research it is not circumscribed by limits of time or national frontiers: educational research often has transferable qualities that enable academics from very different backgrounds to communicate their shared interests without difficulty. Impeding some of this sharing of educational interests are the differences in ideological loyalties held by educationists. This can easily be illustrated by the following résumé of widely held ideological positions.

First, there is the reconstructionist position in which the functions of education are perceived to be the critical appraisal of contemporary phenomena, the consideration of reform processes and the definition of a new order. A second position is held by those who consider education to be concerned with cultural transmission, with identifying those ideas and phenomena which constitute our cultural heritage and devising ways of ensuring that these are transmitted to new generations. A third position is narrowly vocational in scope, where the focus is utilitarian in character and the emphasis is on the preparation of learners for some clearly defined roles. Here, as with reconstructionism, the focus is upon the future, though it is the future of the individual that takes pride of place. Fourthly, there is the learner-centred position, sometimes referred to as progressivism, in which the focus is on the learner in his or her own personal, individualistic, terms. By contrast, there is, fifthly, the subject-centred, or discipline-centred, position where the focus is on worthwhile learning framed by the classical academic subjects, disciplines and fields of study which go to making up an enduring curriculum in academic institutions.

In this chapter I have chosen to explore the expression 'European dimension' which has become increasingly used in educational discussions, especially as 1992 approaches. I shall discuss some of the difficulties which are generated by the use of this expression and in so doing illustrate the eclectic nature of educational research and demonstrate the complexities which result from the ideological variety to which I have just referred.

Defining Europe

If you wish to delay the start of any conference, seminar or discussion convened to discuss aspects of education in Europe, you have only to ask the simple question, 'What do we mean by Europe?' Gaining a consensus on an answer to this is far from simple. Answers come from many sources including geography, history, politics and economics. The question is translated into other forms: 'Where is Europe?' 'What is Europe?' 'When was Europe?' or 'When will Europe be?'

It is difficult to disagree with Professor Mead's assertion that 'the distinctiveness of Europe lies in its physical geography, its ethnography, its technology, its values and its territorial organization'.[1] He sought to define the spatial limits of this 'geographical expression' and focused, as all commentators seem to do, on the eastern border. Mead asserts:

> One fact is certain. Europe embraces the metropolitan part of Russia. The cultural imprint of Russia is European rather than Byzantine: the technology is indisputably European.[2]

For Dostoevsky, Russia was a 'better Europe, purged of the disharmonies and defects of a materialistic west'. There is a contemporary resonance in these views in the recent references by President Gorbachev to 'our common European home'.[3]

If we can agree that the eastern limits of Europe are defined more precisely by a limit running north to south approximately along the line of the Urals, accepting by so doing the spatial disaggregation of the Soviet Union, then we are likely to be more content than simply accepting the straight lines drawn by atlas editors.

From the outer limits one moves inwards to the centre or core of Europe. Geographers are not alone in exploring the metaphor of core and periphery in spatial areas. We can turn to the detailed and provocative essays of Immanuel Wallerstein to assist in clarifying these concepts.

Wallerstein has written about economic and political polarization and refers to 'core processes' in 'core areas' and 'peripheral processes' in 'peripheral areas'. To this conception of core and periphery he has added the concept of hegemony, asserting:

> If hegemony is defined as a situation in which a single core power has demonstrable advantages of efficiency *simultaneously* in production, commerce and finance, it follows that a maximally free market would be likely to ensure maximal profit to the enterprises located in such a hegemonic power.[4]

From Wallerstein's writings I would take one paragraph which has particular significance in the search for an understanding of the spatial definition of contemporary Europe. He writes:

> States in which core-like activities occur develop relatively strong state apparatuses which can advance the interests of the bourgeoisies, less by protection (a mechanism of the medium-strong seeking to be stronger) than by preventing other states from erecting political barriers to the profitability of these activities. In general, states seek to shape the world market in ways that will advance the interests of some entrepreneurs against those of others.[5]

For my purposes, these statements lead in three directions. First, there is the spatial translation of the metaphor of core and periphery to the continent of Europe. A neat summary of this was provided in a map drawn by Russell King which illustrates the amalgamation of different, empirically defined core areas.[6] In this spatial translation the concept of hegemony is highlighted. The tensions between those states to the east and west of the Lotharingian axis and the position of the United Kingdom with regard to France and Germany are particularly relevant to this.

The second direction concerns an alternative definition of core. Geopolitical and economic considerations lead to one set of definitions derived from statistical indicators. More elusive is the concept of core defined by qualitative, humanistic criteria. In the search for the definition of a cultural core of Europe one has to accept the notion of peripheral or marginal cultures and also a cultural hegemony. Where is the cultural heart of Europe? Where is European culture to be experienced at its most authentic? Is this European-ness to be sought in notions of cultural heritage expressed, for example, in the Mozart celebrations of this year or in the annual selection of a European cultural city — Glasgow in 1990 and Dublin in 1991?

Thirdly, the very title of one of Wallerstein's books, *The Politics of the World-Economy*, in which the hyphen between 'World' and 'Economy' is highly significant, is a reminder that in too sharp a focus on Europe and the European dimension there lies the danger of Eurocentricism. Locating Europe in its global position is probably a more important task for educationists than is the hunt for a consensual definition of the spatial limits of Europe.

It would be easy to avoid these spatial aspects and turn to a simple definition of Europe as an agglomeration of nation states. All one needs to do is to add together those nation states which are contained within a loosely defined continental Europe. Historians of nationalism and nation states have demonstrated how slippery such a conception is. The recently published collection of essays by Hobsbawm[7] is particularly interesting in seeking to understand the notion of a European dimension. He writes:

> I do not regard the 'nation' as a primary nor as an unchanging social entity. It belongs exclusively to a particular, and historically recent, period. It is a social entity only insofar as it relates to a certain kind of modern territorial state, the 'nation-state', and it is pointless to discuss nation and nationality except insofar as both relate to it.

He goes on to quote from Gellner:

> Nations as a natural, God-given way of classifying men, as an inherent ... political destiny are a myth: nationalism, which sometimes takes pre-existing cultures and turns them into nations, sometimes invents them, and often obliterates pre-existing cultures: that is a reality.[8]

Hobsbawm goes on to write:

> In short, for the purpose of analysis nationalism comes before nations. Nations do not make states and nationalisms but the other way round.

For my purposes this suggests that Europeanism comes before the definition of the European territory. The spirit of Europe and European identity is a prerequisite for a definition of Europe. From this we can assert that Europeans will forge the new Europe, Europe will not produce Europeans. The history of continental Europe has been distinguished by shifting national boundaries as states and alliances have sought to gain control over peoples and territories. The result has been that Europeans have been able to shift allegiances between nation states and other social structures, such as religion and political ideology, as it suits them. Just as there are social and regional variations within political boundaries regarding levels of national consciousness, so there are variations with regard to European consciousness.

It is Britain's membership of a number of powerful international organizations which has forced public attention in Britain on Eurocentric matters. Of these, the major ones are the Western European Union, the Council of Europe and the European Community. To these can be added two organizations with roots in Europe but whose membership extends beyond the frontiers of Europe — the North Atlantic Treaty Organization and the Organization for Economic Co-operation and Development. Both the Council of Europe and the European Community have been active in promoting the notion of a European dimension in an educational context.

Discussions about education in the framework of the European Community have been restricted by the strict reading of the Treaty of Rome. Whereas the Council of Europe works in a variety of fields, including health, social welfare, education, culture, sport, the environment, local government and justice, the work of the European Community is circumscribed by economic, and especially, common market, considerations. It is in the signing of the Single European Act in 1986, which aims to create 'an area without internal frontiers in which the free movement of goods, persons, services and capital is ensured', that the possibilities for a more active participation by community member states in trans-national educational initiatives have been opened up.

Behind this unified, single market lies a division of Community leaders into two camps. On the one hand there are the so-called 'maximalists' who advocate European federalism and a broad expansion of the scope of European Community activities, backed by procedural, political reforms focusing particularly on increasing the power of the elected European Parliament. On the other hand there are the 'minimalists' who are sceptical of federalism and parliamentary reforms and they focus their attention on a pragmatic and gradualist approach to unification which stops well short of full economic and political union. The agenda for the maximalists, spelled out by Delors, has four central issues: monetary co-ordination, political and defence co-operation, institutional reform, and internal market liberalization. The importance of 1992 lies in the progress made towards achieving the latter two. The recognition of this divide between maximalists and minimalists is of fundamental importance for educationists seeking to respond to initiatives under the broad umbrella of the European dimension.

The divide is not confined simply to economic and political considerations. There are social considerations also. These are clearly seen in the European Community's social policy and particularly in the contentious Social Charter. This Social Charter has grown out of Article 118 of the Treaty of Rome which refers to the promotion of

> close co-operation between Member States in the social field, particularly in matters relating to:
> — employment;
> — labour law and working conditions;
> — social security;
> — prevention of occupational accidents and diseases;
> — occupational hygiene;
> — the right of association and collective bargaining between employers and workers.

Out of this has come two notions: the Community's 'social space' and the 'People's Europe'. Both find embodiment in the Social Charter. This has extended the list from Article 118 to include for Community citizens the right to freedom of movement, the right of workers to information, consultation and participation, the protection of children and adolescents, elderly persons and disabled persons, and, of particular relevance in the context of this discussion, the right to vocational education. The Social Charter serves to extend the definition of the European citizen within the confines of the Community. It is an important ingredient in the emergent civic culture of the new Europe. It cannot be ignored in any consideration of the European dimension in education.

A Young Persons' Europe

Just as the People's Europe can be used as a clarion call for giving the Community a human face so also can the idea of a 'Young

Persons' Europe' act as a starting-point for a closer consideration of the European dimension in educational institutions. From an early age children begin to receive knowledge, develop skills and acquire attitudes relevant to international understanding. Through processes of political socialization in which a number of agencies are involved, including the family, the mass media and the school, young people become more or less international, and, in a European context, more or less European.

In 1983 I collaborated with colleagues from the Free University of Amsterdam, the Royal Danish School of Educational Studies and the University of Stuttgart in a study of international behaviour.[9] We selected a sample of schoolchildren aged 12–13 from schools in the cities of Amsterdam, Copenhagen, Manchester and Stuttgart. There were 730 children in the sample drawn from 24 schools: 5 schools in Amsterdam, 6 in Copenhagen, 6 in Manchester and 7 in Stuttgart. By chance the sample was roughly divided into equal numbers of boys and girls. We designed a questionnaire which we distributed to the pupils in their schools. One of our questions asked the pupils to name the European countries which they had visited and the results are shown in Table 1. It is interesting to note the high percentages of these young adolescents who had travelled to foreign countries and also the pattern of countries visited. Not surprisingly, they reflect proximity, holiday destinations and countries which pupils may have visited as part of a school-organized study excursion.

Included in our questionnaire were questions which sought to identify those countries to which the pupils had positive and negative dispositions. A summary of the response is given in Table 2.

These were just two of the questions which we posed in our study. In our overall conclusions we stated:

> The most striking and, possibly the most predictable, pattern which emerges from our study is the demarcation of Europe into east and west. This is evident in children's travel experience, their penfriends, their dispositions towards particular countries and what they would like to know about countries. Broadly, they divide between a political east and a tourist west. It would be wrong to over-emphasise this distinction. To do so would be to overlook the references to Ireland and to Turkey by pupils. Terrorism and immigration are important themes to place alongside ideology and holidaymaking.

This study should be viewed as a snapshot of the international behaviour of a small sample of adolescents and, given the dramatic

Table 1: European countries most visited by pupils.

City	Five most visited countries in Europe	Percentage of pupils in the sample from each city
Amsterdam	Belgium	78
	Federal Republic of Germany	76
	France	53
	Spain	38
	Austria	32
Copenhagen	Sweden	81
	Federal Republic of Germany	80
	Norway	46
	Spain	25
	Italy	25
Manchester	France	41
	Spain	34
	Italy	13
	Federal Republic of Germany	11
	Greece	8
Stuttgart	Austria	78
	Switzerland	64
	Italy	61
	France	48
	Yugoslavia	26

changes in eastern Europe in the last few years, we ought to expect that the 'private geographies' of young people will have changed also. This concern with international behaviour is the backcloth against which to consider the proposals which have been made by the European Community for promoting the European dimension in education.

The 1988 resolution on the European dimension

In May 1988 a resolution on the European dimension in education was signed by the Council of the European Communities and the Ministers of Education meeting within the Council (Document 88/C177/02). This grew directly from the 'Solemn Declaration on

Table 2: Rank order of countries liked and not liked by pupils in the four countries.

Countries receiving the most 'like' responses (rank order with percentage of responses)

Rank	Boys		Girls		Boys and Girls	
1.	France	(13%)	France	(17%)	France	(15%)
2.	F.R.G.	(10%)	Spain	(13%)	Spain	(10%)
					U.K.	(10%)
3.	Austria	(9%)	U.K.	(12%)	Italy	(9%)
	U.K.	(9%)				
4.	Denmark	(8%)	Italy	(11%)	F.R.G.	(8%)
	Italy	(8%)				

Countries receiving the most 'not like' responses (rank order with percentage of responses)

Rank	Boys		Girls		Boys and Girls	
1.	U.S.S.R.	(13%)	U.S.S.R.	(12%)	U.S.S.R.	(12%)
2.	D.R.G.	(12%)	Ireland	(11%)	Albania	(10%)
					D.R.G.	(10%)
3.	Albania	(11%)	Albania	(10%)	France	(7%)
					Ireland	(7%)
					Poland	(7%)
					Turkey	(7%)
					U.K.	(7%)
4.	France	(8%)	D.R.G.	(8%)	F.R.G.	(6%)

European Union' of Stuttgart (June 1983), the conclusions of the European Council in Fontainebleau (June 1984) and the 'People's Europe' report adopted at the European Council in Milan (June 1985).

This resolution[10] had four objectives:

to strengthen in young people a sense of European identity and make clear to them the value of European civilization and of the foundations on which the European peoples intend to base their development today, that is in particular the safeguarding of the principles of democracy, social justice and respect for human rights;

to prepare young people to take part in the economic and social development of the Community and in making concrete progress towards European union, as stipulated in the European Single Act;

to make them aware of the advantages which the Community represents, but also the challenges it involves, in opening up an enlarged economic and social area to them;

to improve their knowledge of the Community and its Member States in their historical, cultural, economic and social aspects and bring home to them the significance of the co-operation of the Member States of the European Community with other countries of Europe and the world.

In the resolution a list of measures was proposed for implementation at member state level and Community level. Member states were encouraged to make every effort to implement changes in the following areas:

Incorporation of the European dimension in educational systems through the formulation of policies;

Inclusion of the European dimension explicitly in school programmes [i.e. curricula] and teaching;

Arranging for teaching material to take account of the common objective of promoting the European dimension;

Giving greater emphasis to the European dimension in teachers' initial and in-service training;

Promoting measures to boost contacts between pupils and teachers from different countries.

Complementary measures included reference to colloquia and seminars, the promotion of school initiatives and extra-curricular activities, the participation of schools in activities organized as part of Europe Day (9 May), the participation of schools in the European schools' competition and similar competitions, and increased co-operation between the member states in the area of school sports.

Having signed this resolution the Department of Education and Science invited the National Curriculum Council to offer advice to assist in framing a response to it. They produced a definition of the European dimension which was extended by a statement of aims. The definition reads:

The major purpose of the European Dimension resolution is to strengthen pupils' sense of European identity; to prepare them to take part in the economic and social development of the Community following the European Single Act; to improve their knowledge of the European Community and of its member states; and to inform them of the significance of the co-operation between those states and the other countries of Europe and of the world.

The European dimension in education should enable pupils to live and work with a degree of competence in other European countries, to reflect critically on experiences in them so as to give an informed understanding of the predicaments and aspirations of other Europeans in order to reflect critically on or challenge existing perceptions.

The aims of promoting the European dimension for pupils would be to:

inform the whole curriculum and act as a focus point for pupils' acquisition of knowledge and skills acquired in various curriculum areas;

promote a sense of European identity, including the provision of first-hand experience where appropriate;

help pupils to acquire a view of Europe as a multicultural, multilingual community which includes the UK;

enable pupils to acquire knowledge, skills and experiences which enable them to live and work in Europe comfortably but not uncritically;

prepare young people to take part in the economic and social development of the community and make them aware of opportunities and challenges;

develop knowledge of economic and social aspects;

encourage awareness of the variety of histories, geographies and circumstances;

further an awareness of European development past and present with 1992 only a stage;

promote an understanding of common European ideals while developing an awareness of Europe's interdependence with the rest of the world.

With these statements from the Council of Ministers and the National Curriculum Council (NCC) in England and Wales we can return to what I wrote in the introduction to this chapter. There I referred to the five ideological positions held by educationists. In the resolution of 1988 and the NCC definition, we find evidence of a reconstructionist position in the emphasis on the need to prepare young people to take part in the economic and social development of the Community and in making concrete progress towards European union. However, as I asserted earlier, when referring to the maximalist and minimalist positions, there is no consensus within the Community at the highest levels as to what European unity means. We have only to trace the debates about the European Community in the British Parliament to detect the obvious splits within the parties and between the parties. Further, there is the alarm expressed by British political leaders about the hegemony of the French and German governments. The Lotharingian axis, referred to earlier, has taken on greater significance since German unification and the roles which France, Germany and the UK will play in the changing eastern Europe remains to be seen. Educationists may speculate on the future of Europe and, should they wish to introduce the European dimension to their students, they will need to consider carefully their own political predilections. What is clear is that the children entering our schools now at the age of five will leave school in at least eleven years' time and the Europe they will encounter then will be very different from the Europe we know today. For those dealing with students in higher education the same question about the political and economic shape of a new Europe is equally important. It is easy to view greater European unity as a panacea for solving the pressing problems already with us, which are likely to be intensified in the future — ecological ruin, a fall in the standard of education, a deterioration in the quality of urban life associated with drug addiction and violent crime, the problems of the elderly, the problems of homelessness and poverty. To these should be added the recent anxiety stemming from the potential migration of substantial numbers of Russians and other eastern Europeans to the west and the migration of citizens from third-world countries also to western Europe.

The resolution also referred to the need to make clear to young people the value of European civilization. Here we see evidence of an ideology which emphasizes cultural transmission. It is easy to be romantic about European civilization. In European conferences attended by educationists it is not unusual to find people searching for a definition of European civilization which embraces the achievements of Greece and Rome, medieval Christendom and the Reformation, the Renaissance, the Age of Exploration and the Age of Revolutions, the Industrial Revolution and the rise of European nationalism. There is also the view of Europe as the birthplace of the great '-isms' — humanism, liberalism, Marxism, Fascism, and Nazism. Some draw attention in a Eurocentric way to cultural attitudes. Thus in a conference organized by the Council of Europe to consider the place of Europe in school curricula, one speaker[11] referred to four polarizations or dilemmas fundamental to any culture. These polarizations were liberty/security; materialism/

spirituality; rationality/emotionality; nature/production. Notice the statements about European culture which go alongside these polarizations:

> Europeans can be typified by their general desire to live within well-ordered societies in which they feel that their well-being is secured. However, they demand freedom of choice in everyday things and set great store by privacy and the right to order their own personal lives.

> Although at present tarnished by the materialism engendered by the consumer society and the struggle to attain ever more ambitious economic goals, European man [sic] remains fundamentally an idealistic and spiritually-minded creature searching for a utopian society based on Christian, liberal or socialist principles.

> The importance placed on reason is one of the most fundamental aspects of European culture. . . Europeans are beginning to realize that reason, with all its worth, needs to be tempered by the emotions and that room needs to be left for the free play of intuition and imagination if the European, creative spirit is to be preserved.

We do not need to look far back in history to see how biased are these assertions. Tracing and defining our cultural heritage is far from being a simple task. Just how difficult it can be within the confines of one member state of the Community can be gauged from the controversy surrounding the attempt to write programmes of study for history in the National Curriculum in England and Wales. This can be highlighted by the recent letter (14 January 1991) from the Department of Education and Science inviting responses to the draft order for history in England (this does not apply to history in Wales). It reads:

> The Secretary of State has accepted the NCC's recommendations in respect of the attainment targets and programmes of study, subject to one change of substance. His reservation concerns the course of modern history that forms part of the programme for key stage 4 (pupils aged 14–16 years). He recognises that from time to time teachers have to treat matters, in history and other subjects, which are topical and controversial. He is confident that they will handle these with care and sensitivity and with regard to their duty to offer a balanced presentation of opposing views on political issues. However, the Secretary of State considers that it would not be right for him to make the study of events up to and including the present day a statutory requirement as part of National Curriculum history. His view is that programmes of study should not prescribe teaching about contemporary events and people, many of whom are still living, because of the difficulty of treating such matters with an historical perspective. The Secretary of

State believes that it is right to draw some distinction between the study of history and the study of current affairs.

Accordingly the programme of study for key stage 4, and some of the examples which illustrate the statements of attainment, have been adjusted so as to focus on the first half of the 20th century, with reference to events from the turn of the century to the 1960s.

Given that the place of history in the curriculum of pupils aged 14–16 years is still unclear (though all the evidence suggests that it will become either optional or part of some integrated or correlated arrangement with geography), it is obvious that pupils would have little opportunity to study in history the evolution of the European Community. Despite the Secretary of State's signature being appended to the resolution of 1988, the notion of a European dimension would lack for school pupils the kind of serious consideration which could only be given in the context of the study of recent history. It appears that crucial opportunities for improving pupils' 'knowledge of the Community and its Member States in their historical, cultural, economic and social aspects' and bringing 'home to them the significance of the co-operation of the Member States of the European Community with other countries of Europe and the world' have already been lost. Obviously, history has no monopolistic position with regard to the European cultural heritage. Music, art, modern languages, literature, geography and other subjects all have a role to play. History, however, has conventionally been the subject with the greatest responsibility for education for citizenship and it is in this context that the letter from the Secretary of State is most important with regard to the promotion of the European dimension.

The third ideology was narrowly vocational in scope. The second objective of the resolution was to 'prepare young people to take part in the economic and social development of the Community' and this was extended by the National Curriculum Council to 'enable pupils to acquire knowledge, skills and experience which enable them to live and work in Europe comfortably but not uncritically'. The Commission which took office in January 1989 placed education and training at the top of its priorities. Investment in training was seen as 'both an essential link between economic and social policies and a key element in the promotion of the free movement of ideas'.[12] It is the mobility of ideas and persons which underpins the initiation of a number of schemes which are referred to by their acronyms, for example, ERASMUS, COMETT, LINGUA, PETRA, EUROTEC-

NET and IRIS. ERASMUS and its extension to eastern Europe via TEMPUS is designed to promote student mobility and co-operation in higher education; COMETT is concerned with training in technology in order to meet industry's requirements for a qualified work-force; LINGUA aims to promote an improvement in foreign-language competence; PETRA is the programme for the vocational training of young people and their preparation for adult and working life; EUROTECNET aims at developing vocational education in the new technologies; and IRIS is the Community network of training programmes for women. All of these varied programmes constitute tangible components of the European dimension in education. They are pioneering and ambitious even though the funding allocated to them by the Community represents a miniscule fraction of the national education budgets of the individual member states. In all of these programmes British participation rates are high, as befits a net contributor to the Community budget.

The fourth ideological position focused on the learner. It is this position which serves as a reminder that any proposals for promoting a European dimension must be located in the learning career of pupils and students. Whatever the definition of a European dimension, if it is to fit into the curricula of educational institutions it must take into account the state of readiness of the individual learner and acknowledge that structures for the learner to acquire greater knowledge, understanding and skills and to modify or change attitudes have to be built. For the school curriculum in England and Wales the European dimension has to be located within the list of areas of experience which have been identified as the basis for the whole curriculum, and this requires close consideration to be given to the place of the dimension in the evolving National Curriculum. With regard to the learner, consideration must be given to differentiation and progression, to balance, depth and relevance at each of the four key stages through which all pupils must pass.

The principal vehicles for carrying the European dimension in schools are the subjects which constitute the curriculum. What has run as a thread through this chapter is the controversial nature of the European dimension. It is bounded by value judgements and runs into difficulties concerned with stereotyping, bias and prejudice. I have already referred to the difficulties of teaching recent and contemporary issues under the banner of history. Currently, there are several references to the European Community in the draft standing order for geography, including an example of an attainment target which reads:

> review the pattern of agricultural or industrial output, and regional development programmes, at the European Community level and within selected areas of the European Community; discuss the role of physical, economic, technological and political factors in explaining the patterns.[13]

From this and other examples in the same document it would appear that geography has the potential to play an important part in promoting the European dimension but, like history, its position in the crucial Key Stage 4 has not yet been decided. What is clear is that geography teachers will not be able to provide the historical context necessary for a thorough understanding of the development of Europe. Other subjects have their parts to play, not least modern languages, though their contribution will inevitably be circumscribed by the limits set for the acquisition of linguistic skills and the geographical limits set by the language of study. Despite these limitations, it is through modern languages that many pupils will gain their first-hand experience of mainland Europe in a formal educational setting. The definition accorded to school subjects by examination boards and teachers as they seek to domesticate the National Curriculum will have the most powerful impact on the transmission of the European dimension in schools.

Conclusion

In this chapter I have chosen initially to consider difficulties in defining Europe before going on to discuss briefly the way proposals for promoting the European dimension in educational institutions fit into differing educational ideologies. What emerges is that there are various European dimensions and that the proposals emanating from the European Community are simple to state but difficult to implement. That there are successes to record in terms of student mobility, collaborative projects and the communication of ideas across frontiers there can be no doubt. However, to find evidence of substantial change is difficult and rendered more difficult by the current proposals for the implementation of the National Curriculum in England and Wales.

As 1992 approaches we shall find an increasing use of the expression 'European dimension'. It will be on the lips of politicians, economists, academics and teachers. What Meyer wrote about the German idea of 'Mitteleuropa' can just as easily be written about Europe:

> Geographers sought to give it definition; economists, politicians and journalists manipulated it; and idealists caressed it with romantic devotion. The more current the expression became in Germany and abroad, the more vague, ambiguous and emotional was its use.[14]

Put another way, when trying to make sense of the European dimension one can follow Bevin's mixed metaphor which he used to describe the proposed European Assembly in the 1940s: 'Once you open that Pandora's box, you'll find it full of Trojan horses.'[15]

REFERENCES

1. W.R. Mead, 'The discovery of Europe', *Geography*, 67 No. 3 (1982), 193–201.
2. Ibid.
3. M.S. Gorbachev, *Towards a Better World* (London, 1987).
4. I. Wallerstein, *The Politics of the World-Economy* (Cambridge, 1984).
5. Ibid.
6. R. King, 'Southern Europe: dependency or development', *Geography*, 67 No. 3 (1982), 221–34.
7. E.J. Hobsbawm, *Nations and Nationalism since 1780: Programme, Myths, Reality* (Cambridge, 1990).
8. E. Gellner, *Nations and Nationalism* (Cornell, 1983).
9. M. Williams, O. Biilmann, R. Hahn and J. Van Westrhenen, 'A cross-national study of children's attitudes', in *Perception of People and Places through Media*, Vol. 1 of the Proceedings of the Geographical Education Commission, Congress of the International Geographical Union (Freiburg, 1984).
10. *Resolution of the Council and Ministers of Education meeting within the Council on the European Dimension in Education 1988*, printed in the Official Journal of the European Communities (Brussels, 6 July 1988).
11. H. Janne, 'Europe's cultural identity', quoted in D. Peacock (ed.), *Europe in Secondary School Curricula: Aims, Approaches and Problems* (Council for Cultural Co-operation, Council for Europe, Strasbourg, 1982).
12. Commission of the European Communities, *Guide to the European Community Programmes in the Fields of Education, Training, Youth* (Commission of the European Communities, Brussels, 1989).

13. Welsh Office *National Curriculum: Draft Statutory Order for Geography* (Welsh Office, Cardiff, 1991).
14. H.C. Meyer, *Mitteleuropa in German Thought and Action 1815–1945* (Netherlands, 1991).
15. Quoted in C. Russell, 'The Council of Europe – forty years on', *New Europe*, 3 No. 1 (1990), 15–19.

Index

Aberdare, Lord 70
Aberdare Report (1881) 30, 32, 41
Abergavenny Grammar School 32
Aberystwyth Rural Policy Group 7
ADAG (TVEI) 226; *see also* Technical and Vocational Education Initiative (TVEI)
addysg Gymraeg 217–30
addysg uwchradd ddwyieithog 121–38
adventure schools 13
Advisory Committee on the Supply and Training of Teachers (ACSET) 192, 196
Advisory Committee on Studies in Education at the Open University 5
Advisory Committee on the Training and Supply of Teachers (ACSTT) 192, 196
Allsobrook, D. 78
Ambrose, G.P. 167
Anderson, Sir John 64
Anglesey County Arts Fund 67
Anglesey Music Club 67–8
Anglo-Welsh Review, The 65
Arolygwyr E: Mawrhydi (AEM) 131, 132, 222; *see also* Her Majesty's Inspectorate (HMI)
Area Training Organizations (ATOs) 155, 161–2, 171, 175, 189
Armytage, W.H.G. 189
Arnold, Thomas 45, 53
Arts Council of Great Britain 4
  Art in the Red 66
  Brighter Prospect, A 66
  Struggle for Survival, The 66
  see also Welsh Arts Council; Welsh Committee of the Arts Council
Asiantaeth Hyfforddi 226–7
Association for Promoting the Education of Girls in Wales 42
Association of University Teachers 208
Audit Commission 213, 214

Bains Report 206
Baird, A. 80
Baker, C. 125
Baker days 148
Bangor Diocesan Congress 39
Bangor Grammar School 32
Bangor Normal College 172
Barke 125
Barnard, H.C. 60
BBC Welsh Orchestra 71
Beaumaris Grammar School 32, 33, 34, 37, 38, 39
Bell, A. 110
Bell, Revd Andrew 8
Beloe Committee 86
Bessey Report 139, 140
Better Schools 210, 212
Bevan, Archdeacon 15
Bevan, Madam 12, 13
Bevin, Ernest 247
Bickersteth 19
Biggs, Edith 142
bilingual education 3, 7, 8, 80, 103–6; *see also* addysg Gymraeg, addysg uwchradd ddwyieithog
Bloom: *Taxonomy of Educational Objectives* 168
Board of Education 153, 164
  Welsh Department 30
Botwnnog School 36
Bowen, Professor E.G. 29
Boyson, Sir Rhodes 215
Briscoe, Dr, Vicar of Holyhead 39
British and Foreign Schools Society 12, 13
British Council 7
Bruner 168
Bryce Commission 46, 47, 54

Burnham Report (1925) 153–5, 159, 160, 165
Butler, R.A. 155
Butler Act 204, 205
Button, Dr Leslie 140–1
Bwrdd yr Iaith Gymraeg 229, 230

Callaghan, James 196, 207
Campbell, Bishop of Bangor 39
Canolfan Astudiaethau Addysg (Aberystwyth) 218, 221
Canolfan Astudiaethau Iaith (Bangor) 219, 222
Canolfan Uned Iaith Cymru (Trefforest) 222
Canolfan yr Adran Gymraeg (Caerdydd) 222
Cardiff Intermediate School for Boys 45, 54–7, 60
Cardiff Training College 156, 158, 167
Carnarvon and Denbigh Herald 34, 36, 38, 40
Cartrefle College of Education 142, 160
Central Welsh Board 30, 57
Certificate of Education 103
Certificate of Secondary Education (CSE) 86, 87, 94, 101
Charity Commission 30, 31, 32, 39, 41
Chartist movement 31
child-centred education 214
Church schools 13
Church Union Society 12
Clarke, Sir Kenneth 64, 213
COMETT 244, 245
Commins, Nigel 24, 25
Committee of Council on Education 12, 16
comprehensive education 89–91
Confederation of British Industry (CBI) 208
Conway, H.T. 7
Council for National Academic Awards (CNAA) 162, 163, 174, 194, 199

Council for the Accreditation of Teacher Education (CATE) 5, 22, 164, 174, 179, 184, 193, 197, 198
Council for the Encouragement of Music and the Arts (CEMA) 63, 64
Council of Europe 235
Cowbridge School 78–9
Cowie, Revd B.M. 20
Crosland, Anthony 97, 192
Cross, Tom 65, 71
Cross Commission 153
Curriculum Council for Wales 143; *see also* Cyngor Cwricwlwm Cymru
Curriculum Study Group 86, 87
Cwmcarn School 212
Cwmni Theatr Cymru 4
Cwricwlwm Cenedlaethol 107, 122, 129, 131, 134, 135, 136, 218, 221; *see also* National Curriculum
Cyd-bwyllgor Addysg Cymru 122, 125, 134, 219, 229; *see also* Welsh Joint Education Committee
Cymdeithas y Dysgwyr (CYD) 228
Cyngor Canol ar Addysg 132, 136
Cyngor Cwricwlwm Cymru 135, 229–30; *see also* Curriculum Council for Wales
Cyngor Ysgolion 125; *see also* Schools Council

David Hughes' Charity 32, 33, 34, 36, 37, 41
Davies, Emily 31
Davies, John (Master of Model School) 24
Davies, John (student) 18
Davies, Robert 37
Davies, S. Kenneth 63
Davies, Thomas 18
Davies, Sir Walford 64
Davies (Gregynog) collection 2
day schools 13

Deddf Addysg; *see also* Education Act
  (1980) 134
  (1988) 122, 228
Delors, Jacques 236
Department of Education and Science (DES) 104, 150, 153, 162, 163, 169, 178, 179, 189, 191, 192, 194, 199, 200, 240, 243
  Circulars
    10/65 90, 205, 206
    10/70 206
    3/84 197
    7/73 171, 172, 173
    9/78 196
    88/C177/02 238
DES/ATO 144
DES/ATO Letter 2/70 143
Dodson, Professor Carl 7, 125, 217
Dolman Theatre, Newport 70
Durnford, R. 39, 40, 41

Edmunds, Revd William 14–15, 18–20, 21, 22, 23, 24
Education Act; *see also* Deddf Addysg
  (1918) 154
  (1944) 85, 88, 155, 157, 168, 189, 190, 191, 203, 204–5, 214
  (1980) 209, 211
  (1986) 190, 210, 211
  Reform (1988) 82, 180, 196, 211
Education (Teachers) Regulations Act (1982) 196
Education: Framework for Expansion, A 170, 178, 195
Edwards, Sir Owen M. 3, 30, 79
eleven-plus examination 87
Endowed Schools' Act (1869) 31, 32, 33, 39, 42
Endowed Schools Commission 30–9
ERASMUS 244, 245
Ethical Union 47
Europe, education in 231–47
European Community 235, 241, 244–6
EUROTECNET 244–5

Evans (Curate of St Peter's) 15
Evans, Clifford 70
Evans, Sir Emrys 63

Festival of Britain (1951) 65
Field, Mr (tutor) 18–19, 23
Findlay, Dr J.J. 45–60
  Arnold of Rugby 58
  Demonstration Schools Record, The 60
  Principles of Class Teaching 60
Findlay, Mrs 53
Fleure, Professor H.J. 29
Foat, Dr 59
Forde, Professor C. Daryll 29
Forster 78
Friars' School, Bangor 32
Froebel 47, 48–9

Galton, Maurice 109
garden city education 46, 57–9
Gellner, E. 234
General Certificate of Education (GCE) Ordinary Level 86
General Certificate of Secondary Education (GCSE) 103, 149
General Teaching Council 199, 200
Gittins, Charles 3
Gittins Report 108, 157, 161, 170, 190
Gladstone, William 41
Glamorgan College of Education 163
Goode, Misses 20
Gorbachev, President Mikhail 232
Gordon, Alex 63
Gosden, Peter 177
grammar schools 30, 77, 78, 86
grant-maintained schools (GMS) 211–12
grant-related in-service training (GRIST) 147
Grants for Education Support and Training (GEST) 147
Graves, Professor Norman 181
Great Debate 207, 208, 209
Griffith, Wyn 64
Griffiths, B.J. 140

Guest, Lady Charlotte 31
Gulbenkian Foundation 67
Gwlad y Basg 136
'Gwreiddiau' (prosiect cwricwlwm) 107–19

Hahn, Dr Kurt 140
Halliwell, Revd Principal 2
Hammond, J.L. 34, 35, 37
Harlech, Lord 64
Harris, J. 80
Her Majesty's Inspectorate (HMI) 164, 192, 208; *see also* Arolygwyr Ei Mawrhydi (AEM)
Herbart 48
Hereford, Bishop of 53, 58
Heseltine, Michael 213
Hirst, Paul 180
Hobsbawm, E.J. 234
Hogan, Jim 140
Hoggan, Dr Frances 31
Howard, Ebenezer 57
Howells' Charity School (Denbigh) 34, 41
Hughes, David 39
Hunt, Sir John 140
Hunter, Bob 2

initial teacher training courses (ITT) 179, 180–1
in-service education 139–51
in-service training (INSET) 178, 182
Institute of Manpower Studies (IMS) Report 182
International Monetary Fund 207
International Theatre Institute 66
IRIS 245

James, Lord, of Rusholme 162, 170, 172, 177, 195
James, Dan Lyn 217
James Committee and Report 5, 153, 157, 161–5, 177, 178, 181, 195
Jenkins (student) 18
Jenkins, Warren 69
John, Dr D. Dilwyn 63

Jones, Evan John 3
Jones, Glyn Saunders 218
Jones, Griffith 12
Jones, Gruffydd 75
Jones, Professor Gwyn 63, 64
Jones, Professor Idwal 2
Jones, J.O. 67, 68
Jones, L.G.E. 188
Jones, Philip 71
Jones, R.M. 217
  Cymraeg i Oedolion 227
Jones, Dr Thomas 63
Jones, W.R. 125
Jones' Charity School, Monmouth 32, 41
Joseph, Sir Keith 190, 196, 210

Kay-Shuttleworth, Sir James 188
Keynes, Lord 63
Khlief, B.B. 81
King, Russell 233
King Alfred School Society, Hampstead 46–54, 57
Kogan, M. 191

Labour movement 31
Lawton, D. 196
  Tightening Grip, The 179
Letchworth Garden City education 57–9
Lewis, Saunders 70, 82
Lewis, W.J. 2
Lewis School, Pengam 42
LINGUA 244, 245
Literacy and Numeracy 102
Llanllwch School 15
Llanrwst School 36
Llewelyn-Jones, Eileen 63
Llewelyn-Williams, Alun 63
Lloyd, Selwyn 66
Lloyd, Wynne Ll. 63
local education authority (LEA) 203–15
  Training Grant Scheme (LEATGS) 147
Local Government Act
  (1948) 66
  (1972) 206

Index

London School Board 47
Longland, Jack 140
Longueville Jones, Revd H. 11, 23, 26
Loosmore Report (1981) 80
Losing an Empire, Finding a Role: The LEA of the Future 213
Lowe 78
Lowndes 79

MacMillan, Lord 63
McNair Report (1944) 153, 154, 155–9, 160, 164, 165, 167, 169, 189
McRobert, M.J. 63
Madras system of education 8
Magnus, Sir Philip 56, 57, 60
Master of Education degrees 146–7, 150
Mead, Professor 232
Memorandum of Association and Incorporation (King Alfred School Society) 47, 48
Meyer, H.C. 247
Miall, F.W. 48
Miall, Professor Louis Compton 47, 48
Ministry of Education 159
mixed-ability teaching 92, 93
Model School 23–6
Model Voluntary Aided School 24
Moral Instruction League 47
Morgan, Kenneth O. 79, 82
Moseley, Revd H. 20–1, 22, 25
Mudiad Ysgolion Meithrin 135, 225
Mullins, Alice 48
Mullins, Roscoe 48
Murgatroyd 81
music festivals 65

National Advisory Council on the Supply and Training of Teachers 192
National Association of Schoolmasters/Union of Women Teachers (NASUWT) 184
National Consumer Council (NCC) 208
National Curriculum 82, 143–5, 147, 149–51, 175, 182, 184, 212, 243, 245, 246; *see also* Cwricwlwm Cenedlaethol
National Curriculum Council 240, 241, 244
National Eisteddfod 82
National Society 12, 13, 24
   Welsh Education Committee of the 11, 13, 16, 25–6
National Union of Teachers 154, 208
Newsom Report 86
Niblett, W.R.: *University Connection, The* 189
Nonconformity 77
Normal College, Bangor 158
North Atlantic Treaty Organization 235
North Wales Arts Association 68
Nuffield Secondary Science 88
Nunn, Percy 59

ORACLE 109
Organization for Economic Co-operation and Development 235
Orme, Dr 40
Owen (Nonconformist) 19

Packwood, T. 191
Parry-Williams 125
Parry-Williams, Dr D.E. 63
Parry-Williams, Lady Amy 63
pastoral care 95–7
Patey, Revd Dr Edward 140
Pease, C.A. 59
People's Europe Report 239
Pestalozzi 47
PETRA 244, 245
Petts, John 71
Phillips, J. 19
Phillips, Sir Thomas 13, 14, 16
Piaget 168
Pinsent, Arthur 8

Plowden Report 161, 170
Polytechnic of Wales 163, 173
Powell, Rachel 17
Powell, Thomas 17
Powell, Walter 17
Presswood, Robert E. 63
Primary Education in Wales 190
PRISMS 109
progressive school movement 46
Prys Davies, Gwilym 228
Pugh of Abergwili 15
Purdom, C.B. 59
Pwyllgor Datblygu Addysg Gymraeg (PDAG) 134, 219, 224, 225, 227–9

raising of the school-leaving age (RoSLA) 87, 88, 95, 144
Reed, Revd (later Canon) William 18, 19, 21, 24
Rees, Alwyn D. 29
Rees, Frances 63
Regional Advisory Council (RAC) 172
Reynolds, D. 81, 82
Rhieni dros Addysg Gymraeg 135
Rice, Charles 54–5
Richmond, Douglas C. 42
Robbins Committee and Report (1963) 153, 159–61, 164, 169, 189, 194
Roberts, C. 124, 125, 132
Ross, A.M. 189
Royal Society of Arts 86
Russell, John 55, 58, 59

Sadler, Dr Michael 48
Saer 125
St David's Trust 70
St Mary's College of Education 5, 173
Salisbury, Marquess of 39
Saunders, Mrs 20
Schon, Donald 181
school-leaving age *see* raising of the school-leaving age
Schools Council 87, 168, 169; *see also* Cyngor Ysgolion

Enquiry: Young School Leavers 88
Committee for Wales 88
RSLA: Another Year—To Endure or Enjoy? 88
Secondary School Examinations Council (SSEC) 86
Seddon 1
Shakoor, A. 154
Sharp 125
Sharp, Cecil 48
Sherman Theatre, Cardiff 70
Short, Edward 161
Sigsworth, A. 110
SIMS 145
Single European Act (1986) 235, 239, 240
Smith 125
Smithers, Professor 183
Social Charter 236
Society for Promoting Christian Knowledge (SPCK) 12, 13–14
Solemn Declaration on European Union 238–9
South Wales and Monmouthshire Training College *see* Trinity College, Carmarthen
Spencer, Herbert 47
staff, senior, role of 97–100
Stones, E. 181
streaming 93
Sunday schools 13, 77
Swyddfa Gymreig 107, 130, 134, 218, 220, 223, 227–9; *see also* Welsh Office
Symonds, J.C. 17

Task Group Assessment and Testing (TGAT) 82
Tasker's Charity School, Haverfordwest 32, 41
Taylor, Mary 142, 160
Taylor, Sir William 163, 197
Taylor Report 208, 209
teacher education 5–6
control of 187–200
in the 1990s 177–85

non-university 167–76
university 153–65
Teaching Quality 196
Technical and Vocational Education Initiative (TVEI) 144, 147, 210; see also ADAG
TVEI-related in-service training (TRIST) 147
Thatcher, Mrs Margaret 81, 177, 194, 196, 206
theatres 70
Theatr Clwyd, Mold 70
Theatr Fach, Llangefni 67
Theatr Gwynedd, Bangor 70
Theatr Hafren, Newtown 70
Theatr Harlech 70
Theatr Taliesin, Swansea 70
Theatr y Werin, Aberystwyth 70
Thirlwall, Bishop 15, 25
Thomas, Sir Ben Bowen 68
Thomas, Gwyn 228
Thomas, J.B. 189
Thomas, William 22–3
Thornycroft, Sir Hamo 48
Tomlinson, George 87
Torch Theatre, Milford Haven 70
Trades Union Congress 208
Treaty of Rome 235, 236
Treharne, Sir Cennydd 70
Trinity College, Carmarthen 2, 11–26, 158, 172
  curriculum 23
  entry requirements 16–17
  opening day 16
  recruitment of students 17–18, 25
Trusts of the South Wales Training Institution 15–16
Tuck, J.B. 189

underachievement 100–3
Universities Council for the Education of Teachers (UCET) 182
University Board for Training Colleges 154
Urdd Gobaith Cymru 224

Voysey, C.F.A. 48

Walden, George 212
Wales Advisory Body (WAB) 174
Wallas, Graham 48
Wallerstein, Immanuel 233
  Politics of the World-Economy, The 234
Wallis, E. White 48
Wallis, Isobel White 48, 49
Walburton, Canon 153, 165
Watkin, Mrs Auriol 3
Watson, Professor Foster 30
Waugh 53, 54
Weaver Report 170, 171
Webster, J. Roger 1–10, 217
  on Arts Council 65, 66, 69–70
  career 2–9
  research 3, 29–30, 76
Welsh Advisory Board 163
Welsh Arts Council 4, 73
Welsh Committee of the Arts Council 2, 4, 63–73
Welsh Intermediate and Technical Education Act (1889) 30
Welsh Intermediate Education Act (1889) 32, 45, 46, 56, 76, 78
Welsh Joint Education Committee (WJEC) 101–2, 103, 105, 140, 163; see also Cyd-bwyllgor Addysg Cymru
Welsh-medium teaching 6, 7, 8, 82
Welsh National Opera 4, 65, 66, 69, 72
Welsh Office 104, 105; see also Swyddfa Gymreig
Welsh Schools' Council 80
Welsh Theatre Company 4, 67, 69–70, 72
Western European Union 235
Western Mail 31
Wheldon, Huw 64, 140
William, G.G. 14
Williams, C. 124, 131
Williams, Gwyn A. 76, 79, 83
Williams, Iolo Aneurin 63
Williams, Professor Jac L. 5, 8, 30, 217

Williams, Shirley 208
Williams, Sir William Emrys 63, 70, 72
Williams' School, Dr, Dolgellau 41
Williams-Bulkeley, Sir Richard 35
Williams-Ellis, Amabel 48
Williams-Ellis, Clough 48
women and girls, education of 30–42

Woods, Alice 48
Wragg, E.C. 181
Wrexham Training College 158, 159, 167

Young Person's Europe 236–8
Yr Arloeswr 2
Ysgrifennydd Gwladol Cymru 134, 220, 228

COLEG GWENT
L.R.C. - EBBW VALE
TEL: 01495 333078